M000095728

A PRACTICE ALMOST PERFECT

The Early Days at Arnold, Fortas & Porter

Norman Diamond

University Press of America, Inc.
Lanham • New York • London

Copyright © 1997 by
University Press of America,® Inc.
4720 Boston Way
Lanham, Maryland 20706

12 Hid's Copse Rd.
Cummor Hill, Oxford OX2 9JJ

Library of Congress Cataloging-in-Publication Data

Diamond, Norman
A practice almost perfect : the early days at Arnold, Fortas & Porter /
Norman Diamond.
p.   cm.
1. Arnold, Fortas & Porter--History. 2. Law firms--Washington
(D.C.)-- History. I. Title.
KF355.W27D53   1997 340'.06'0753--dc21   96-47284 CIP

ISBN 0-7618-0627-X (cloth: alk. ppr)

♾™ The paper used in this publication meets the minimum
requirements of American National Standard for information
Sciences—Permanence of Paper for Printed Library Materials,
ANSI Z39.48—1984

For

My Wife Luna
My Son Monty
My Daughter Sarah
My Grandson Alex

Thurman Arnold striding to his office

CONTENTS

FOREWORD

Norman Diamond succeeds admirably in this book in recapturing the atmosphere -- the intellectual excitement, the vitality, the gaiety, and the camaraderie -- that characterized Arnold, Fortas & Porter in the first two decades of its existence. For those of us like me who were young lawyers in the firm in those years, it was always springtime.

The three founding partners -- Thurman Arnold, Abe Fortas, and Paul Porter -- were each in their own way remarkable men, who miraculously complemented one another's capabilities in forming a great law firm. As Norman recounts, Judge Arnold was the *pater familias* of our firm. He presided over the firm with wisdom and humor. He rejoiced together with the young lawyers in our moments of triumph. He encouraged and cajoled us when we were defeated and disappointed. Above all, he taught us what it means to be a lawyer. He inspired us, in Justice Holmes' famous phrase, to live greatly in the law. He did so with a total absence of humbug and pretense.

Arnold would not have thought of himself as a symbol or as part of the folklore of the law. Yet, he became just that. As Hugh Cox, who had been Thurman's first assistant in the Antitrust Division in the Department of Justice, once remarked, Thurman's impact was like that of a fresh wind blowing across Medicine Bow in Wyoming.

The marvelous anecdotes about Judge Arnold that Norman relates convey to the reader a sense of the extraordinary man that Arnold was. Norman has undertaken to answer in depth a question concerning Judge Arnold that I touched upon in a talk about him that I gave in October 1991 on the occasion of his 100th birthday. I said:

> "What was it like to work with Judge Arnold? I find it difficult to do justice to a description of the intellectual excitement that one experienced in working together with him, to his marvelous imaginative insights and creativity and resourcefulness, to his ability to cut through legal doctrines and rhetoric and to perceive things as they really are, his irreverence towards figures of authority and his delight in puncturing platitudes, his boundless energy and enthusiasm, his gaiety and his puckish wit, his generosity of spirit."

As Norman points out, Abe Fortas was a superlative legal craftsman -- he was an artist in the law. I believe that Fortas was one of the greatest lawyers of his generation. His skill and versatility in handling a broad range of issues were simply dazzling. He had no peers as an all-around tactician or as an appellate advocate. Numerous businessmen and government officials (including President Johnson) relied upon him as an advisor on many business and political problems, as well as their legal counselor.

In the office Fortas was an exacting taskmaster. To the young lawyers in the firm he sometimes seemed to be impersonal, if not harsh. However, Fortas cared deeply about the firm. To this day the partners are the beneficiaries of the things he did.

In a penultimate chapter, Norman writes of the circumstances surrounding Fortas' resignation from the Supreme Court in 1969. He finds it puzzling that, in a time of crisis, Fortas did not promptly retain Judge Arnold as his attorney. Norman thinks Abe should have done so immediately upon *Life* Magazine's partial revelation of his relationship with Louis Wolfson. He was a Wall Street operator of dubious character, then under scrutiny by the SEC for violations of securities legislation. In Norman's view, Arnold would have promptly disclosed the full arrangement and successfully countered *Life*'s innuendo that it involved the illegal practice of law by a member of the judiciary. Conceding that Abe's conduct was highly improper, Norman notes that it was not unlawful, and believes Arnold's prestige would have enabled Abe to weather the storm.

Perhaps so, but there is considerable room for doubt. There was widespread antagonism on the part of the Nixon Administration and numerous conservatives, including southern Democrats, resentful of the Warren Court in general and Fortas in particular. Their feelings were generated by the Court's decisions regarding racial issues, promoting civil liberties and extending unprecedented protection to criminal defendants. The Republicans were motivated by the added incentive of a Supreme Court vacancy by ousting Fortas.

I agree that Fortas' dissembling about his highly improper financial arrangement contributed substantially to his forced resignation. Certainly his evasiveness worsened his position by allowing the full details to be exposed by the Department of Justice. In the total circumstances, he may well have strengthened the anti-Fortas sentiment to the point that it could not have been resisted. But I'm not as certain that in the totality of the circumstances, even Judge Arnold's magnificent character and ability could have saved Abe's seat.

Norman's vivid portrait of the third of the founding partners, Paul Porter, is the best account about him that I have ever read. As Norman recounts, Paul had extensive knowledge and a keen understanding of the way in which the government functions. He had a legion of friends and acquaintances. The anecdotes and stories about Paul that Norman sets out bring to life Paul's warmth, common sense, decency, and wit.

The law firm that these three men built was a special place. The firm became justly celebrated for the excellence of its work and its indomitable courage, plus its strong spirit of collegiality. The firm was a partnership in the best sense of that term. The ethos of the firm is that lawyers in private practice are not simply guns for hire and that they have a responsibility to aid those who are disadvantaged or oppressed by government power. As Norman narrates, during the McCarthy era the firm represented, without compensation, many government employees and private citizens who were victims of the anti-communist hysteria. I agree with him that the firm's activities in those years deservedly rank among the finest hours of the legal profession in recent times.

Norman's book has one major gap: It neglects the tremendous contribution that Norman made to the law firm over a period of five decades. During the years he focuses upon, Norman was one of the key partners; he had responsibility for significant projects involving some of the firm's most important clients, such as Kroger, Federated Department Stores, and Lever Brothers. Norman is renowned for the meticulous care and attention he devoted to his client's affairs and for his unwavering commitment to producing a first class work product. The English language is the tool of lawyers, and Norman has always insisted that briefs and opinion letters be written with accuracy and clarity and precision.

Among the young lawyers, he was regarded as a demanding mentor who had little patience for shoddy work -- to work with him was to be "Diamondized." But he was also known for his generosity and his concern for the welfare of the young men and women in the firm. His thoroughness, his tenacity, and the attention he has given to every aspect of difficult legal matters are among the legends of the firm. Some of his cases that he describes -- for example, those involving the fight by Masters against resale price maintenance and the FTC proceedings against Kroger -- rank among the firm's most memorable triumphs.

Norman's book is replete with anecdotes about his colleagues, but there are precious few about him. One could devote several lengthy chapters to choice stories about his raucous discussions with Judge Arnold, captured so well in the delightful poem by Reed Miller. Much could be written about his fervent love of the Brooklyn Dodgers and the University of North Carolina basketball teams, not to mention his exciting and sometimes quixotic experiences as an owner of racehorses.

Two incidents may give a hint of the richness that has been omitted. On one occasion, he and I were scheduled to fly to Atlanta on Delta airlines for a client meeting. At the time, Delta widely advertised: "Delta is ready when you are." When we arrived at the airport, the airline agent at the gate informed us that the flight was overbooked and notwithstanding our reservations there was no seat for us. Norman at once demanded a face-to-face meeting with his superior. "I'm going to complain to the Federal Trade Commission that Delta is engaged in false and deceptive advertising," Norman growled. "What do you mean?" the startled supervisor asked. "Well," Norman declared, "you advertise that you're ready when your passengers are. I'm ready, but you're not!" And he stomped off.

In the span of five minutes, Norman delivered one of the greatest oral arguments in the history of the firm. In the mid-1950s, we were representing a client in a matter before the old Court of Claims. Judge Arnold agreed that he would leave Norman twenty minutes for our rebuttal argument. It was the last case on that day's docket, following lunch. The day the case came up was a steaming July afternoon. The courtroom was unbearably hot. Further, either air-conditioning was lacking or was not functioning.

After hearing the previous case, all seven justices on the court were dozing off, unable to keep their eyes open. When our case was called by the Clerk at 3 p.m., even Judge Arnold couldn't get their attention. Throughout the argument by Judge Arnold and opposing counsel, Norman had scribbled furiously on a legal pad, page after page. Unwittingly Arnold had left only five minutes for Norman's presentation. When the moment arrived for his remarks, he strode swiftly to the lectern and proclaimed in a booming voice: "I have fifteen points." He proceeded to recite them one-by-one, speaking forcefully and in rapid fire machine gun fashion, to be sure he covered all of them. The somnolent judges stirred to life and stared at Norman in a dazed state. In five minutes, Norman completed all fifteen points and triumphantly sat down. His performance moved the Clerk of the Court to say: "Anyway you woke them up." Maybe that's why we lost the case despite Norman's bravo performance.

Some years ago, *The New Yorker* published profiles of "The Most Memorable Person I Have Known." Norman would be a wonderful candidate for such a profile.

Abe Krash
August 1996

PROLOGUE

My purpose in writing this book is to portray three remarkable men -- Thurman Arnold, Abe Fortas and Paul Porter -- and the character of the law firm they founded fifty years ago. The original name of the firm was Arnold, Fortas & Porter (changed to Arnold & Porter upon the appointment of Abe Fortas to the Supreme Court in 1965). I am still with the firm. The emphasis of this book is on the halcyon days when those three men were active in its practice.

The genesis of my endeavor was a persistent thought that a single volume should assemble for all time the distinctive personalities, extraordinary achievements and unrecorded anecdotes, plus one sad *denoument*, which marked them and their professional careers. This reflects a repudiation of one of Arnold's memorable comments. Somebody once told him that a remark he had just made should be recorded for posterity. With his characteristic whimsy, the Judge replied: "Posterity has never done a thing for me. I don't see why I should do anything for posterity."

Photographs of the founding fathers hang on the walls of my office. Hardly a day goes by that I don't recall an event involving at least one of them. I doubt that any law firm has ever had three men of their stature on active duty at the same time. Many other able lawyers have served the firm. But none has ever matched the range of talents which characterized each of them.

Arnold, Fortas & Porter was established just after World War II. None of them had a background in the service or locale of any big time law firms. Thurman Arnold came from Laramie, Wyoming; Abe Fortas from Memphis, Tennessee; and Paul Porter from Winchester, Kentucky. The sum of their accomplishments was astonishing. When they founded the firm, they collectively comprised two law school faculty members; a town mayor; a state legislator; three public servants who had performed in various New Deal capacities; one journalist and part-time diplomat with the rank of Ambassador; a best-selling author; an Assistant Attorney General; an Under Secretary of the Interior; a Director of the Office of Price Administration; and a Judge of the United States Court of Appeals for the District of Columbia Circuit.

The three name partners were simultaneously active in the practice of the firm for almost a quarter of a century. From its inception, it earned a notable reputation for the excellence, integrity and courage of its service to its clients and the happy environment in which it functioned. For them and the colleagues they hired, monetary considerations were almost incidental. I can only recall hearing of them when Abe would express concern about meeting the next month's expenses. He had a sense of insecurity about money. I don't know why; we were never in the red.

All three shared a fearlessness for the defense of civil liberties against government encroachment. Arnold, Fortas & Porter was preeminent among all law firms in defending the victims of the red-baiting frenzy that infected the legislative and executive branches of the federal government in the early 1950s. Unlike their cowed contemporaries in the profession, Thurman, Abe and Paul fought the forces of repression in the full glare of relentless publicity, well aware of the financial risks to their firm.

To quote Gene M. Gressley in his illuminating essay on Judge Arnold:

> "It is difficult, if not impossible, to recreate for those who did not live through it the violence of emotions, the national paranoia, the morbid excitement of the McCarthy era. Even for those who experienced this time of madness, the feverish convulsion of those years is blotted out. The horror and insanity has been cauterized, but scars on the body politic remain. . . ."[1]

The absurdity of that idiotic period is attested by the omission of a single reference to McCarthy or to the Loyalty program in J. Edgar Hoover's book on Communist infiltration of the United States.[2] This is instructive in light of the major role played by the FBI in the Administration of the Loyalty program.[3]

Neither Thurman nor Paul had any interest in law firm management or administration. That was Abe's dish of tea. Thurman and Paul kept the office loose and relaxed with their humor and wit. They always expressed satisfaction and gratitude for the assistance provided by their younger colleagues. The readers will note a total absence of criticism about either of them. There was simply no basis for an adverse word. Abe was different. He was the stern taskmaster. He saw to it that everyone toed the mark to ensure that the firm's work was done to perfection.

There were several synergies which bonded them. Perhaps most importantly, they liked and respected each other. As Lewis Cassels -- a United Press reporter -- wrote in an article for *Harper's* Magazine in November 1951:

> The morale of the office is exceedingly high. The visitor gets the feeling that everybody there likes everybody else, and that all of them are intensely proud of being on the Arnold, Fortas & Porter team.
>
> This is especially true of the principal partners themselves. They get along famously despite their totally dissimilar personalities, and they obviously have a high degree of mutual admiration.[4]

Everybody, including staff, was on a first-name basis with everyone else. A lawyer was fortunate if a secretary remembered to call him "Mr." if she stuck her head into his office while he was in conference with a client. To this day the word "sir" is unknown at the firm. Arnold and Porter simply did not know the meaning of the word "protocol." Their doors were always open to everyone from the newest messenger to the oldest professional. It was not uncommon for either of them to offer help to a younger lawyer.

It became a daily custom of the firm, lawyers, plus clients who were on hand, to take a break from work -- even if heavy night labor lay ahead -- by repairing to what became known as the Garden Room at about 5:45 p.m. In part, the reason for this daily ritual was to watch the television news, while enjoying the luxury of a libation. But most of us were more eager to hear the observations which Judge Arnold and Paul Porter injected while the newsmen plied their trade.

One comment of Judge Arnold's is typical of the kind of spontaneous insights that lit up that room. The House Unamerican Activities Committee was making hay for the Republicans with widely reported charges of disloyalty within the Democratic executive departments, especially at the State Department. President Truman retaliated by promulgating Executive Order 9835 establishing a loyalty program within the executive branch.[5]

When that was carried on the evening newscast -- coupled with a statement that the President had asked for an appropriation of

$11,000,000 to conduct the program -- the group in our Garden Room, like Democrats generally, enthusiastically approved. The thinking was that the President had "stolen the ball." Arnold differed. He remarked: "It's the worst mistake he ever made." Someone asked: "What makes you say that, Judge." He replied: "When you ask for $11,000,000 to conduct a witch hunt, you've got to find witches." As usual, subsequent events proved the accuracy of Arnold's vision. Years later, the President conceded it was a "bad mistake."[6]

I also want to set some things straight about the legal profession. Not much good has ever been said about lawyers. Shakespeare long ago voiced a popular notion when he wrote: "First thing we do, let's kill all the lawyers."[7] With the passage of time, the public's view of the profession keeps sinking. Today lawyers are generally regarded as smooth-talking characters, not much better than medicine men, relentlessly concerned with the accumulation of personal wealth. Who hasn't picked up the paper to read about one lawyer or another filing groundless lawsuits designed to shake down an innocent defendant? Who hasn't also watched a TV news show critical of lawyers for extracting exorbitant fees at the expense of hapless clients?

While lawyers in general are considered disreputable, the Washington lawyer has been singled out as particularly odious. There is a widespread belief that Washington lawyers are principally engaged in lobbying Congress and the executive agencies to obtain undeserved benefits for special interests with deep pockets. I hope that those notions will be dispelled by my description of our practice while the name partners were active participants -- a period which spanned the challenging times of McCarthyism.

Along the way, it's my further hope to expand the public's understanding of the scope of the law beyond the parts they usually experience through the media or personal contact. Those are typically matters involving criminal sanctions, product liability, personal injury, domestic relations and, more recently, spousal abuse.

A collateral purpose will be to provide realistic insights about the ways in which lawyers and judges actually function. I trust that fellow lawyers will understand that those undertakings will entail the explanation of some rudimentary concepts. In doing so, I'll try to avoid Arnold's lament that the function of lawyers is to make simple things appear so complicated that ordinary people can't understand them.

ACKNOWLEDGMENTS

This volume owes its publication to the assistance of two of my partners at Arnold & Porter and the unflagging cooperation of members of its staff. The full text was read by two outstanding lawyers who are truly leaders of our firm: Duane (Bud) Vieth and Abe Krash. Bud was for many years Chairman of our Policy Committee, on which Abe served a lengthy term.

Richard Palmer, one of the firm's superb librarians, consistently tracked down essential sources of outside materials. I'm still marveling at the ingenuity he invariably displayed in ferreting such items from unlikely sources.

During the eight-year incubation of the manuscript, three secretaries lent their skills to the project: Barbara Moylan -- herself a talented writer -- helped for several years, until she was lured by another firm at a significantly higher salary; Helen Kidwell for more than a year, until she retired; and Janet Rowland, an exceptionally gifted woman, who is presently working with me.

Most of all, I must express my fervent appreciation to the exceptional group who serve as our Word Processing unit. Its remarkably capable and dedicated Manager, Kathleen McManus, arranged for production of the manuscript. Veronica Hansborough, the Unit's talented Coordinator, oversaw the actual production, taking pains to avoid interference with the firm's regular work.

I would be remiss if I did not pay special tribute to Sue Zimmerman. The initial draft was completed by partial texts from several different specialists. Sue was then assigned by Kathleen the sole responsibility for printing the ultimate manuscript, to the exacting specifications of the publisher. Under our computer setup -- with different applications and multiple conversions -- this proved, as expected, a complex undertaking. Sue solved the difficulties by dint of her rare combination of extraordinary intelligence and superior technical skills. While executing her difficult assignment, she somehow discerned and alerted me to flaws or repetitions in the text. She has been the project's indispensable woman.

The indispensable final, camera ready manuscript could not have been prepared without the exceptionally competent work of Bonnie Smith. She literally saved the day.

Finally, but by no means last, I must extend the full measure of my gratitude to my editor, Lynn Haney. Already the author of ten books, she taught me the writing techniques that would attract a publisher's attention. They were all new to a novice like me. As this book attests, she succeeded. She read every word I wrote with a critical eye for its suitability in the book world -- from the standpoints both of the publisher and the readers.

Lynn provided much of the information about the book required by the publisher. She anticipated the publisher's need for the identities of future events and their locations, for use as distribution centers. In a word, she was fully sophisticated in the ways of the publishing world.

She kept me going whenever my enthusiasm waned or my will faltered.

Part I - How We Happened

A rare portrait of Thurman Arnold, at his ease
and immaculately attired

CHAPTER ONE

THE FOUNDING FATHERS AND ME

The fathers of our firm were a perfect blend. Before establishing it, they shared other background features, besides their origins in localities far from the nation's metropolitan centers. Arnold and Fortas served simultaneously on the Yale Law School faculty. All three men served the alphabet agencies of the New Deal throughout the Great Depression and World War II, on occasion working together at the same one. Each achieved a high government post. However, such commonalities do not solely account for the unique harmony that marked their relationship as law partners.

This is not to say that they shared a common outlook on life or that they had similar roles in their law firm. In fact, their differences strengthened the organization. For every divergence, one or the other had a complementary attribute.

Thurman and Abe co-founded the firm of Arnold & Fortas in January 1946, after resigning from their government positions. Thurman had served four years as Assistant Attorney General in charge of the Antitrust Division in the Justice Department before serving two years as Judge of the United States Court of Appeals for the District of Columbia Circuit, the nation's second highest court. Abe was Under Secretary of the Interior Department for three years before casting his lot with Thurman. When they formed their partnership, Thurman was 56 and Abe 20 years his junior.

At age 46, Paul Porter joined his friends in May 1947, after serving in numerous capacities as a New Deal trouble shooter. His last post before helping to found the firm was as special envoy to Greece with the rank of Ambassador. In that post he oversaw Truman's support program which saved that country from Soviet domination.

Thurman embodied the essence of the man of the great American West. When he entered the office each morning, he looked like an eager cowboy striding into Dodge City, looking for action. His appearance was rumpled, his manner bluff and hearty. Standing slightly below six feet in height, he had a sturdy build, with a contour showing a slight middle age bulge. His face was strong and a bit ruddy -- somewhat suggestive of an aging Marlboro man. It was topped by dark gray hair, with a matching mustache.

Arnold typically appeared reflective, suggesting a mind always at work. Then, if the discussion took a lively turn, his expression would quickly shift to animation. Strong of voice, the Arnold sound would sometimes rise to a stentorian level. It might occur when he emphasized a point during a court argument or when highlighting a point during a serious speech. He might even become vociferous when debating a legal issue with an office colleague. But there was never a bite in his bark.

I served under Arnold for a brief period at the Department of Justice when he was Assistant Attorney General in charge of the Antitrust Division. Although both of us were on the same floor, his office was as far as it could be from mine. Holmes Baldridge, Chief of the Litigation Section, was my neighbor. One morning about 9 a.m. I walked by as someone stuck his head into Holmes' office and asked: "Holmes, have you seen Thurman this morning?" Holmes replied: "Hell, I haven't even heard him."

My career has included work with and against many lawyers and the observation of many others. Lots of them were able; some brilliant. If I had to select the best of them all, it would be Arnold. Besides his knowledge of the law and his marvelous writing skill, he had two rare and unmatched talents. They were extraordinary creativity in the application of standard legal principles, and most of all, unmatched perception of the realities of present society and of the future impact of current events.

Although his background as a teacher, author and public servant caused many to regard him as an academic or philosopher, Arnold had few, if any, peers as an imaginative, pragmatic and fearless lawyer. An Arnold biographer recites Arnold's legal talents, as analyzed by Abe Fortas, during a personal interview on July 19, 1971:

. . . Abe Fortas recalled that he found Arnold extremely useful in two ways: First, Fortas would go to Arnold with a seemingly impossible legal puzzle. After a few minutes of highly stimulating conversation, Arnold was likely to produce several ideas that at first blush appeared absolutely inane. However, after being exposed to one of Arnold's intellectual gypsy sessions, Fortas found himself several days later discovering that Arnold's deductions made sense. Arnold simply possessed an unfathomable depth of resourcefulness and imagination. Secondly, Fortas, particularly in the McCarthy years, found Arnold's courage a tremendous bulwark. A certain comfort and reassurance came from having ten feet down the hall an individual who plainly refused to be intimated by the hysteria of the age.[1]

In looks as well as in aura, Abe was totally different from Thurman. He was fascinating to study in repose. He reminded me of a gymnast at the instant he was to start his routine -- intense and totally focused. He was of average height and trim stature; very neat in appearance. His features were regular, his expression taut but somehow communicative. You knew where you stood with him just by the way he looked at you. Normally his manner was quiet and serious, if not reserved. At work, he was detached and deeply absorbed -- rarely affable. He could turn ice cold in a split second whenever someone or something disturbed him.

Abe's skill as a lawyer was universally recognized. In comparing him to Arnold, Cassels had this to say:

". . . Fortas is equally brilliant, but in an entirely different way. He is the logician, the meticulous craftsman of the law, who analyzes a problem as a chemist analyzes a strange compound. He thinks far more slowly than Arnold, but is in a much better position to defend his conclusions.[2]

I'm not so sure about Abe's far slower thought processes or the superiority of his ability to defend his conclusions. There are no calculators for such intangibles. I would describe them as the original thinker and the superb artist. To put it another way, Arnold was an authentic genius, the best all-around lawyer I ever knew. Abe's artistry included a remarkable capacity to make other people think he was a genius.

Abe's abilities need no endorsement from me. But I must mention one incomparable talent. I never heard his equal as an appellate advocate in any court, anywhere, any time.

Paul brightened a room just by his sunny presence. He had a way of making everyone around him feel better. When introduced to a younger lawyer's spouse, he'd invariably say: "Like we say down in Kentucky, you outmarried yourself." That made both the bride and groom feel good. It's said of Will Rogers that he never met a man he didn't like. I'm sure that Paul was liked by every man he ever met.

Physically, Paul stood about six feet, four inches, perfectly built -- neither lean nor husky -- and good looking. His manner was invariably friendly and cheerful. His voice was pleasant, almost mirthful. His moods ranged from congenial to jolly. He was fun to be around and easy to work with.

Cassels affirmed Porter's outstanding legal ability, although in more racy terms than I would have used. After attesting to Paul's personal charm, he said:

> Though Porter is unquestionably astute, no one would describe him as an intellectual. His great asset is a gift of gab that makes him a persuasive conversationalist in private and an eloquent advocate in court. His arguments, even before the august Supreme Court, are liberally seasoned with wit. That may be one reason why the word-weary justices usually compliment Porter warmly for his presentation -- even when they rule against him.[3]

Cassels was right on target in recognizing Paul's professional expertise. It was exceptional, though I suspect Paul felt a sense of academic inferiority compared with his partners. He had studied law at the University of Kentucky, while they were Harvard and Yale graduates.

In all the time I knew them, I never heard an unkind word from any of the founders about either of the others. In her biography of Fortas, Laura Kalman notes an illustrative incident. It arose during the McCarthy scare, while Arnold was defending Owen Lattimore, a leading scholar on far eastern affairs of state. He had been indicted for alleged perjury in the course of Senate hearings. These were held after the infamous Senator McCarthy had labelled Lattimore as the top Soviet agent in the United States. Abe Fortas had agreed that we would represent him *pro bono* and had personally appeared for him during two sets of extensive Senate hearings.

Arnold took over during the subsequent criminal proceedings. Our Bill Rogers, then an associate -- later to become Under Secretary of State for Henry Kissinger -- was assisting Arnold. He reported to Fortas that Arnold kept mixing up Manchuria and Mongolia, to the distress of Lattimore and his wife. Bill evidently expected Abe to correct the problem.

According to Laura Kalman's biography of Fortas, he explained to Bill:

> . . . "Thurman is a genius, and you've got to let him be a genius in his own way and not tug on his sleeve and constantly try to keep him within the strict bounds of the truth and accuracy." For Rogers, that good advice reflected Fortas' respect for Arnold and his sense that "Thurman's idiosyncrasies were part of a great mind."[4]

The modest compensation which each had earned in government service contributed to a mutual sense of values about the conduct of a law firm. It freed them from the hunger for money which was a way of life in other prominent law firms. In such situations, avarice made competitors as well as colleagues of the firm members -- inevitably a source of internal friction. Thurman, Abe and Paul were equal partners and close friends. They remained that way throughout their active participation in the affairs of Arnold, Fortas & Porter. Of course, I don't mean to imply that they lived modestly. The firm quickly prospered to the point where each enjoyed an up-scale lifestyle.

As I have mentioned, all three of them were passionate in the defense of civil liberties against government oppression. Their battle against that plague lasted eleven years, from 1947 to 1958. It began with rumblings on Capitol Hill, particularly the House side, about the infiltration of government by Communists. Almost immediately, ten State Department employees were summarily dismissed with prejudice, without charges or hearing, on the ground that they were "potential security risks." However, three were soon permitted to resign "without prejudice".[5]

The other seven remained subject to the stigma. On notice that it would be communicated to prospective employers, they turned to Arnold, Fortas & Porter. On August 6, 1947, the firm submitted a petition to the Department of State Loyalty Committee asking for an immediate hearing. Only an acknowledgment of the petition was received. On October 4, 1947, the partners sent a letter to the Secretary of State requesting that the subjects be permitted to resign without prejudice. It emphasized that otherwise the taint of disloyalty would permanently prejudice their economic futures. Alternatively, it was proposed that the employees be furnished with charges and an opportunity to rebut them. Neither request was granted.[6]

While these efforts to obtain relief for the State Department victims were going nowhere, Arnold spoke at one of the annual forums held by the *New York Herald Tribune* on current events. He sat next to Mrs. Ogden Reid, owner of that great newspaper, always Republican oriented. He excited her indignation when he told her of the arbitrary conduct of the Department. As a result, she assigned the paper's Washington Bureau Manager, Bert Andrews, to probe the matter. Beginning November 2, 1947, he addressed it in a series of front page stories in the *Herald Tribune*.[7] He did such a thorough job that major institutions and individuals of the print and radio media, plus letters from the public, expressed such widespread outrage that the prejudice attached to the dismissals was rescinded. The facts are recited in Andrews' previously cited book -- at note 5 -- revealing in full detail all that he had learned. The book won a Pulitzer Prize. All seven found other employment.[8]

Nevertheless, the attention focused on the Department's personnel may well have caused other injury to its staff. The damaging loyalty publicity may conceivably have been compounded by a common belief that the government in Washington, and particularly the State Department was a haven for homosexuals. The effect of that impression actually stimulated a Congressional investigation of the subject.[9]

Subsequently, Senator Joseph McCarthy of Wisconsin became the Congressional version of "Attila the Hun" in leading the assault on civil liberties, purportedly to cleanse the government and the nation of rampant Communism. His ruthless, unscrupulous and scurrilous tactics introduced the defamatory term "McCarthyism" into the English language, defined as follows:

> 1.   the practice of making accusations of disloyalty, esp. of pro-Communist activity, in many instances unsupported by proof or based on slight, doubtful, or irrelevant evidence. 2.   unfairness in

investigative technique.   3.   persistent search for and exposure of
disloyalty, esp. in government office.[10]

Beginning in 1950 when the firm undertook the representation of
Owen Lattimore, we fought McCarthyism and its concomitant
trampling of civil rights for eight long years.   In the course of that
conflict the founders each handled many cases to which they personally
devoted countless hours, without recompense, in opposition to patent
violations of rights guaranteed by the Constitution.   Among them were
two outrageous cases which were brought before the Supreme Court.
But as narrated in the succeeding CHAPTERS THIRTEEN and
FOURTEEN, the Court deadlocked in one and decided the other for
our client on a trivial technicality.   In my opinion, the Court simply
lacked the fortitude to decide the constitutional issues.

Finally, in litigation known as the "Fort Monmouth" case,[11]
McCarthyism met its judicial Waterloo.   That case was brought by six
scientists employed at Fort Monmouth against the Secretary of the
Army.   They prevailed on appeal from an adverse district court
decision, which had sustained the Army Department's termination of
their employment as "security risks".[12]   In that case, besides denial of
any hearing, even the names of the persons who had ruled against the
unfortunate individuals were withheld from them.

The ground of the appeals was that the dismissals were accomplished
by a procedure in which the Army's Security Review Board failed to
follow its own rules.   According to those rules, after a hearing of the
issues, the employee would be sent a letter "advising him of the
[Board's] findings."   However, the only notice given to five of the
plaintiffs was a summary statement that "your continued employment
*** would not be clearly consistent with the interest of national security
under the provisions of Executive Order 10540." [13]

One of the employees received a letter paradoxically stating that "the
Security Hearing Board had found that his continued employment could
be clearly consistent with the interests of national security . . . but that
the Security Review Board had tentatively concluded that his continued
employment 'would not be clearly consistent with the interest of
National Security under the provisions of Executive Order 10450.'"[14]
(Incredible as it sounds, that is not a misstatement.   "You kin look it
up," as Casey Stengel, the celebrated baseball manager of the New
York Yankees and New York Mets, was wont to say).

The appellate court rejected the argument that those notices constituted the necessary "findings" of the Security Hearing Board. It held that they were "a mere conclusory statement, notifying the employee that he is a 'security risk'". When Arnold demanded the findings, the Army declined to furnish them on the ground that the names of the authors of the finding would be disclosed, to the government's detriment. When Arnold offered to take the findings with the names deleted, disclosure was still refused.

The government then agreed to the entry of judgment for the plaintiffs and their reinstatement, plus back pay, on the sole condition that they would immediately resign. As Judge Arnold stated: "Since nothing short of a draft would have induced the defendants in the Fort Monmouth trials ever to work for their government again, this was an easy condition to meet."[15]

It is my conviction that the unremitting and fearless fight of the founding fathers against the evils of McCarthyism constituted the noblest cause pursued by the profession during my experience. It may be no exaggeration to state that it was among the finest hours in the entire history of the bar. Referring to a statement by Justice Douglas on the appropriate process for handling subversive problems, Bert Andrews said:

> Why did Justice Douglas speak out?
>
> At a Washington social gathering, he heard a prominent lawyer agree vigorously in theory that something ought to be done to forward the battle for civil liberties and to protect minority groups against hysterical attacks. He heard the same lawyer, asked to take the leadership in one such battle, accept at first and then back away because of fear that he might lose important clients if he did so.[16]

United as they were in their passion for civil liberties, the founders were distinctive in other ways. Actually there may have been more differences than similarities in their outlooks on life and their roles in the law partnership they created. But the differences among them strengthened the firm. As previously noted, for every divergence, one or the other had a complementary attribute.

Although they were personally close, the founders' social milieus were altogether different. So were their attitudes towards their friends. Thurman and Paul conducted themselves just as they did in the office.

Abe's outside manner was altogether different. He was extremely warm and gracious towards those whose company he favored, almost to the point of sycophancy.

Judge Arnold's social contacts were diversified, embracing judges, intellectuals, neighbors and just plain folks. Abe socialized primarily with important clients, high government officials and a broad spectrum of prominent people in all walks of life, ranging from music to business to finance. Paul mingled chiefly with the movers and shakers of Washington, particularly at the Burning Tree Club in nearby Maryland, an all-male golfing bastion where they regularly congregated.

Thurman's eclectic friendships included Charles Pickett, a scion of the Confederate General -- George Pickett -- who led the historic confederate charge at Gettysburg. Pickett was an ultra-conservative. He became the foil for Thurman's wit following the Supreme Court's decision in *Brown v. Board of Education*, 347 U.S. 483 (1954). It was the historic case which ruled that state-mandated separate schools for black and white children violated the Equal Protection Clause of the Fourteenth Amendment to the Constitution. This moved the Virginia legislature to enact a statute, called "The Gray Plan." It incorporated what became known as "massive resistance" to the integration of Virginia's public schools. In brief, it provided that any time a court ordered integration of any such school, it would be shut down.

One night Arnold and Pickett were at a dinner party where the subject came up. Thurman promptly expressed his hearty approval of the legislation, but questioned whether it was adequate. This moved Pickett to state enthusiastically: "Thurman, I'm glad you've seen the light at last, but tell me what brought you around and what else do you have in mind." Thurman replied: "The statute makes absolute sense -- but it doesn't go for enough. I would close all of the public schools in Virginia because it's a complete waste of the taxpayer's money to try to educate Virginians."

Abe's preference for the "rich and famous" is illustrated by the following passage from Kalman's biography:

> . . . A cultural individual who was equally comfortable in the drawing room, music room, boardroom and courtroom, he possessed immense appeal for clients. Further, he courted them . . .

> . . . In the 1960s Fortas once told the investment banker John Loeb that he had invited "some of your friends" to dinner. The Loebs arrived and

were sitting around the pool with Fortas and Carol Agger when Lynda
Bird Johnson and Chuck Robb arrived, followed by Robert and Margy
McNamara. A few minutes later President and Mrs. Johnson appeared,
and the four couples settled in for the evening. It showed Loeb, who
later became a client, how intimate Fortas and Johnson were, "because
after all," he emphasized, "you can't deliver the President unless you're
very close to him."...[17]

Paul was party to a legendary incident that happened at Burning
Tree during the loyalty hysteria in which he was the target of a
putdown. It has often been told by reporters and authors, but never
accurately. In particular, to my knowledge, the identity of the man
who tried the putdown has never previously been revealed. As Paul
reported it to me immediately after the event, this is what happened:
As he entered the Burning Tree bar one afternoon, John McClure, a tax
lawyer for Coca Cola -- which we represented on other matters --
spotted Paul and asked: "Is your firm still representing pinks and
queers?" This was at the height of McCarthyism. Paul didn't bat an
eye in responding, "Sure John, why? Are you in trouble?"

The mistaken reports typically had the putdown artist asking, "Hi,
Paul, are you still representing homosexuals and communists?" --
hardly normal rhetoric for such a dialogue. One foolish author had a
United States Senator putting the question to Paul -- with Paul
answering: "That's right Senator, what can we do for you?"[18] Anyone
with a remote knowledge of Paul would know he would never offend
a Senator under any circumstance.

Whether because of, or despite, their deviations, the combination of
the Judge, Abe and Paul embodied all the necessary elements -- internal
and external -- prerequisite to a skilled, successful and satisfying law
practice. Beyond that, while they were present, the practice was
pursued in a uniquely pleasurable ambience. It once occurred to me
that the firm's atmosphere could be likened to a congenial repertory
company in which the lawyers were the performers and the cases
comprised the productions.

Frequently, when my mind wonders back to the firm's incubation
years, I wonder how all the forces came together which enabled me to
join the firm. I believe the script starts with my Mom. She was from
New Haven. But for that Yale would have been just another school.
As it was, no sooner was I old enough to be aware of the world around
me, than I became conscious of Yale. Mom used to sing us Yale songs

as lullabies. By the time I reached school age, I was a Yale booster, rooting hard for its teams in every athletic contest in which they participated, especially football. Yale was then an athletic powerhouse. Along with Harvard and Princeton, it comprised "The Big Three." As soon as I could read, the newspaper reports of each game were mother's milk. Yale rarely lost. I remember the legendary football coach of the 20s, T.A.D. ("TAD") Jones, and such old-time players as Ducky Pond and Albie Booth.

During my senior year at the University of North Carolina, at Chapel Hill, I decided to go to law school. I thought of and applied to only one -- Yale -- because of my boyhood attachment to it. I knew nothing of its relative academic standing or its admissions policy. It was only after my arrival that I learned of the limitation of its basic first year students to 100 students -- a handful compared to other Ivy League schools. (In addition, for a short time, there were 25 places for a combined four-year course with the Harvard Business School, where that group of enrollees spent one year).

I had no idea of the brilliantly unorthodox faculty which Robert Hutchins -- later the famed President of the University of Chicago -- had assembled during his three-year term as Dean of the Yale Law School, in the late 1920's, starting when he was 26 years old. During my time that faculty included Arnold and Fortas. I took both of their courses.

I've always believed that an item I wrote for a student publication called the *Yale Law Journal* was responsible for my career at Arnold, Fortas & Porter. The *Journal* was a learned magazine published and written in major part during the school year by 16 or so selected students comprising its "Board of Editors". Each of the eight issues featured articles by leading scholars of the day, book reviews by experts in the field, and most importantly, contributions authored by students called "Notes" and "Comments." The "Notes" generally dealt with the meaning and implications of recent cutting-edge judicial decisions. The "Comments" dealt at greater length with broader legal topics of current interest.

During the depression years -- 1935 to 1938 -- when I attended the law school, selections for the limited places were based upon an actual writing competition among the top 32 students in the class, based on their grades. This was conducted by the existing Board members who chose their successors by evaluation of their drafting and analytical skills in composing Notes and Comments. When assigning a project to a competitor, the Editor named a faculty member who would be available for consultation. Beyond their introduction, there was rarely any contact between them.

So far as I know, the competition for places on the Law Journal Board was unique to Yale. Comparable student publications at other schools -- typically called "Law Reviews" -- selected their editors solely by grade ranking. Today I understand that any willing student can write for them. In my year 16 competitors were successful

Of those 16, the top five served, respectively, as Editor-in-chief; 2 Comment Editors and 2 Note Editors. They primarily reviewed student work, contributing content suggestions and criticisms. Of the next two, one served as Articles Editor. He elicited and edited longer legal commentaries from prominent legal scholars, usually law school professors. The other was the Book Review Editor. His function was to procure critical analyses, from similar sources, of recent legal publications. The 16th served as Business Manager, soliciting paid subscriptions to the *Journal* and overseeing collections. The in-between eight continued to write Notes and Comments for the *Journal*. I was one of those.

I came to Abe's attention because of a comment I wrote for the *Journal,* while a member of the Board. But for that, I doubt that he would have known me. His course was all lecture -- no student participation.

My comment appeared in the December 1937 issue of the *Journal.* It was entitled "Protective Committees and Reorganization Reform."[19] 47 Yale L.J. (1937-38) at 229 *et seq.* It relied, in part, on a Congressional document.[20]

Corporate reorganization is a remedy designed to enable a corporation which cannot pay its debts on time to stay in business and ultimately survive. The process entails the development of revised terms for satisfying the interests of the corporation's creditors and stockholders. It is started by a Petition For Reorganization filed with the appropriate United States District Court, each of which has jurisdiction over bankruptcy matters.

Upon acceptance of the Petition, creditors of the corporation are stayed from pursuing collection efforts, while the debtor remains in business, usually under its same management, and endeavors to work out a plan for resolving its credit problems. This typically involves a significant extension of time to do so and a reduction in the amounts

ultimately payable. Protective committees were organized to represent
the various parties who held claims against the debtor corporation.

Meantime, unbeknown to me, Abe had played a major role in the
study by the Securities and Exchange Commission which eventually led
to the above-cited Congressional Report. His work on the study and
the unethical practices of the insiders who dominated the protective
committees are outlined in a book about Fortas by Robert Shogan. In
his words:

> Fortas meanwhile was completing work on the bankruptcy
> reorganization study, which had been his first assignment at the SEC.
> The three-year investigation produced a detailed report demonstrating
> that the so-called protective committees of company officials and
> creditors who took over bankrupt companies were, in fact, often
> protecting no one's interest but their own. The majority of investors
> were left out in the cold. The report called for specific action to correct
> these abuses, and Congress, in the Bankruptcy Act of 1938, adopted its
> most important recommendations. The new law required, among other
> reforms, the appointment in substantial bankruptcy cases of an impartial
> trustee who would oversee reorganization and make certain that the
> interests of all investors were considered.[21]

My piece included several suggestions besides those contained in the
Committee Report. They apparently impressed Abe. That doubtless
accounted for his proposal that upon my graduation in June 1938, I join
his future staff in Washington, where he had assumed a full-time
government job. Knowing of his hard-nosed reputation, I was flattered
and immediately accepted.

Subsequently, with Abe's o.k., I first worked one year in the office
of Thomas E. Dewey, the newly elected District Attorney of New York
County. That job gave me priceless litigation training. At the end of
the year, I left for Washington and got in touch with Abe. He was
then about to move from another government agency to take charge of
the Bituminous Coal Division of the Interior Department. That meant
a six week delay before he could hire me.

Needing funds, I took a temporary job under Arnold at the
Department of Justice which I've already mentioned. I next went to
work for Fortas on schedule, and spent two years in the General
Counsel's Office of the Coal Division. After two more years of
civilian service at other government agencies, I obtained an

appointment as an officer in the United States Naval Reserve. And that, by a quirk of fate, led to my career at Arnold, Fortas & Porter.

In brief, I served the Navy in Washington for about 2½ years. During that period I kept in contact with Abe, who was Under Secretary of the Interior. Among other things, because of my access to the Navy Post Exchange, I was able to provide him with "goodies" unavailable to civilians. My Navy discharge, due in March 1946, came just as the brand new law shop formed by Thurman and Abe was warming up. By sheer coincidence, when I started thinking about a civilian job, I received a telephone call from Abe asking that I meet with him. I did so and accepted his offer to serve the embryonic firm of Arnold & Fortas as an associate.

CHAPTER TWO

THURMAN ARNOLD
A Singular and Plural Mind

I heard about Arnold before I ever saw him. On my first day at the Yale Law School -- in September 1935 -- before classes started, someone told me this anecdote: Thurman and his close friend, Charles Clark -- Dean of the school -- joined up for a barbershop visit. Their haircuts were finished at the same time. The proprietor then offered Clark a dab of cologne. After sniffing it, he said: "No thanks. If I came home smelling like that, my wife would think I'd been to a whorehouse." When it was offered to Arnold he said: "Sure, put it on. My wife doesn't know what a whorehouse smells like."

Arnold's personality was informal - unaffected and uninhibited. He personified Popeye's message: "I am what I am." What you saw was what you got. His attitude toward his students was one of equality rather than a master and disciples relationship.

Thurman was easily the most exciting member of the Yale faculty. No one could have been less professorial. Laughter was a constant in his classes. His exceptional sense of humor and whimsy were always topical, sometimes ironical, often instructive, never personal.

Arnold's presence dominated every group in which he was active. This is exemplified in the autobiography of Justice William O. Douglas' earlier years. He was then a colleague of Arnold's on the Yale faculty and his bosom companion at New Haven. The incident occurred at a faculty meeting called by Dean Clark, who was somewhat prissy. It concerned the report of a night watchman that a woman had been seen in the dormitory room of a leading student after midnight, toward the end of his last semester at the school.

15

Clark called a faculty meeting to consider this violation of the school's code of behavior. He felt that expulsion was in order. So did eight other faculty members. Douglas disagreed and then recounted Arnold's exposition of the matter:

> It was Thurman Arnold who tossed the big bomb. Thurman had talked with the student and learned that the girl was dancing in a chorus that was performing locally. She had come to the dormitory for a quiet and decorous hour. The student played Tchaikovsky's *Nutcracker Suite* for her. Then they played a few hands of gin rummy and the young lady was sent back to her hotel.
>
> Thurman addressed the faculty as follows: "All the evidence is in. The campus policemen examined the suite of rooms where all this occurred and have assured us that nothing untoward went on; a victrola and records were in the center of the room; cards were on the floor; there was no evidence of any wrongdoing. Everything is exactly as the boy represented. Now, gentlemen, we have a case here of a perfectly normal, healthy young man who escorted to his dormitory room at near midnight a lovely young lady from the Paramount Chorus. They remain there for an hour and a half. And what do they do? They play Tchaikovsky's *Nutcracker Suite*. That's what they did, and that's *all* they did. In light of this, I say again that we don't really need this boy at Yale, and I say this not because of what he *did* do but because of what he *didn't* do!"[1]

The student was not expelled. He went on to graduate with honors, and before many years, headed his Bar Association.

The incident reflected Arnold's gift for discerning, and his ironical talent for exposing, absurd human behavior without personally disparaging the actor. In the dormitory incident, someone else, feeling as Thurman did, would likely have described the other faculty members as a bunch of damned fools.

Arnold's view of the law school curriculum was that three years was too long; two would do. He also believed that there was an excessive concentration on abstract legal principles. In his mind, the school failed to educate the students about the way the judicial system functioned. In particular, it neglected to introduce the students to the litigation process.

Arnold decided to do something about it. So he introduced a supplement to the first year curriculum studies called "The Moot Court of Appeals" (now known at Yale as the "Thurman Arnold Moot Court of Appeals"). This was a paradigm of real life in the law. Its purpose was to provide concrete experience about the legal process in action -- *i.e.*, the way real cases were conducted.

This is how it operated. The records of actual trials were utilized for arguments before the court. Two students would be assigned to each record. One would be designated to argue for the appellant, the losing party at the trial, the other to defend the decision for the winning side. On the scheduled date, the students would appear to present their arguments.

The court was sometimes comprised in part by real judges; at others by practicing lawyers and faculty members. Arnold, himself, frequently participated, often as the presiding judge. The judges were encouraged to pepper the student litigants with probing questions.

While I was at the law school, two memorable incidents occurred when Thurman presided. One happened in a domestic relations case. The student who appeared for the appellant had been in a squash game accident on the previous day. He came to the court on crutches, with his foot in a cast. In the course of his presentation, he made a point which moved Thurman to inquire: "Counsel, have you got any authority for that proposition?" The student answered by referring to his supporting precedents in the approved judicial manner (*i.e.*, stating the names, jurisdictions and dates of the cases upon which he relied). This sort of dialogue then ensued. Student: "Yes Sir, your Honor, I have *Brown v. Brown*, Georgia, 1861." Thurman next asked: "Have you got anything else?" The student responded: "Yes Sir, *Smith v. Smith*, Virginia, 1862." "Is that all you've got?" Thurman inquired, apparently exasperated. "No Sir, I have one more case -- *Williams v. Williams*, Alabama, 1864." This moved Thurman to exclaim: "What in hell are you anyhow -- a civil war veteran?"

Another Moot Court matter involved the use of a square piece of aluminum in a can of beans instead of the usual round piece. The plaintiff had lacerated his mouth by accidentally including the square piece of metal with his first mouthful of the beans, which he had evidently heated in the can. The student defending the cannery concluded his argument this way: "And I submit, your Honor, the difference between a round piece of tin and a square piece of tin in a can of beans is the difference between Tweedle Dee and Tweedle

Dum." Whereupon Arnold observed: "Counsel, if my memory serves me right, Tweedle Dee and Tweedle Dum were both round."

Arnold's classes were undoubtedly the most popular in the law school's three-year term. They were a continuous source of entertainment for several reasons. First and foremost was his irrepressible talent for pungent, meaningful and often instructive wit, almost always elicited when a student responded to his queries.

Next was the informality of his classes. Arnold simply could not affect the posture of the dominant professor *vis a vis* subordinate students. His classes seemed more like a college bull session among equals.

Finally, and most important, there was his unorthodox teaching style. His method was neither the typical lecture type nor the Socratic method of firing rapid questions around the classroom, designed to test the students' knowledge of assigned materials.

Instead Arnold framed carefully camouflaged questions which could not be answered by the rote system of memorizing the contents of the case book or other materials pertaining to the course. He would posit an intricate problem and call on someone to provide the solution. Thoughtful, analytical responses were required. His inquiries often led to off-the-wall incidents. On one occasion -- during a class on Evidence -- following a student's proffered solution, Arnold declared: "No, No, No -- that's just the very thing you wouldn't do." This moved the student, Clive DuVal (later a respected Virginia State legislator) -- ordinarily quiet and respectful -- to rise to his feet and exclaim: "Ah, the Hell you wouldn't!" No one thought that was out of order. It certainly didn't ruffle Arnold, who simply went on to the next problem.

In another evidence class Arnold was expounding on the dangers of cross-examination, noting that it was unwise to take on an impressive adverse witness. The sooner he was off the stand, the better. But, Arnold said, there might be exceptions. He then told of an incident which occurred in the course of a homicide trial in Laramie during Prohibition days. The defendant was a federal revenue agent, stationed in Colorado. He had chased a well-known bootlegger across the state border and shot him. In defense he called the Governor of Colorado as a character witness. After a question identifying him, he was asked to state his occupation. He answered: "Fortunately, I happen to be the Governor of the great state of Colorado." He then attested to the sterling character of the defendant. Thurman was assisting in the prosecution. To his astonishment, the Wyoming prosecutor undertook to cross-examine the Governor. He asked: "What did you say your occupation was? Again the Governor repeated: "Fortunately, I happen to be the Governor of the great state of Colorado." The prosecutor then asked: "Fortunately for whom?"

Some students played a game connected to Arnold's reputation for an inability to connect names and faces. As he once put it, "There are three things I can never remember; names, faces and I forget the third." This was the game: when Arnold called on X, Y would answer in his place. This was a source of much amusement. My guess is that Arnold was on to the sport, but never betrayed his awareness.

In his mind, there wasn't any magical expertise prerequisite to teaching any particular course. He would take on any subject for which there was a teaching need. However, there was one first-year course which was taught exclusively by Arnold. It was mistakenly made a mandatory first-year course. Called *"Trials, Judgments and Appeals,"* it was actually devoted to litigation strategy and tactics. As such, it was way beyond the comprehension of law school freshmen. It should have been a third year course. Its value was only realized after graduation by students who became trial lawyers. Arnold was probably the only regular faculty member who had engaged in litigation and could effectively teach the subject. It was dropped soon after he left to join the Department of Justice.

Arnold abhorred case books, then and now the standard teaching material at the nation's law schools. These consist of extracts from appellate opinions supposedly incorporating immutable legal principles. He thought such principles could be more readily taught by a textbook and felt that most appellate judges -- lacking litigation backgrounds -- never grasped the significant features of the cases they reviewed.

Nevertheless, since convention dictated that a case book accompany every course, he compiled one with the assistance of J.W. Moore, a young colleague on the law school faculty. It bore the same name as the course -- *"Trials, Judgments and Appeals."* It was unconventional in the sense that it contained an unusual amount of plain-spoken legal commentary, plus carefully chosen opinion excerpts, written in direct, simple language. It was the only one I kept after graduating.

Arnold also detested the arcane, supposedly learned vernacular which so commonly infected legal verbiage. At the outset of almost every one of his courses, he would illustrate the point by quoting the inscription on the main United States Post Office: "Neither snow nor rain nor heat nor gloom of night stays these couriers from the swift completion of their appointed rounds." He would then observe: "All that means is mail will be delivered even if it's raining." (As the blizzard of '96 demonstrated in Washington, D.C., Arnold somehow foresaw that mail might not be delivered even if it's snowing).

The irresistible appeal of Arnold's courses was best exemplified by the students competing for one of the limited places on the Editorial Board of *The Yale Law Journal*. Particularly in the depression years -- when I attended the law school -- 1935-1938 -- selection for the Editorial Board was intensely prized. It could readily mean the difference between a post at a top law firm and a lesser job. This was especially true for Jewish students, like me. With extremely rare exceptions, their worthwhile job opportunities were limited at the time to the very few notable Jewish firms or the government.

Consequently, almost everyone who qualified for the *Journal* competition immediately dropped class attendance to focus on his or her *Journal* assignments. The one exception was Thurman's classes. Their fun and games atmosphere was better than a vaudeville show. Few of us skipped them.

The oddity was that Arnold didn't think much of the *Journal*. As I've noted, each competing student was assigned a faculty consultant. In my year, the student who drew Professor Arnold was really excited, expecting a particularly learned dialogue with Thurman. Instead, Thurman said: "Write whatever you like. You'll find cases that support whatever you say." The student was dumbfounded. He had believed the law to be as definitive as the Ten Commandments. At the time realism was a scarce commodity at the nation's law schools.

Arnold considered the *Journal* part of "legal inflation." In his mind that included the almost incessant stream of legal dissertations and treatises, mostly authored by law professors, and especially the American Law Institute's *"Restatement of the Law"*. That was a huge project, supposedly consisting of scholarly expositions of the governing principles in every field of the law, complete with case citations. They were chiefly written by professors from various law schools. The Institute met every year to ensure that its disquisitions were up to the minute in terms of accuracy. Arnold was right. For all the effort devoted to the Restatement project, my experience indicates that judicial opinions pay precious little attention to them.

Much more important than Arnold's performance on the law school faculty was his magnificent mind, the unparalleled breadth of his knowledge, and his uncanny capacity for discerning the true characteristics of the human condition. This was demonstrated when he published *The Folklore of Capitalism,*[2] while still a member of the Yale faculty, which quickly became a national best seller.

It proved the unparalleled quality of Arnold's capacity to perceive the ways in which the interplay of social ideas, politics and economics creates the organizations which enable society to function. *"Folklore"* is not an attack on capitalism. It is, rather, a penetrating analysis of how the system actually functions.

This is what the peerless book reviewer of the *New York Times*, Ralph Thompson, had to say, among other things, in his review of *Folklore*, on December 21, 1937:

> . . . Some one has already called the book the greatest contribution to political thinking since Marx. Whether it is that or not, it is certainly one of the most penetrating and exciting political studies since Veblen's "Theory of the Leisure Class" appeared in 1890. Mr. Arnold is a professor at the Yale Law School, and known to the public as author of "The Symbols of Government," published last year.

In a continuation of his review of *Folklore*, on December 22, 1937, Thompson said, among other things:

> American myths and rituals, says Mr. Arnold, center about the business man. He is our national hero quite as the scholar was the hero in ancient China and the soldier in imperial Germany. Whatever seems to have an adverse effect upon him will therefore be considered bad and even sinful, indecent and destructive of the national morale.

Following that recognition of the centrality of the American businessman, Arnold made this statement -- of eerie relevance in today's political dialogue:

> . . . A businessman balances his budget. Hence the unbalanced budget which was actually pulling us out of the depression was the source of greater alarm than administrative failures which were actually much more dangerous."[3]

Arnold next voiced this astonishingly prescient comment, considering today's confrontation between our two political parties:

> Coupled with the national heroes in every institutional mythology is the national Devil. Our Devil is governmental interference. Thus we firmly believe in the inherent malevolence of government which interferes with business. Here are people who are not to be trusted -- they are the bureaucrats, the petty tyrants, the destroyers of a rule of law . . . .[4]

Arnold's treatment of the Prohibition Era in *Folklore* exemplifies his talent for recognizing the realities of human affairs. During that "noble experiment," ordinary citizens viewed the crime war between revenue agents and bootleggers as a game of "Cops and Robbers" -- the good guys against the bad guys. "Speakeasies" were supposedly places where illicit beverages were available for partying by racketeers and their "molls."

Actually, respectable pillars of the community were most of their patrons. West 52nd Street in New York was populated by a string of speakeasies featuring highly popular musicians and clienteles of law-abiding citizens. Today's fashionable Club 21 started as an illicit and elite watering hole known then as "Jack and Charlie's." Such establishments could also be found on or near the premises of almost every fraternal organization and college campus.

Arnold, however, saw the bootleggers for what they really were: An economic institution essential to support the national pretense that the public was abstaining from the sin of consuming alcohol. As Arnold explained the paradox:

> NATURALLY, there had to arise some machinery which would keep the spiritual and temporal government marching in step. Such machinery had to be placed behind the scenes, because the elaborate ritual which went on in front had nothing to do with the realities of the situation. This may be illustrated by looking back at the prohibition experiment. When men wanted to pretend that the nation was dry, a vast and complex organization of bootleggers became a necessity in order to meet the demand for liquor. There was a practical task before the social organization which had to be accomplished, *i.e.*, the distribution of liquor. There was also an elaborate ceremony to be celebrated, *i.e.*, that the nation was dry. It was the duty of the spiritual government to denounce the liquor-distributing organization as sinners

and to put a few of them in jail, without however going to such extremes as to stop the actual business of supplying alcohol.

For this duty, the myths of the time were completely adequate. The conceptions of freedom, individualism, and so on, became sacred things which justified the purely ceremonial enforcement of prohibition which the demands of the time required. When it again became recognized that the distribution of liquor was legitimate, the machinery for that purpose became much less complicated. Ritual, learning, literature disappeared. Bartenders, a comparatively decent and law-abiding class, were substituted for bootleggers. The business was done better and more efficiently.[5]

For many years Philip Morris, the world's leading tobacco manufacturer, has been a client of the firm. Our representation of its interests has elicited frequent criticism. Among them was a letter from Professor Sturtevant of Yale to Judge Arnold. Under date of July 1, 1969, Arnold's reply stated in part:

*   *   *   *

I was myself a professor at Yale for eight happy years. I know from experience some of the consequences when a professor gives up hope for a decent society. He becomes morose and irritable. He exhibits a tendency to thumb his nose at people with whom he disagrees under the delusion that this will put them in their place and make them ashamed of themselves. His point of view becomes narrow and even may affect his teaching. I feel, therefore, an obligation to Yale to give you such mental therapy as I can; hence this letter.

One of the great achievements of American constitutional law is the fact that every litigant either before a court or before Congress is entitled to be represented by an attorney. The duty of an attorney is not towards society but towards his client. An attorney is not ethically permitted when presenting his client's case to give his own opinion as to the merits. His duty is solely to make the best presentation he can. . . .

*   *   *   *

Whatever be the ultimate solution of the cigarette problem it will not be furthered by establishing the principle that in any sort of legal controversy either side should be deprived of the services of the best counsel he can obtain.   Your idea is a dangerous doctrine.   Once established, it will sap the very foundations of the American ideal of a fair trial.

Letters like yours which attack the theory of adequate representation by counsel on both sides without judgment as to the merits represent a dangerous tendency which reached its height in the McCarthy era when even University presidents refused to support professors in their right to a fair hearing.[6]

Arnold left Yale in 1938 to become Assistant Attorney General in charge of the Antitrust Division of the Justice Department. During his tenure of "five years, he undertook 215 investigations and launched nearly half of the antitrust litigation since the Sherman Act's inception".[7] He next served two years as a judge of the United States Court of Appeals for the District of Columbia Circuit. He resigned that post in 1945.

After a short stint in private practice with a transportation expert named Arne Wiprud, he persuaded Abe Fortas in January 1946, to form the brand new law partnership of Arnold & Fortas. When Paul Porter joined them in mid-1947, the firm's name became Arnold, Fortas & Porter.

Not long after the firm was founded, the value of Arnold's broad conversance with history and the world in which we live was displayed in an unlikely context. It was a case in which the Judge represented *Playboy Magazine*, then in its infancy. Although Arnold doesn't mention it in his autobiography, I recall a statement -- perhaps from the attorney who referred the case to Arnold -- that it was precipitated by the town leadership of the site of Grace Metalious' "Peyton Place," at the time considered a lascivious work, in the hope of regaining its respectability. Along with several more risqué publications, *Playboy* was carried by a Vermont newsdealer. He was indicted for violation of a Vermont statute prohibiting pornography. It condemned the "publication" or "circulation" of "a magazine . . . which contains obscene, lewd or indecent . . . pictures". On behalf of *Playboy*, Arnold promptly filed a motion to dismiss, which the trial court just as promptly certified without opinion to the Supreme Court of Vermont.

His brief for *Playboy* was a classic. It consisted entirely of his personal output. No one else in the office contributed as much as a

comma. He shamed the Supreme Court into remanding the case to the
trial court on technical grounds, without venturing an opinion. At that
point the Attorney General *"nolle prossed"* the indictment (*i.e.*
withdrew it). In short, Arnold won the case without a trial, or even a
stated reason for its termination.

What Arnold's brief did was first congratulate the state prosecutors
for their previously unbroken history of forbearance from the
prosecution of obscenity cases:

> We think it is a tribute to the civilized tolerance of Vermont
> prosecutors that this Court has never before been called on to define the
> standards of obscenity and to differentiate between risque or daring
> literary material and obscene material. The decision of such an issue is
> fraught with such danger to free speech and creative literature that
> elsewhere it has often resulted in absurd censorship.[8]

Arnold then argued that because "obscenity statutes represent a
moral taboo, rather than a rational process, the field of pornography is
full of curious contradictions".[9] These he proceeded to outline at some
length:

> . . . For example, distinguished artists are not prone to committing or
> assisting in the commission of ordinary crime. But the literature of
> obscenity contains some of our greatest names. Mark Twain, whose
> dialogue called *"1601"* is today widely but secretly circulated, wrote to
> a Cleveland librarian, "If there is a decent word findable in it is because
> I overlooked it." Great painters have lent their talents to producing
> erotic material so extreme that it had to be secretly circulated. Such
> names include Hogarth, Rowlandson, Aubrey Beardsley, Rubens,
> Rembrandt, Jan Steen, Michelangelo, Raphael, Tintoretto, Titian,
> Boucher and Rodin. In music Gilbert and Sullivan produced an obscene
> musical play called *"The Sod's Opera"*. Yet Sullivan was the man who
> wrote *"Onward Christian Soldiers"*. The list could be extended
> indefinitely. One of the most widely read pornographic articles was
> written by Benjamin Franklin; another star in this galaxy was Eugene
> Field.
> There is a certain high comedy in the contradictions which roam
> throughout the area of pornography. At the same time that men insist
> on suppressing obscene literature and punishing those who write it they
> enthusiastically go on collecting it and preserving it in libraries of
> priceless value. The Catholic Church is a leader in the fight against
> obscenity. Yet it maintains in the Vatican library the most famous

collection of erotica in the world, consisting of 25,000 volumes and 100,000 prints. Ralph Ginzburg in his recent book states that among libraries the Vatican erotica "is probably most accessible to the nonprofessional bibliophile". Erotic material was collected by that good church man J.P. Morgan. Henry E. Huntington, the railway magnate, had the greatest collection in the West. Yale, Princeton and Harvard have collections of erotica.

Access to this material is ordinarily made difficult. But this is not true of the Library of Congress which has the largest collection of erotica in the United States. Anyone over sixteen may see the books. In addition, the Union catalogue of the Library of Congress publicly lists existing erotica works giving information which could be used by any pornographic bookseller. Logically it might seem that the Library was contributing to the crime of obscenity but no sensible man would want to change its present practices. Thus the moral problem of obscenity is as full of inconsistencies and contradictions as was another moral crusade, i.e., the enforcement of prohibition where good citizens wanted liquor and prohibition at the same time.[10]

The unorthodox, humanistic approach of the *Playboy* brief reflected Arnold's normal method of dissecting a legal problem. It was another demonstration of his extraordinary insight of the ways in which man's ideas, talents, and political practices interface to form organizations which gratify his moral, social, artistic and physiological needs.

I should add that but for Arnold, Fortas and Porter, *Playboy* might have faded into oblivion. Shortly after the magazine started publication, it applied for a temporary second-class mailing permit. The Post Office Department soon intervened by a unilateral action, without hearing, in which it declared *Playboy* "unmailable" by reason of obscenity. This revoked its temporary second-class permit and precluded issuance of a regular permit of that class. Without a second-class permit, which carries the lowest postage rate, a magazine cannot prosper, if it can survive at all. Absent such a permit, no publication can marshall a sufficient number of subscribers to attract enough advertising revenue to make a go of it.

A Chicago attorney, Maurice Rosenfield, brought *Playboy's* problem to Judge Arnold, who turned it over to Bill McGovern, an outstanding trial lawyer who had served with him at the Antitrust Division. Bill promptly filed suit and obtained a temporary restraining order prohibiting the Postmaster General from interfering with *Playboy's* access to second-class mails.[11] Since restraining orders are valid for only ten days, Bill simultaneously filed a motion for a preliminary injunction which, upon entry, is valid until final judgment. Following a series of protracted formal and informal proceedings on that motion, in and out of court, *Playboy* received the necessary permit in August of 1958. The complaint was accordingly withdrawn.

There was one drawback to the case. Rosenfield had promised that if we got the second-class permit, the centerfold star of the issue first blocked from the mails would attend our Christmas party. She never showed up.

Besides his extraordinary perception of contemporary reality, Arnold also had an uncanny vision of the future effect of the introduction of innovative ideas or events. The first investigative hearings to attract a national audience on public television were conducted by a Special Senate Committee to Investigate Organized Crime in Interstate Commerce.[12] It became known as "The Kefauver Crime Committee," after the name of its chairman, Senator Estes Kefauver of Tennessee.

It was designed to put on a sensational show which would attract a wide audience. It proved a spectacular success. Noting that it paved the way for the infamous McCarthy hearings, Arnold addressed the pernicious nature of the practice with uncanny foresight in a June 1961 article for *Atlantic Monthly*.[13]

In light of the *Menendez Brothers* and *O.J. Simpson* trials, and the Iran/Contra hearings, the article has startling pertinence today, notably these excerpts:

> The production put on by the Kefauver Committee on crime is unquestionably the best show of the year. My introduction to it was during the examination of Mr. Frank Costello. I missed an entire morning at the office, fascinated and at the same time appalled by the dramatic quality of this new form of public inquisition.

> Mr. Costello was not visible. Instead the camera focused on his hands, which constantly moved and twitched in a decidedly guilty way . . . . It soon appeared that Costello had started as a bootlegger. It became equally apparent that the questions were not for the purpose of finding out anything. The committee already had the information. . . .

*   *   *

Trials in our courts of justice are public but the audience is so limited that the ordinary housewife cannot see the show because, as we go to press, cameras are still banned. I suggest that if this rule cannot be changed, all the judge has to do is to hold a trial like that of Alger Hiss in Yankee Stadium. By this method, while the judge could not get television rights he would still have quite a crowd in any *cause célèbre*. And since judges do not have to run for office as often as Senators, this minor disadvantage creates no real injustice.

*   *   *

Today the utility of this device in getting rid of subversive ideas on the screen, in the theater, on college campuses, is as yet unexplored. Anyone who has been on television knows the camera fright involved in a first appearance. College professors are shy and retiring folk. When their opinions are inquired into before twenty million listeners by an investigator experienced and skilled in television showmanship, millions of American housewives are going to enjoy the entrancing spectacle of seeing them go to pieces before their eyes with twitching hands, nervous voices, hesitating answers, and similar evidences of guilt which made the ancient trial by ordeal the effective instrument that it was.

*   *   *

Yet in spite of these many and obvious advantages, I am prepared to argue that the entire show should be taken off the road and that hereafter no investigator should ever be permitted to use the long arm of a government subpoena to force any witness, however unsavory, to confess (or discuss) his sins before twenty million people. . . .

The thing which I believe is overlooked by those who argue that television is a legitimate extension of our traditional public hearing is this. The reason that a criminal trial is public is not to obtain the maximum publicity for judges or prosecutors. It was not intended to make a *cause célèbre* out of criminal prosecutions. It is public for the protection of the accused against star-chamber methods, and for the protection of the public against secret deals and alliances. The notion that since a criminal trial is usually entertaining it should be so staged as to provide the greatest entertainment to the greatest number is not an American tradition. A criminal hearing should not be a star chamber. It is equally important that it should not be a circus.

*   *   *

The vice of this television proceeding is not in the way this particular committee conducted it, but in the proceeding itself. Any tribunal which takes on the trappings and aspects of a judicial hearing, particularly where there is compulsory examination of witnesses, must conform to our judicial traditions, or sooner or later it will develop into a monstrosity that demands reform. Those traditions are:

1. It must be public and at the same time not a device for publicity.

2. It must protect the innocent even at the cost of letting the guilty escape.

Television has no place in such a picture. For witnesses it is an ordeal not unlike the third degree. On those who sit as judges it imposes the demoralizing necessity of also being actors. For the accused it offers no protection whatever. Former Federal Judge Simon H. Rifkind recently said that our judicial procedure, "forged through the generations to the single end that issues shall be impartially determined on relevant evidence alone, works fairly well in all cases but one -- the celebrated cause. *As soon as the cause célèbre comes in, the judges and lawyers no longer enjoy a monopoly. They have a partner in the enterprise, and that partner is the press.*" I would add that when television is utilized in investigations or trials, *causes célèbre* will increase like guinea pigs and still another partner will be added - to wit, the mob.[14]

* * *

The lesson which Arnold taught should be learned by today's proponents of televising courtroom proceedings. But I doubt that it will. As the Simpson trial demonstrated, the process holds too much promise of rewards for the participants and the media. Who will ever forget the televised chase of the white bronco along the Los Angeles freeway? National Public Radio recently reported that 50 books have already been published by everyone and anyone remotely connected to the Simpson case, with more on the way. Actual and prospective authors range from jurors and peripherally related characters on up to the lawyers on both sides. The temptations flowing from the presence of cameras in the courtroom of a notorious trial are irresistible.

One of Arnold's notable talents as a courtroom lawyer was his adroit use of irony to put the issues of his case in perspective. It is well known that *Peters v. Hobby*, 394 U.S. 331 (1955) was the only case in which the Supreme Court wrote an opinion about the monstrous loyalty program enforced during the Truman and Eisenhower administrations. As outlined in the succeeding CHAPTER FOURTEEN, the Court ruled for Peters on a trivial technicality which did not address the grave constitutional issues it involved, much to the disgust of Arnold and Porter, who had shared the argument in the case.

Peters specialized in nutrition and metabolism as a professor at the Yale Medical School. He became a consultant to the Surgeon General, devoting approximately ten days a year to that function. The facts of the case were a travesty of constitutional requirements of due process of law. The only testimony of record was highly favorable to Peters, reflecting the experience of a host of witnesses who knew him well. Nevertheless, for some unfathomable reason, on the basis of worthless, undisclosed evidence, Peters was suspended from government service for three years on the ground that there was "reasonable doubt" of his loyalty to the United States.

After summarizing those facts, Arnold began his Supreme Court argument with the following observation:

> ". . . . Thus the Department of Health, Education and Welfare was saved in the nick of time from a danger that had existed, apparently since 1949. They were saved by a secret informant or secret informants, some of whom were unknown even to the Board. It was apparent that Dr. Peters had the ability to fool the eminent people he had known all his life, and without this secret informant, he might still be pouring Soviet theory on metabolism and nutrition into the attentive and gullible ear of the Surgeon General of the United States."[15]

There was no limit to Arnold's gift for wit and humor. He was not only infused with an inimitable and unorthodox sense of whimsy but was a master of the ad lib. In retrospect, I can't recall that I ever saw him laugh or even smile. No matter what he said, he was always deadpan. There was just a frequent twinkle in his eyes.

Arnold's flair for whimsy came into play in 1946 at an inaugural dinner to start the Yale Law School Alumni Association of Washington, D.C. Lloyd Cutler and I were asked to organize it. For a major drawing card, we immediately chose Arnold to preside as toastmaster. To enlarge the audience, the invitation also advised that wives, husbands and friends of alumni were welcome. It worked. We had a full house. The evening was a roaring success. Judge Arnold was at his best. He opened the proceedings by announcing: "We are gathered here tonight to perpetuate the myth that higher education is possible at Yale." Next a quartet of four former Whiffenpoofs, a world renowned Yale singing group, entertained a delighted audience with familiar college favorites. After hearing the quartet, Arnold observed, "It might have been better to arrange that our four scheduled speakers deliver their remarks simultaneously."

The principal speaker was Justice Douglas. In presenting him, Arnold referred to a Supreme Court opinion issued a week earlier -- Douglas writing for the Court. The case had ruled that the exclusion of women from grand juries was unconstitutional. Characterizing the opinion as a landmark in the law, Arnold called particular attention to one sentence of "immortal significance" and urged the audience to listen carefully as he quoted: "The truth is that the two sexes are not fungible."[16] Arnold then declared, absolutely poker-faced: "Now, any of you who have been entertaining any different ideas had better get unfunged."

Not long afterward, Arnold was to deliver the main address at an important luncheon function held at New Haven on the law school premises. Abe, his wife, Carol Agger, and I accompanied Thurman. He drew a giant crowd. His speech consisted solely of verbatim readings from the Law School's curriculum. This described the courses offered, from the first to the third year, and the Professors who taught them. Arnold read the text without changing a word, but with interspersed inflections, pauses and emphases. From start to finish every single person in attendance was convulsed with uncontrollable laughter. He had a way of injecting absurdity into ordinary narrations if they were infected by the slightest innuendo of overstatement or self-importance.

Arnold was a superbly educated man, wholly apart from his schooling. In the course of numerous conversations with him, it became evident that he had read and absorbed an astonishing body of significant books written from classical to modern times. Not that he made a fetish of demonstrating his knowledge. Quite the contrary. It just emerged from conversational references. Knowing that he was a full-time hands-on lawyer who personally wrote the briefs in many of his cases, I asked how he managed so much outside reading. He said he was usually up with a book at 4 a.m. each morning.

The depth of his familiarity with the evolution of civilization is illustrated by another excerpt from *Folklore*. He there spoke of the seventeenth-century condemnation of the use of a newly discovered anti-fever drug -- quinine -- by the University of Paris medical faculty. The faculty then occupied a position in medicine not unlike the position of the Food and Drug Administration in government today. As Arnold stated:

> The remedy for fever established by the learning of the time was the art of bleeding to rid the body of those noxious vapors and humors in the blood which were the root of the illness. Of course, patients sickened and died in the process, but they were dying for a medical principle, so it was thoroughly worthwhile. To depart from that principle would have the same effect on human health as the failure to shoot strikers occupying the plant of an industrial concern in a sit down strike, or as the tampering with the Supreme Court of the United States has today on social well-being.

*   *   *

> Such were the attitudes of those learned in medicine in 1638 when the Jesuits in Peru discovered quinine. The cures which were accomplished by the use of this drug were marvelous, due in part to its own merit and in part to the fact that patients escaped the bleeding process. It was natural that such a radical departure from established precedent should be viewed with alarm. Therefore, it was not surprising that the University of Paris declared the use of quinine unconstitutional and banned the drug as dangerous.

*   *   *

> However, it was more than a medical problem. It was a moral problem which affected the character, the freedom, and the homes of everyone. Fortunately, the unlearned people of the time, like those of today, were constantly forgetting the great moral issues of the future for the practical comfort of the moment. Hence the use of quinine eventually became common. The significant thing, however, was that it had to be introduced by a quack who concealed it in a curious compound of irrelevant substances.[17]

Because of his authorship of *Folklore*, and his economically creative administration of the Antitrust Division, Arnold enjoyed some esteem as an economist. One day, shortly after the end of World War II, I was in the Judge's office when he answered a phone call.   In concluding the conversation, he said: "I haven't the faintest idea but one thing I will guarantee; all the economists will be wrong."

I asked him what that was all about. He said someone from Time Magazine had asked for his estimate of the extent of unemployment following World War II. There was genuine concern that it would be extensive when the round-the-clock war plants were converted to civilian production. Some economists' predictions of the anticipated unemployment ranged as high at 15,000,000 people. Arnold's comment proved to be 100% accurate. The pent-up demand for civilian goods was so intense that a labor shortage developed.

Among his other skills, Judge Arnold's marvelous way with verse would have been envied by W.S. Gilbert. I quote below a delightful example he composed while a student at Harvard Law School in 1914. The verse addresses the most esoteric subject in the entire common law, known as Conflict of Laws.   Its principles are supposed to determine the applicable law when an issue involves disputes between persons in different jurisdictions or transactions crossing the lines of two or more jurisdictions, each with differing rules on the legal questions. Arnold poetically wrote of the resulting confusion:

CONFLICT OF LAWS

Conflict of Laws with its peppery seasoning,
Of pliable, scarcely reliable reasoning,
Dealing with weird and impossible things,
Such as marriage and domicil, bastards and kings,
All about courts without jurisdiction
Handing out misery, pain and affliction,
Making defendant, for reasons confusing,
Unfounded, ill-grounded, but always amusing,
Liable one place but not in another,
Son of his father, but not of his mother,
Married in Sweden, but only a lover in
Pious dominions of Great Britain's sovereign.
Blithely upsetting all we've been taught,
Rendering futile our methods of thought,
Till Reason, tottering down from her throne,
And Common Sense, sitting, neglected, alone,
Cry out despairingly, "Why do you hate us?

> Give us once more our legitimate status."
> Ah, Students, bewildered, don't grasp at such straws,
> But join in the chorus of Conflict of Laws.

CHORUS

> Beale, Beale, wonderful Beale,
> Not even in verse can we tell how we feel,
> When our efforts so strenuous,
> To over-throw,
> Your reasoning tenuous,
> Simply won't go.
> For the law is a system of
> wheels within wheels
> Invented by Sayres and Thayers and Beales
> With each little wheel
> So exactly adjusted,
> That if it goes haywire
> The whole thing is busted.
> So Hail to Profanity,
> Good-bye to Sanity,
> Lost if you stop to consider or pause.
> On with the frantic, romantic, pedantic,
> Effusive, abusive, illusive, conclusive,
> Evasive, persuasive, Conflict of Laws.[18]

Although he consciously tried not to display any sentimentality, Arnold was in fact the kindest and most generous of men. He had no reverence for money. By way of example, after my first three years with the firm my wife and I realized we needed a larger home. We were then renting a tiny one-bath home for ourselves and our first child, plus a live-in housekeeper and a dog. Closet space was so limited that cartons absorbed every inch of otherwise unused space. Another baby was on the way. A more spacious house was an absolute necessity. We decided to buy one.

Lacking the cash for a down payment, I decided to try my luck at obtaining financial help from the firm. This led me to tell Judge Arnold that I was thinking of buying a house. He said: "Fine, wonderful, good idea." I cut in: "I'm not sure you understand, Judge, I'm thinking about the possibility of borrowing the down payment from the firm." He replied: "Oh, don't bother Abe and Paul. Let's see, I can put a mortgage on my ranch in Wyoming and I can borrow some money on my life insurance. Sure, go ahead!" He meant every word of it. But, of course, I couldn't accept his incredibly kind offer. I managed to borrow the needed funds at a bank.

I recall two comments illustrative of his attitude toward money. "The peculiar thing about money is that the people who need it most never seem to have any." and "I never saw the day when I couldn't live on 10 percent more than I was making." In a word, Arnold just lacked interest in the accumulation of material wealth. It may not be a stretch to think that his attitude toward monetary matters subliminally permeated our office during his time with us. If so, it may have been the shield that protected us from the internal conflicts about compensation which so often afflicted other firms.

I don't mean to imply that Thurman had no understanding of money. Acquiring it was just not one of his passions. He readily invested in the stock market, usually on the recommendation of a friend of his in Richmond, Virginia. This afforded another illustration of his generosity. Whenever the Judge had a tip, he passed the information on to his colleagues, including me. Whenever possible, I would buy a little of whatever he recommended. One of his recommendations proved extremely rewarding. So much so that I paid a special visit to the Judge to tell him how grateful I was for the profit I had made. The Judge replied: "That's good but I lost money on it." I asked: "How did that happen?" He replied: "I didn't buy enough."

Arnold's kindness and humor were not limited to the office. When I hosted a surprise party for my wife, Luna on our 25th anniversary, Mr. and Mrs. Arnold were, of course, among the invited guests. Their gift to us was an exquisite, antique silver teapot. In presenting it, he said; as nearly as I can recall:

> "We would be so grateful if you would take this off our hands. We've been wasting so much time and energy trying to find a place for it in our house, but we just can't find one. Please do us this favor.

At the same function, Paul presented Luna with a Croix de Guerre. She had been proclaiming for years that she deserved it for tolerating me.

As I think back on Judge Arnold, I'm reminded of a comment by Dean Acheson -- then Secretary of State -- when he served as a Toastmaster at a District of Columbia fund-raiser for President Truman

Frances Arnold in her treasured garden

during the 1948 campaign. In the course of his introduction of the President, Acheson said:

> The remarkable thing about Harry Truman is that he can look at the world and see what he is looking at.

The same was true of Thurman Arnold, perhaps in fuller measure.

Arnold's most important legacy was his everyday, natural way of life. It set a standard of decency for human behavior. When working on a project with others, give them credit for the good things that happen; take the blame for those that turn sour. Never pass the buck. Never cry over spilled milk. Never expect human beings to be any better than they really are. Of course, thinking of those concepts as a code for living and practicing them do not necessarily coincide. But they are surely worth trying.

It's impossible to write about Judge Arnold without mentioning his wonderful relationship with his wife, Frances. Dinner at their house was a coveted invitation. It always meant an evening of pure pleasure. Mrs. Arnold was gracious and gifted with a bland imperturbability, plus a wit of her own. This was usually displayed in gentle banter with the Judge -- a source of amusement for whoever was in their company.

I remember one incident after she mentioned how much they had enjoyed dinner the evening before at the British Embassy. This moved Thurman to comment that he hoped those present had taken notice of the fact that they moved socially within the highest diplomatic circles. Her reply went something like this: "You needn't have mentioned it, Thurman.   Everybody who's anybody knows we're invited everywhere."

Following Judge Arnold's death, she moved back to Laramie. To my surprise, she and Luna then carried on a correspondence which lasted until Mrs. Arnold's recent death. She was 99 years old. Her letters were handwritten and completely lucid to the very end.

Abe Fortas in his typical office mode

CHAPTER THREE

ABE FORTAS
Elder Prodigy

Although the youngest faculty member at the Yale Law School, Abe was not open to friendship with the students. Some professors, among them Harry Shulman, Myres ("Mac") MacDougall, Fred Rodell and Thomas ("Tommy") Emerson related to students on a first-name basis. I doubt that any student ever established such a relationship with Abe.

What he lacked in amiability, Abe made up for in brilliance. As I've said, he was an incomparable appellate advocate. The judiciary knew it as well as the bar. This was evidenced in two renowned cases which he argued on assignments by the courts. *Gideon v. Wainwright*[1] and *Durham v. United States*.[2] Abe's unsurpassed intellect, sensitivity and resourcefulness in the appellate arena were captured in a single sentence of his argument in *Gideon*. The question was a defendant's constitutional right to counsel in all state felony prosecutions. The Sixth Amendment of the Constitution expressly guarantees such a right only in the federal courts. At the time, federal constitutional law guaranteed that right only in state capital cases.

Clarence Gideon, a penniless defendant had been denied counsel during his trial in a Florida state court on a felony charge of breaking and entering. Over his objection, he had been forced to represent himself. After his conviction was affirmed by the Florida Supreme Court, he personally drafted and filed a petition for review by the Supreme Court of the United States. The Court agreed to hear the case and assigned Fortas to appear for Gideon.

A minority of the Court led by Justice Hugo Black had been pressing the proposition that the "equal protection" clause of the 14th

37

Amendment -- the post-Civil War provision aimed at racism -- guaranteed everyone the full panoply of protection in relation to state action that the Bill of Rights -- the first ten amendments to the Constitution -- afforded *vis a vis* the federal government. During the Gideon argument, Black tried to induce Fortas to make that proposition the essence of his claim that Gideon was entitled to counsel. Fortas declined, stating:

> I like that argument that you have made so eloquently. But I cannot as an advocate make that argument because the Court has rejected it so many times. I hope you never cease making it.[3]

Abe won the case on the more limited ground that the right to counsel was guaranteed by the incorporation of the Sixth Amendment in the due process clause of the 14th Amendment, without reference to other elements of the Bill of Rights.

Abe's reputation had earlier been recognized in the *Durham* case by the Federal Appeals Court for the District of Columbia. It involved the criteria for an insanity defense to a criminal charge. At that time, the almost universal requirement for establishing such a defense was the mid-19th century English precept known as the McNaghten Rule. It required proof that the defendant did not know right from wrong.

Durham had been charged with breaking and entering. His record disclosed three incarcerations in the District of Columbia's mental hospital, St. Elizabeth's. He was nevertheless convicted in the face of psychiatric testimony that he was "medically insane," but not necessarily unaware of the difference between right and wrong. He received a sentence of three to ten years imprisonment.

On appeal another attorney had argued that reversal was necessary because the trial court should have required the prosecution to prove sanity beyond a reasonable doubt because the proof showed "some mental disorder." The court then ordered the case reargued and assigned Fortas as Durham's counsel.

Fortas had a keen interest in psychiatry. He was Vice President of the Washington School of Psychiatry and a Trustee of the William Allanson White Foundation. He argued that the McNaghten Rule was obsolete in light of modern psychiatric medicine. The court agreed. It adopted Abe's argument that an accused could not be convicted "if his unlawful act was the product of a mental disease or a mental defect."[4]

The decision aroused considerable public and professional criticism. There were visions of hordes of criminals turned loose on the streets of the nation's capital as a result of this decision.[5] As usual, Arnold's reaction was more realistic. He predicted that the decision would have no effect on the administration of criminal law, and that Durham, an habitual criminal, would be back in jail within a year. He proved right on both counts.[6]

Within the firm, Abe had an interest in its administration. Neither Arnold nor Porter cared one whit about that phase of the organization. Nor were their talents suited for it. That made Abe the unquestioned manager of the firm. As I wrote for the *Yale Law Report* in an issue memorializing Abe:

> His partners recognized Abe as the firm's leader from the day it was founded in 1946 until he left to join the Supreme Court in 1965. His ability to organize and direct a law firm was almost uncanny. He had never previously been associated with one. However, Abe just seemed instinctively to know how to conduct relations with clients; the way in which the work of the firm should be processed; and how its internal business affairs should be conducted.[7]

Like his partners, Abe's motivation in the practice of law was not dominated by mercenary considerations. Principle invariably dictated his decisions. As I further wrote in the same article:

> Principle was never compromised by material considerations. At least one large client severed relations with the firm because of hostility to the firm's repeated defense of victims of the "loyalty" program fomented by McCarthy. The deterrent effect on potential clients was readily accepted.

> On a previous occasion, a major client of Abe's had vigorously criticized Paul Porter for accepting President Truman's designation as spokesman for the reinstitution of wage/price legislation (following the President's famous Turnip Day speech at the 1948 Democratic Convention). Paul consulted Abe about it. Abe told Paul to respond with a vigorous message that the retention of our services did not carry with it any censorship privileges.

> The continuing priority of principle over prosperity was manifested many years later when LBJ was in the White House. One of the

nation's largest corporations had been brought under criminal investigation by the Antitrust Division. The target soon offered Abe a handsome retainer. He promptly undertook discussions directed towards its representation in relation to the grand jury proceedings. When told that such representation would not be his function, Abe called a meeting of three of his younger partners, including me. He described the situation and asked for our opinion. We all sensed that a pipeline to the White House was the object of the proffered retainer. Each of us reacted negatively. Abe said, "I feel exactly the same way." That ended that matter.[8]

These instances demonstrate that Abe's concern about the firm's finances and, perhaps his own, was secondary to his instinct against compromising the firm's integrity for material gains. Nevertheless, regardless of the firm's continued prosperity, I doubt that he ever overcame his underlying financial anxiety about money. Unlike Thurman, he never exhibited any interest in investments. I recall one indicative example of that aspect of his persona. On his desk there was a large stack of $25.00 U.S. Baby Bonds, carrying a modest interest rate, but guaranteed by the federal government. The pile was high enough to represent a fairly sizable sum.

Outside the law, Abe's passion was music. Kalman made the point eloquently:

> . . . Fortas was at his most likeable with musicians. Carol Agger [Abe's wife] and her brother, a musicologist, had persuaded him to begin playing the violin again after the war, and he numbered Isaac Stern, Alexander Schneider, and Walter Trampler among his closest friends. "I remember seeing this urbane . . . gentleman have an entirely unurbane and unabashed enthusiasm for music," Stern recalled. "It was such a passionate and wholly unambiguous, unashamed love affair with music. . ."[9]

Space limitations force me to exclude many recollections of the founding fathers. However, I've got to mention one only indirectly related to the firm, because it yielded so much pleasure to my wife, Luna. Abe's influence with LBJ is hard to minimize. It has been written about so often and in such depth that it would be redundant for me to dwell on it.

It's common knowledge that Abe was responsible for LBJ's establishment of the National Council On the Arts in 1965 and the selection of Roger Stevens, Abe's friend and client as its head.[10] What is not public knowledge is that Abe was responsible for the selection of my wife to serve as Secretary to the Council. Abe not only liked her, but knew of her sure grasp of Washington's political ways. She had served Clinton Anderson during his service in the House, in the Cabinet as Secretary of Agriculture, and three full terms in the Senate. For a time, Stevens and Luna represented the entire government complement of the Council. They worked out of the White House, or more accurately, the Executive Office Building.

No job could have better suited Luna. She had always been celebrity conscious. During her ten years with the Council, it included leaders in every field of the visual and performing arts, literature and architecture. Among those I remember were: Issac Stern, Agnes DeMille, Gregory Peck, Charlton Heston, Sidney Poitier, Robert Merrill, Marion Anderson, James Earl Jones and Duke Ellington. Luna loved the job. She became known as the Council's Jewish Mother.

There is one Council episode I must mention. At a meeting in Los Angeles, the hosts were Charlton Heston and Gregory Peck, the incoming and outgoing Chairman of the Screen Actors Guild. They were greeting the attendees as they arrived for the first session. As Luna entered, she breezed past them, exclaiming, "Where's Paul Newman?" Peck nudged Heston and said: "I guess we're not good enough."

Inside the office, Abe's attitude was altogether different -- the pure personification of the totally focused professional man. But in my opinion, Kalman's analysis of Abe's relationships with his colleagues is unjust. She has a penchant for quoting anonymous sources critical of Fortas to depict him as a despot. In her words: "'he ran the place,' one lawyer remembered. 'It was Abe Fortas and Abe Fortas alone . . . . He was managing partner and he was senior partner, he was everything.'"[11] Contrary to her intimation that Abe dictated all hiring by the firm, given his druthers, Abe would not have hired a number of lawyers whom Thurman and Paul sponsored. On her own, Kalman volunteers: "Fortas lacked an inner compunction to treat people with civility."[12]

She uses another unidentified source to emphasize his displeasure when some of the younger partners asked for a "percentage of the firm's earnings -- [h]e said it ruined his Christmas."[13] If that was

really said, Abe may have been speaking in jest. I was among those
younger partners and sensed no such reaction. My recollection is that
Abe agreed and suggested that the percentages be calculated in the
exact ratios of each individual's compensation during the prior year to
the firm's net income. This was acceptable to me.

Kalman next quotes another confidential source as follows:

> . . . "Every law firm has a taskmaster who is a son of a bitch," another
> said and he thought Fortas took on the role. He "would gather all the
> young lawyers and hold little training sessions in which he'd read the
> riot act to us about being careful." A third recalled "He'd lecture us on
> how to do our work."[14]

Anyone who seriously complained about these sessions lacked
perspective about their purpose. They were more in the nature of
exercise classes to keep all of the firm's lawyers on their toes. I
attended many of them. The lyrics might vary but the melody was
always the same: the output of the firm was diminishing; the quality
of our work was deteriorating. We'd better get up to snuff before the
firm lost its reputation for excellence. There was never any talk about
billings, income, or any other material considerations. The meetings
were more like a football coach's pregame pep talks to his team.

Later, after Abe left for the Court, Paul realized that neither he nor
Thurman could maintain the custom. So, he assigned me to write a
"Manual for Associates." It focused solely on the mechanics and art
of practicing law and the methods of making sure that we produced the
best possible product. There wasn't a word about building the firm's
income or developing business.

Kalman seems to me to be more than a little confused in her analysis
of the character, temperament and *modus operandi* of Abe Fortas.
Speaking of him, she said, "No one who knew him professionally . . .
nor any of his friends . . . ever claimed to understand him."[15] Based
on my long-term experience with him, dating back to law school, I
don't think he was all that difficult to understand.   As I saw Abe, what
was deemed to be a distant attitude toward his colleagues was a product
of his elevation to high positions at a very young age. He went directly
from law school to the Yale law faculty. By the time he was 32, he
was Under Secretary of the Interior. In other words, he was a true
"whiz kid." This impelled him to assume an air of dignity when
dealing with subordinates and strangers, usually older than he. This

soon became second nature to him. Add to the mix Abe's sense of infallibility, his perfectionism and aversion to inferior performance and you pretty well have his makeup within the firm.

By way of example, consider Abe's position as General Counsel of the Bituminous Coal Division. He was its actual head, although a man named Howard Gray was its nominal director. The Division's job, prescribed by the Bituminous Coal Act of 1936, was to set binding *minimum* prices for soft coal for every mine in the country.

For administrative purposes, the Act divided the bituminous coal producing areas into 11 geographical districts. Each was represented by a semi-official board. Its members were chiefly mining company executives who were supposed to look after the interests of their geographic constituents before the Division.

The statute was a payoff to John L. Lewis, Chief of the United Mine Workers ("the UMW"), for his support of F.D.R. in 1932 and 1936. The soft coal industry had developed such huge production capacity during WWI that it had an enormous surplus when the war ended. Coal piled up at the mineheads in such huge quantities that it had to be moved out to permit access to the mines. Typically, it was loaded on to railcars and shipped with no specified destination. It became known as "distress" coal which sold for anything a buyer would offer. Of course, this radically reduced the miners' wages. The statute was meant to relieve that hardship.

Abe's job was wicked. The law had a four year sunset provision. When he took over, two years had already been wasted by a seven member predecessor commission. This consisted of the UMW's incompetent designees, who had bungled their price-fixing function by setting prices without prior hearings. This invited a series of court injunctions which had restrained enforcement of the program.

The undertaking confronting Abe was enormous. It was to establish minimum f.o.b. mine prices for every ton of soft coal that moved, by every means of transportation, for every destination and for every end-use. The project was to be accomplished in one monster evidentiary hearing, called General Docket No. 15, after which the prices had to be supported by findings of fact and conclusions of law. At that time the nation's industrial plant was fueled almost exclusively by soft coal.

Because of the agency's mission, representatives of the coal producers and union officials walked in and out of the agency as if it were a candy store. Pretty soon they were on a first name basis with everyone on the staff except Abe Fortas. He kept his distance. All outsiders -- many more than twice his age -- always called him "Mr. Fortas."

The clue to Kalman's misconceived recital that "Abe lacked an inner compunction to treat people with civility" can be found in the earlier passages of her biography addressed to the Division. She speaks as follows of Abe's splendid relationships with his staff at that agency:

> Fortas won from his subordinates the loyalty and commitment that Jerome Frank had received from his underlings at the AAA. Morale in the division was extraordinarily high. "Fortas certainly installed a sense of industry on the part of the guys," Norman Diamond observed. Harold Leventhal thought Fortas "a peerless leader." David Lloyd Kreeger could never reconcile stories that later circulated in Washington about Fortas as a private practitioner with the Fortas he knew at the Bituminous Coal Division. "He would come in, and he'd put his arm around you, and he'd say, 'Dave, how are we doing on that,' because I tended to be a last minute worker under pressure," Kreeger remembered. "Never a cruel boss, never a sharp tongue. He was very nice to work with."

*   *   *

> Fortas's days in the coal division remained special to him, as they did to those who worked with him. "I have never felt more keenly the happiness which comes only through feeling that one's close associates and fellow workers are friends and companions," he told Howard Gray when he left the division. Although he easily slipped into flattery, Fortas was probably speaking truthfully here. The Bituminous Coal Division had provided his first opportunity since the *Yale Law Journal* to serve as absolute boss, and he had exercised his authority without arrogance.[16]

What Kalman overlooked was the difference between Fortas' sense of his responsibility in public life and the burdens he assumed as head of the law firm. As a public servant, his sole obligation was to ensure the quality of the work of the staff and himself. As she says at another point, at Arnold, Fortas & Porter, he felt "that the entire responsibility for the firm's future rested upon his shoulders. He had always seemed older than his contemporaries, and the firm made him older still."[17] In addition, as Kalman was also aware, during Johnson's tenure as Vice

President and President, Fortas carried a heavy load as LBJ's personal advisor.[18]

Perhaps two actual incidents, rather than rhetoric, can best exemplify Kalman's exaggerated notion of Abe's incivility towards his juniors at the office. On my 50th birthday -- on July 15, 1964 -- Abe, just four years older than I, sent me the following card, which I still have:

"For Partner Diamond

Happy Birthday -- welcome to the fifties!

Abe Fortas"

He was then just about one year shy of his appointment to the Supreme Court and up to his eyeballs in extraneous chores for LBJ. I was astounded that he knew, let alone remembered. No one else at the office did. Some of my closest friends did not.

In response to my congratulory note on his appointment to the Supreme Court, Abe wrote this letter to me:

29, July 65

My dear friend Norman-

Your is the most beautiful, moving letter I have ever received. Thank you, my dear friend and colleague. I shall always be grateful for ours years together. Forgive me my bouts of temper and impatience; they were coupled with much affection and the greatest appreciation of your remarkable ability and devotion.

You know, I think, that I would not voluntarily have departed - for any position in the world. I had no choice.

I know now, by specific reports from clients, that we will retain our accounts; and I know that the firm will thrive and grow.

Devotedly,
Abe

To Norman Diamond, a splendid lawyer and a warm friend — Affectionately — Abe Fortas

Abe Fortas, as General Counsel of the Bituminous Coal Division, at a function celebrating completion of General Docket No. 15 which set minimum price for every ton of soft coal mined in the United States

Abe Fortas enjoying his favorite pastime

Paul Porter in his normal congenial mood

CHAPTER FOUR

PAUL PORTER
Toujours L'Ami

Paul infused the office with infectious friendliness. An incorrigible extrovert -- in contrast to the Judge and Abe -- he invariably had the latest gag to tell us, including the source and victim. He seemed like a sponge who instantly absorbed the latest good yarn. I was in Paul's office early one morning -- about 9:00 a.m. -- when his phone rang. From Paul's end of the conversation, I deduced that the caller was Paul Raiborn, a Paramount executive located in Los Angeles. When Porter hung up, I verified Raiborn's identity as the caller. So I said to Paul, "What's he doing ringing you at 6:00 a.m.?" Porter answered, "He wanted to be the first to tell me a new joke." I asked, "Had you heard it?" He said, "Yes." Of course, he didn't let on to Raiborn.

It was always easy, sometimes fun, to have Paul react to a legal problem. If he thought that a document prepared for him had an exaggerated tone, he might recall Andrew Jackson's order to his troops at The Battle of New Orleans during the war of 1812. As they crouched behind their breastworks, awaiting the Redcoats' charge, he bellowed: "Elevate them guns a little lower." He might say, "I felt like the bastard son at the family reunion," if he'd been denied the right to intervene in a lawsuit on behalf of a client whose interests were affected.

Paul just couldn't say anything unkind to anyone in or out of the firm. But his wit and solicitude didn't detract from his professional skills. His extraordinary legal talent was evidenced by his advocacy in the judicial appeals from the outrageous departmental decision dismissing Dorothy Bailey as disloyal. It was displayed in three forums: before the Civil Service Loyalty Review Board; the United States Court of Appeals for the District of Columbia, which sustained the Board,[1] and the Supreme Court where Porter shared the argument with Judge Arnold. The Supreme Court being equally divided 4 to 4 (Justice Clark abstaining), the lower Court's decision was affirmed without opinion.[2]

As elicited by Paul from the Review Board the facts were shocking beyond belief. In Kalman's account she notes:

> In appealing the decision to the U.S. Civil Service Commission loyalty review board, Paul Porter claimed that the charges against Bailey represented "malicious, irresponsible, reckless gossip which . . . stems from an internecine union controversy." The Board's chairman, Seth Richardson, countered that "five or six of the reports come from informants certified to us by the Federal Bureau of Investigation as experienced and entirely reliable." Porter asked for the names of the informants and whether they had been active in Bailey's union. "I haven't the slightest knowledge as to who they were or how active they have been in anything," Richardson replied. "Is it under oath?" Porter asked. "I don't think so," Richardson replied. The loyalty review board upheld the decision to fire Bailey and bar her from government service.[3]

This is Cassels' description of Paul's Supreme Court argument in the *Bailey* case:

> . . . The Supreme Court agreed to review the case and Porter made what many of his colleagues consider the most eloquent argument of its kind since Zola's appeal in the first Dreyfus case. . .[4]

Paul was as quick as lighting with an *ad lib*. Shortly after the six-day Israeli-Arab war in 1967, one of our partners returned from a visit to Israel. He told a group of us, including Paul, some of the war stories he had heard. One of them concerned the practice of Egyptian tank officers upon the approach of an Israeli tank unit, -- later verified in Randolph Churchill's book *"The Six Day War"*. They immediately stripped off their uniforms, put on native clothes and blended into the nearest Bedouin village. Paul unhesitatingly observed: "That's a well-known military tactic. It's called the Gaza Strip."

Paul's gift as a raconteur was legendary. He had a story for almost
every and any situation or occasion. Once, after getting short shrift at
an administrative hearing, he recalled his attendance at a Washington
Senator's ball game in the company of Justice William O.
Douglas (at
the time Chairman of the Securities and Exchange Commission). On
a close play at first base, called against Washington, the Senators'
manager, Bucky Harris, a diminutive figure, charged out of the dugout
and confronted the first base umpire. He was Cal Hubbard, a giant of
a man who had played for many years at tackle for the Green Bay
Packers of the National Football League. As Harris started fuming,
Hubbard ignored the diatribe. He turned his back and folded his arms
across his chest, meanwhile remaining absolutely silent. This impelled
Douglas to remark to Paul: "That's what we call giving them a hearing
at the SEC."

Paul's wit was at his command in any and every environment. If
one of us was worrying about a seemingly insoluble legal problem,
he'd often relate an incident from his past to lighten the atmosphere.
In one such instance, he told this tale of his early days of practice in
Lexington: During a rumpus between two young neer-do-wells over
a girl, one of them picked up a brick and crushed the other's skull. He
was charged with homocide. Assigned to represent him, Paul promptly
sought a plea bargain from the prosecutor, only to be rebuffed. The
prosecutor said: "Paul, I'd like to accommodate you, but I have two
eyewitnesses who'll swear they saw your man do it." "That's no
problem", Paul answered, "I can produce 20 witnesses who'll swear
they didn't see him do it."

I was in the courtroom when Paul successfully argued an antitrust
case -- before the Supreme Court -- for a liquor wholesaler who had
obtained an antitrust damage award against Seagram's on price-fixing
grounds.[5] The case had been referred to us by a law school classmate
of Judge Arnold -- Joseph Daniels, the senior member of Baker &
Daniels, the leading firm in Indianapolis.

It wasn't the most popular cause. The complaint alleged that
Seagram's and its subsidiary, Calvert, had illegally denied product to
the wholesaler. The reason was its refusal to follow the *maximum*
resale prices which the distillers had established when the government's
ceiling prices were lifted following the end of World War II. The
purpose of those prices was to prevent profiteering while supplies of
desirable product were limited.

**Kathleen Winsor Porter in 1944, the Publication Year
of her Best Seller,** *Forever Amber*

The argument preceding Paul's had involved the legality of a local ordinance forbidding the sale of pasteurized milk within Madison, Wisconsin unless it had been processed within five miles of the city.[6] Paul was up first in the *Kiefer-Stewart* case. A jury verdict for his client -- for $975,000 plus attorney's fees of $50,000 -- had been overturned by the United States Court of Appeals for the Sixth Circuit.[7]

Paul opened his argument this way: "I would now like to direct Your Honors' attention to a case involving another beverage, with which I suspect some members of the Court may be somewhat more familiar." Paul was a close friend of Chief Justice Fred Vinson and doubtless on a first-name basis with all of the Associate Justices. The Supreme Court unanimously reinstated the jury verdict, holding that concerted price-fixing was unlawful even when intended to lower prices.

During our long and close association Paul never indicated any interest in money or its accumulation. His only mention of it to me was in a humorous, indirect reference. At the end of the working day I frequently drove Paul to his lovely home on Tracy Place, while en route to mine. He lived there with his second wife, Kathleen (Kay) Winsor -- the author of *"Forever Amber."* From the day that runaway best seller was published in 1944, when she was just 24, the huge royalties may have induced her belief that substantial funds were always available.

Parenthetically, the book sold two million hard cover copies.[8] MacMillan, the publisher, promoted it heavily as another *"Gone With the Wind"*. It represented the results of five years of research about life during the restoration of the Stuart King, Charles II, beginning in 1160, following the end of the Puritan Cromwell Protectorate. Although regarded as salacious when published, it presented an authentic portrait of English mores at the time -- on the order of the "Hippie" era of free love in the mid-20th Century. Charles was known as the "Merry Monarch".   History records that he fathered 14 illegitimate children by various mistresses.[9]

At any rate, Kay transformed their home into a miniature palace, complete with an exquisite garden which she lovingly nurtured. In describing the final cost, Paul said: "I gave her an unlimited budget and she exceeded it."

In buying the Tracy Place home, Paul followed one of his many maxims --"Never buy a house with more lawn than your wife can conveniently mow." Years later in a telephone conversation with a friend who had just purchased a new home, I quoted Paul's maxim and expressed the hope that he had followed it. This evoked such hysterical laughter that it moved me to say: "It's funny, but not that funny." He answered: "Yes it is. My wife is outside mowing the lawn right now."

The law did not monopolize Paul's interest. He was also attracted by journalism, including the broadcast media, and no less so by politics. While studying law at the University of Kentucky, he was City Editor of the *Lexington Herald*. It was then and still is a highly influential publication.

Paul loved to tell newspaper anecdotes. While he served the *Herald* as City Editor, its publisher was an octogenarian -- Colonel Desha Breckinridge. (Colonel Desha -- as everyone called him -- was a close descendant of John Breckinridge, one of the presidential candidates who opposed Lincoln in 1860.) In Paul's time politics was the hottest topic in Kentucky, even outranking horse racing and good bourbon.

As a tight race for the Democratic gubernatorial nomination approached primary day, nothing had been heard from *The Herald*. Every politician in the state was calling Paul, asking where does *The Herald* stand? With three days to go, Paul diffidently entered the Colonel's office and told him his phone was ringing off the hook with that question. He said he couldn't get any work done and needed to know *The Herald's* position. The Colonel said in a soft drawl: "Well, son, I haven't made up my mind yet. But one thing you can be sure of, when I do we're gonna be gol-durned bitter about it."

Another of Paul's tales about the Kentucky press involved Mark Ethridge, Editor of the *Louisville Courier Journal*. It seems that he had an automobile accident one Saturday night while exiting from his town club. On Sunday morning he looked for a report of the item in the *Journal* and found it buried on the inside of the paper. He promptly called the city editor whom he angrily upbraided for neglecting to put it on the front page. Ethridge characterized it as a serious breach of the *Journal's* no-favoritism policy. As Paul recounted the episode to me, the city editor responded: "What makes you think that Mark Ethridge being drunk on a Saturday night is front page news?"

According to Cassels, Paul "was primarily a newspaperman, though he also had a law degree which he had earned at the University of

Kentucky Law School, while working for the *Lexington Herald.*"[10] As
for Paul's early employment, Cassels may have been right. But Paul
chose a career in the law. He joined Arnold & Fortas in May 1947,
when the firm added his name to its title.

Soon after we first met, Paul and I talked about the reasons that
brought us to Washington. He said that after a short try at law practice
in Kentucky, he had become affiliated with a local publication in a
small Georgia town. While in its service, he had written a piece called
"5 Cent Cotton." It had somehow caught the attention of Chester
Davis, head of the Agricultural Adjustment Administration (the
"AAA"). Davis soon offered him a job at the agency in Washington.
Paul accepted. Cassels said this of his subsequent government career:

> He originally planned to stay in Washington only three months and
> he found himself acting as General Counsel (sic) of the AAA. When the
> Supreme Court finally plowed under that ill-fated agency in 1937, Porter
> had succumbed to Potomac Fever. He remained in Washington as
> counsel for the Columbia Broadcasting System. This interlude of private
> practice lasted until the war started, when Porter was called back into
> the government service in a series of emergency agencies . . . . By
> 1944 Porter was so high in Roosevelt's esteem that he was chosen
> publicity director of the Democratic National Committee for the fourth
> Campaign. Immediately after the election FDR appointed him Chairman
> of the Federal Communications Commission. . . . Paul went to Greece
> early in 1947 with the rank of Ambassador to launch the "Truman
> Doctrine Greek aid program which he handled with notable success.[11]

Another Porter tale relates to his Greek experience. The program's
purpose was to head off a Soviet takeover of Greece. Mark Ethridge's
wife, "Willie Snow," had been assigned by the *Louisville Courier
Journal* to cover the progress of the project. At one point a member
of Paul's staff reported with alarm that she had slipped behind the
Soviet lines. Knowing her feisty, charming and resourceful ways, Paul
replied: "If Willie Snow is on the loose in their territory, those
Commies had better look out for themselves." As Paul anticipated, she
suffered no harm.

In her book on Fortas, Kalman recalls an incident during Paul's
tenure with Roosevelt's 1944 campaign. Citing Eric Sevareid as the
source, she wrote:

. . . He could make anything funny.   In 1944, while Porter was chairman of the Democratic National Committee, (sic) the Republicans scheduled a radio campaign speech by Thomas Dewey to begin immediately after a speech by the President. Porter countered by cutting Roosevelt's speech by five minutes and substituting an interim of somber organ music before the start of Dewey's talk. . .[12]

Paul genuinely enjoyed politics. His anecdotes were not limited to Kentucky. He told of Al Smith's first campaign for Governor of New York in 1920 against Nathan Miller, the incumbent Republican. Miller's campaign claimed as its centerpiece that during his first two-year term he had saved the people of the state of New York $50,000,000. Smith's major campaign aide was Robert Moses, then a political newcomer, later to become renowned -- among other things -- as the father of New York's freeway system and director of its great world fair in 1939. As the campaign wore on, Moses became concerned that the governor's money-saving message was catching on. He kept asking Smith to challenge it, only to be told, "Don't worry Bob, I'll take care of it." With only his windup speech to go, Smith had yet to tackle the issue. When Moses forcefully reminded him of the omission, the candidate replied "I'll take care of it tonight." Good as his word, in his final pre-election speech Smith declared:

"Now, the Governor has been campaigning up and down and across the state claiming that he's saved the people of New York $50,000,000. Well if that's so, what I want to know is, where is it and who's got it?"

Paul maintained an active role in politics after he joined our law firm. As Cassels states: "Paul was a New Deal troubleshooter." In 1944 he became Publicity Chairman for Franklin Roosevelt's fourth campaign.

In 1948 he was president of Americans for Democratic Action (ADA). Its membership consisted largely of ex-New Dealers, plus other liberal Democrats. It's common knowledge that in the spring of 1948 the ADA voted to abandon President Truman and try to enlist General Eisenhower as the Democratic candidate, as did other prominent Democrats.[13]

Paul felt humiliated. He characterized the deserters as "having all of the attributes of a cur dog except loyalty." He met with Truman and apologized profusely for the organization's desertion of the President. As Paul told me of the incident, the President replied:

> "Don't worry about it, Paul. They'll be back in November. They'll
> have no place else to go. Any sitting President who can't get his party's
> nomination is just a sh___ss. Even Hoover could do that."

The astonishing revival of the Democrats after Truman delivered his "Turnip Day" acceptance speech to the Democratic Convention and the astoundingly successful campaign that followed are now indelibly inscribed in the nation's election lore.   Incidentally, following his election, Truman resurrected Hoover's stature as an Ex-President.[13]

I can't think of the 1948 election without mentioning the special memories it has for me.   The 1948 Democratic Convention was the only one I ever attended.   I had been invited by Clinton Anderson -- then Secretary of Agriculture -- and sat in the last row of the New Mexico delegation's seats.   Just behind was the South Carolina delegation, headed by then Governor Strom Thurmond.   I heard every word of his advice to what later became the 1948 Dixiecrat Party.

Election night found me at Dewey's headquarters in the Roosevelt Hotel.   By way of background, I had gone to New York on business the Monday before Election Day.   While in the city I called my old boss, Bernie Katzen, under whom I had directly served during Dewey's first term as District Attorney ("DA").   Katzen was Assistant National Campaign Manager during the '48 campaign.   After we exchanged greetings, he suggested that I stay over and join the "old gang" who planned to gather at Centre Street -- the site of the DA's office -- on the afternoon of Election Day.

Thanks to Bernie's invitation, I spent a good part of Tuesday afternoon listening to Dewey's top bananas reminisce for a while. They soon started to vie for the honor of having been the first to realize that the "Chief" -- as his DA staff always referred to Dewey -- would someday be President. After a time the group repaired to the Roosevelt Hotel -- for an early dinner and the sport of listening to the election returns designate Dewey as the new President.

On that same night my wife, Luna, was at the Connecticut Avenue headquarters of the Democratic National Committee.   Her boss, Clinton Anderson had resigned as Secretary of Agriculture to run for the Senate from New Mexico.   She had planted herself at the Committee's headquarters because the returns from all races got there first. Luna would phone the results to Anderson as soon as they came in.

She told me that until about midnight, the highest dignitary present was Les Biffle. He was Secretary of the Senate and had toured the country for Truman, in the role of a chicken farmer, to sound out voter sentiment. The only others, besides Luna, were Loretta Larkin, Secretary of the Committee and a few staff members.

A party atmosphere prevailed at Dewey's headquarters when Election Night began. Katzen was in the inner sanctum with Dewey and his campaign leaders. I was in a large ballroom with rank and file Dewey supporters.

Happy revelers packed that place. All kinds of goodies, including champagne, were plentiful. Nobody was listening to the returns except me. I sat in a remote corner with a small portable radio glued to my ear. The early popular returns surprised me. They showed Truman maintaining a consistent lead of about 1,000,000 votes.

At approximately 11:00 p.m. I noticed Katzen's wife, Florrie, walk through the ballroom. Her face was absolutely white. I asked: "Florrie, what's the matter? Aren't you feeling well?" She answered: "Bernie says the Chief is licked." I said: "I can't understand it. All we have are early returns." She replied: "I'm only repeating what Bernie told me."

About an hour later, Katzen came through the room. As soon as I could, I told him of my conversation with Florrie. I expressed surprise because all the radio reporters were calling Dewey the winner, based on the anticipated returns from rural areas. Bernie answered that he's not running the way he should in cities like Milwaukee, Minneapolis, Denver and Omaha.

As the night wore on his analysis proved accurate. Truman stayed in a horse race throughout, always with a slight lead in the popular vote. Gradually, the Dewey crowd dwindled. At about 4:00 a.m. I walked Bernie home to his apartment where we sat and chatted for about half an hour. I'll never forget his comment just before I left for my folks' place in Manhattan. "Norman, you'll never know how many castles in the air crumbled tonight." I understood exactly what he meant. He was referring to the many men who served during Dewey's terms as DA and Governor and had planned to set up shop in Washington.

My wife's experience at Democratic Headquarters was just the opposite. Ever-increasing numbers of Democrats began streaming in, starting at about midnight. They partied all night long, beyond daybreak. At about 10:00 a.m. Truman became the definite winner when Ohio voted Democratic.

After Truman had named Anderson as Secretary of Agriculture, I got to know all the secretaries of the cabinet officers and Rose Conway, the President's secretary. One Saturday morning, when the President was away, I finally accepted her invitation to visit the Oval Office. Sure enough the little sign that says "The Buck Stops Here" was on his desk. While we talked I asked Rose whether the folks on Truman's famous "whistle stop" train really thought he had a chance. She answered: "Oh, we knew all along we would win." I asked: "what made them think so when all the polls showed Dewey a big winner." She answered: "The President drew bigger crowds than Dewey did every place he went. Nobody on the radio or in the papers ever mentioned that."

Paul's last public chore before joining us was his service in Greece early in 1947. That might have been the occasion for one of his overseas trips, about which he told one of my favorite Porter anecdotes. It seems that he was flying the ocean on a government transport, when it dropped one of its four engines. There were a number of other passengers. The stewardess felt impelled to reassure them that they were in no danger. When she approached Paul, she said, "There's nothing to worry about. This pilot has never suffered a fatality." Paul rejoined: "Neither have I."

Journalism and politics, may have been Paul's favorite activities. However, as already noted, he did practice law in Kentucky for a short while, following his graduation from law school. Naturally, this was another subject for Paul's inimitable anecdotes about southern practice both in and out of Kentucky.

During that period he became associated with a small law office in Lexington. One evening, while Paul and the senior member were preparing an oral argument before the Supreme Court of Kentucky, scheduled for the next day, the older man began to drink heavily. Paul discreetly suggested that the refreshments might interfere with the quality of the argument. The older lawyer quickly put Paul in his place:

"Young man, you have just one function in this case. When I arrive in court tomorrow morning just make sure I'm facing the judge."

Paul also told of a trial in which a Kentucky lawyer was having a hard time putting a critical question to a key witness. After trying it in three different forms, only to have the Judge sustain successive objections, he tried a fourth version. At that point the judge testily remarked: "Counsel, are you trying to show your contempt for this Court?" "On the contrary, your honor," came the response, "I'm doing my utmost to conceal it."

A similar tale involved another prototype country lawyer's appearance as appellate counsel before the highest court of Kentucky. Upon completion of his argument, the Chief Judge inquired, "The Court would like to hear from you on [citing a previous case]. It seems to be directly in point against you. Would you care to comment on it?" "Oh, yes," replied counsel, "I waive that case."

Still another Porter story concerned an old Mississippi practitioner who was making his first argument before the Supreme Court of the United States. He had no sooner voiced the *pro forma* supplication "May it please the court," when Justice McReynolds -- a champion curmudgeon -- was all over him. The Justice demanded to know why counsel's brief did not conform to the Court's Rules for print, style and sequence. He elicited this disarming answer: "Sheer ignorance and neglect, Your Honor, sheer ignorance and neglect."

As he got on with his career, Paul attracted people from all walks of life. He seemed to have a storage bin somewhere in his mind, from which he could summon recollections of them, always at appropriate times. Colonel Matt Winn, the longtime impressario of the Kentucky Derby, was among them. He particularly cherished his bourbon. According to Paul, as the Colonel downed a shot one day, a friend asked: "Colonel, I've always wondered why you shut your eyes whenever you take a drink?" "Well, son," said Winn, "the sight of good bourbon just makes my mouth water and I can't stand to dilute it."

Another member of the "Porter knew him" circle was the famous syndicated journalist and wit, Irwin S. Cobb, also a native of Kentucky. He required a hospital stay to treat a stomach problem. A couple of days after the procedure, he broke wind in the presence of a pretty young nurse. He apologized profusely. "Oh, no," she exclaimed, "don't apologize; it's really a feather in my cap." The next day, as she reentered his room, Cobb said to her: "Open the window, young lady, I'm about to make you an Indian princess."

Paul's friendships were as diversified as they were abundant. They included Toots Shor, the restaurateur-in-chief of the New York sporting scene. He did not achieve celebrity on the basis of his cultural awareness. Nevertheless he assented when invited to a star-studded performance of Hamlet. The group included Paul. During the first intermission, someone asked Toots whether he was enjoying the play. His reply: "I'm havin' a ball. I'm the only crumb in the joint that don't know how it's comin' out."

Bowie Kuhn, the Commissioner of Baseball, was one of Paul's clients. One day Paul sat in the owner's box at Yankee Stadium, along with the Commissioner. Also present was Mickey Mantle's wife. When Mantle won the game with a home run in the bottom of the ninth, the crowd rose to its feet in a roaring ovation. That is, everyone except Paul, who stayed silent and seated. Mrs. Mantle asked: "Wasn't that great, why aren't you standing?" Paul dryly replied: "Isn't that what he gets paid to do?"

C.R. Smith, the pioneer chief of American Airlines was a sometime buddy of Paul's. C.R., as he was known, was a big, burly, no-nonsense kind of man -- the personification of the rugged individualist. He and Paul buddied around when both were divorced. One evening two women acquaintances joined them for dinner at C.R.'s New York apartment. After dinner one of the ladies suggested they go to the theatre. C.R. declined. She next proposed a movie, eliciting another rejection from C.R. When she said they could go dancing, C.R. replied that he didn't like to dance. In frustration, she asked: "Mr. Smith is there anything you like to do?" He answered "I like to f--k and play poker." She replied: "Thanks for putting the ladies first."

Paul's contribution to Arnold, Fortas & Porter was not limited to his role in the firm's work and in maintaining the light-hearted life style of the office. He also seemed to know the inside about everything that was going on besides what was printed or broadcast by the media. It gave everyone in the office a sense that we were really "in the know". Somehow that increased our sense of belonging to a super special institution.

CHAPTER FIVE

THE FORMATION OF THE FIRM

Toward the end of 1945, Arnold and Fortas were both ready for a career change. Each was anxious to remain in Washington.[1] After two years on the bench, Arnold felt caged. He was well aware of its benefits -- a lifetime appointment at full salary until death, even if disabled from performing the prescribed duties.[2] Nevertheless, he found the judicial life unsatisfactory. He once remarked to me that he resigned because "I just got tired of writing those silly little essays for Fed.2d." (*i.e.*, the series that publishes the opinions of the United States Courts of Appeals).[3]

In a more serious vein, he found the judicial role unsuited to his "preference for partisan argument" and restrictive of his interest in "writing or speaking on controversial subjects."[4] By way of example, about twenty years after he co-founded Arnold & Fortas, he became increasingly aggravated by the hostility so rudely exhibited on college campuses and in intellectual circles toward supporters of the Vietnam War. He vigorously expressed his antagonism toward the dissenters in a speech at Valparaiso University on April 28, 1967.[5]

As Arnold doubtless foresaw, the speech elicited an adverse storm from the liberal press and intelligentsia.[6] There are two short sentences in the speech that particularly impressed me at the time and still do. "In a democratic society dissent is not sacred. Only the right to dissent is sacred."[7]

This was not the first instance of Arnold's divergence from the liberal dogma of the time. In his description of Arnold's tenure following his appointment as Assistant Attorney General in the late '30s, Cassels stated:

During the next five years, Arnold became the greatest
trust-buster in American history. He filed 230 suits against alleged
conspiracies in restraint of trade - more suits than had been filed in
the entire previous fifty-year history of the Sherman Act. Making his
own precedents has he went, Arnold waded fearlessly into such giants
as the American Medical Association, Standard Oil Company of New
Jersey, Associated Press, and finally, to the horror of Democratic
politicians, the building trade unions of the American Federation of
Labor.

Overturning precedent, the Supreme Court rejected the
union cases. I remember them best for a laugh resulting from the
case against the Carpenters Union. One day I had a lunch date with
Ken Debevoise, a law school classmate, who worked for a white
shoe Wall Street firm, headed by Charles H. Tuttle, a leading
Episcopal layman. Ken was feverishly working on a document when
I arrived at his office. He told me it was the Supreme Court brief
for the Carpenters. Astonished, I expressed surprise that his office
represented labor organizations. Ken replied: "When Thurman filed
the case, Charlie Tuttle said: God! that man Arnold, he should be
canonized.

Arnold resigned from the Court of Appeals in June 1945.
The Chairman of the Coca-Cola Company, Robert W. Woodruff,
soon guaranteed him a $25,000 annual retainer. He had become
friendly with Woodruff during his antitrust days. In particular, while
Arnold headed the Antitrust Division, he identified Coca-Cola in
answer to a congressional challenge to his interpretation of antitrust
legislation -- i.e., "to name one big business that violated neither the
letter nor the spirit of our antitrust laws."

Arnold revolutionized the procedure for policing the
antitrust laws. In his time as Division head the Sherman Act had no
compulsory process by which to elicit testimony or compel the
production of documents in civil antitrust cases. (This has since been
rectified by legislation authorizing "Civil Investigative Demands.")
That led Arnold to make widespread use of the Sherman Act's
criminal sanctions. By this process, grand jury subpoenas became
available, backed by contempt citations for failure to comply.
Indictments for antitrust violations frequently followed, putting real
teeth into the antitrust laws.

Arnold's invocation of the grand jury's powers created a
real stir among American industrialists. Indulgent Republican
administrations, had been virtually indifferent to the necessity

of antitrust compliance. Now, as indictments started to flow from the Antitrust Division, complaints from the business community were registered with the Attorney General Robert H. Jackson. Although a former head of the Antitrust Division, he was not an enthusiastic proponent of the laws it enforced. The complaints led Jackson to ask Thurman what he thought he was accomplishing by the indictment of leading American businessmen. In a seemingly serious vein, Thurman replied: "I'm not sure I know exactly, Bob, but one thing I'll guarantee you; they're sure as Hell answering their mail a lot faster."

To get back to Thurman's serious answer to the congressional inquiry: What sparked his identification of Coca Cola was his profound animus toward absentee ownership.   This attitude was traceable to his Laramie roots where he became aware that all of the leading enterprises in town were owned by eastern bankers, with the resultant drain of the local economy's purchasing power.[11]

The Judge selected Coca-Cola because the company's role was confined to selling its highly popular syrup to independent local bottlers whose profits were retained in their local communities. In many localities, Arnold said, the Coca Cola bottler was "the richest man in town" and the major source of financing for local charities and vital community services, such as hospitals and educational institutions. (Not long ago, Woodruff made what was then the largest single gift to an American university, when he contributed $100 million worth of Coca Cola stock to Emory University in Atlanta.)

Parenthetically, I am often amazed by the misstatements that characterize so many books on current personalities and events. In his book on Fortas, Bruce Allen Murphy -- a professor of political science at Penn State -- wrote that James Farley -- mistakenly described as President of Coca Cola -- retained Arnold for this reason:

> [a]fter seventy-five years the patent on the formula to the drink was running out, and soon new competitors would be springing up everywhere at the company's expense. So Farley hired Arnold hoping that he might extend his practice of law to the practice of some politics. Could he lobby old friends in Congress and get a renewal on the patent? Of course he could, said Arnold, for the right fee. So, in a pattern used by the firm in many of its later actions, litigation was avoided in favor of lobbying in other areas for the rules of the game to be changed.

When the effort succeeded, Coca Cola became one of the cornerstone clients of Arnold's new firm. . . .[12]

This was utter nonsense. Patents have historically been issued for only 17 years from the date of issuance. (In the future, they will run for 20 years from the application date.) I can't recall a single instance when Arnold engaged in lobbying during his Washington practice. Incidentally, Farley was President of Coca Cola Export Company for a time, not the parent Coca Cola Company. Bob Woodruff was President and CEO of the Coca Cola Company.

Most importantly, a patent on a food product can only be obtained if its ingredients are fully disclosed. From the time of its founding, Coca Cola has vigorously and successfully fought to maintain the secrecy of its formula.[13] As noted in the cited book on the subject:

> Woodruff's attitude toward the formula was more than just a matter of careful stewardship of one of the most valuable trade secrets in American business. He gloried in the process of secrecy itself, setting up elaborate procedures that seemed to be designed to call attention to the formula as much as they were to protect it. At Woodruff's direction, the company established a rule that no one could see the formula without the formal permission of the board, and then only in the presence of the chairman, president, or corporate secretary. Furthermore, the rule said, only two company officials would be allowed to know the formula at any given time, and their identities were never to be disclosed for any reason. The company then publicized the policy.[14]

Besides Coca Cola, Arnold's fledgling practice was fortified by two Cleveland entrepreneurs, Robert R. Young, CEO of the Chesapeake and Ohio Railroad, and Cyrus Eaton of Otis & Co., a leading Cleveland brokerage firm. They retained him to represent their interests in bidding for the acquisition of the Pullman Company's service unit. It had been divorced from Pullman's car manufacturing division in an antitrust case originally brought by Arnold while he was head of the Antitrust Division. The case had succeeded in its purpose to break up Pullman's ownership of both sleeping car manufacture and the related service facilities required by every railroad in the nation offering overnight passenger service.[15]

Pullman had elected to retain its manufacturing unit when given the choice of which one to divest. The service unit was then put up for sale to a buyer approved by the Court.

Eager to acquire the service unit, Young offered Arnold a $12,500 retainer from his railroad company and Eaton matched it for Otis & Co. Otis would be the underwriter of a public stock offering if Young's bid was accepted. Arnold formed a law partnership with Arne Wiprud, a transportation specialist from the Antitrust Division to present their proposal to the Court.[16] A competing bid was submitted by the American Association of Railroads. It proved successful, notwithstanding Arnold's argument that the railroad combination itself violated the Sherman Act.[17]

The closing argument of opposing counsel at the trial level -- after all the evidence was in -- included a memorable exchange. The railroads were represented by the illustrious former Senator from Pennsylvania, George Wharton Pepper. His argument came first. At its conclusion, he informed the Court that his opponent would doubtless make what would seem an eloquent and persuasive argument. Pepper then admonished the Court to resist Judge Arnold's brilliant oratory and keep its mind on the issues. Arnold responded that he was grateful for Senator Pepper's compliment, but nevertheless felt distressed, stating: "I had been hoping to catch the Court off guard." Incidentally it was Pepper who rejected a Supreme Court appointment because "I'd rather make my living talking to a bunch of damn fools than listening to a bunch of damn fools".[18] (The comment is sometimes misattributed to Arnold).

Later, after founding Arnold & Fortas, Arnold argued the case on its appeal to the Supreme Court. I heard the argument. It could fairly be described as thrilling. In a completely unorthodox presentation, Arnold made no mention of legal issues. Instead he spoke of the unexploited educational and romantic potential of railroad travel -- opening the glories of the western landscapes to sightseers from all parts of the U.S.A. and foreign nations. No one expected Arnold to receive a single vote. He lost when the case was affirmed without opinion by an equally divided court, which voted four to four.[19]

Arnold and Wiprud had dissolved when the *Pullman* case was lost at the trial court level. This is Gressley's explanation of the reasons:

In his autobiography, Arnold remarked that at this juncture, with no other transportation business in sight, "Arne Wiprud, whose sole interest was in transportation law, dissolved our partnership to pursue his own specialty." Most of Arnold's friends today regard the divorce of Arnold and Wiprud as destined. The firm represented a merger of dissimilar talents and temperaments. Had there been no preoccupation with a legal specialization, the two partners probably would have eventually gone their separate ways.[20]

That left Arnold with a small suite of offices at the Bowen Building, 821 15th Street, N.W., but without a partner. Thinking about a replacement for Wiprud, he learned that Fortas was considering resignation from his post as Under Secretary of Interior. He offered a partnership to Abe.[21]

Abe and his wife, Carol Agger, enjoyed life in Washington. She was in active law practice with a tax firm. However, he was concerned about his ability to attract clients if he entered private practice.[22]

As already noted, while stationed in Washington, during my Naval service, I had stayed in touch with Abe. My discharge was set for March 1, 1946. Just before it came due, I met with him. He told me that he had an offer to start a law firm with Thurman Arnold and was considering it. I said, "It's a good idea." He replied: "But I also have an offer for a full professorship at Yale Law School." I told him: "Hey, you've already been around those bases." He asked: "Well, where would I get any clients if I went into practice?" I said: "Abe, if you can't get any clients, I'll starve to death because I'm not going back to the government. I'll hang up a shingle if I have to."

That was the whole conversation. I don't know whether I influenced his decision. Anyway, he joined up with Thurman, notwithstanding his genuine concern about "where he would find clients if he entered practice".[23]   According to Kalman, Abe confided to Douglas:

> "My only specific project thus far is the American Molasses connection," Fortas confided to William O. Douglas. "The proposal there is that I become a Director and Treasurer of the Company as well as special counsel. But the retainer offered is only $500 a month."[24]

The establishment of Arnold & Fortas was a logical and almost inevitable development. They knew each other well. They had served together on the Yale Law School faculty and at times in the New Deal.

As already noted, their wives liked Washington life and both men were ready for a major career change.

Perhaps equally important in their decision to establish Arnold & Fortas was the shift in the government's emphasis from domestic problems -- the war had brought prosperity -- to all-out concentration on the Cold War. Neither of them had any significant background in foreign affairs. Consequently, even if they had been so inclined, they had little prospect of high office in the global struggle with the Soviet Union. Certainly, there were other men of ability with more impressive qualifications for such positions.

However, talented and knowledgeable as they were, each could surely have found gainful employment providing adequate incomes. Consequently, their decision to strike out on their own took some real courage. They had no guarantee that the firm of Arnold & Fortas would prove successful, either overnight or long-term.

Arnold & Fortas started out with the barest minimum of background in private practice. Fortas had none whatever. Arnold's consisted solely of two phases of his pre-Washington career, neither of any use for a Washington law practice. The first was two years in Chicago, following his graduation from Harvard in 1914, until the beginning of his military service in 1916. The other phase consisted of some nine years as a practitioner in Laramie after his Army discharge. In accordance with the necessities of life as a small lawyer, he entered politics and successively served as Mayor of Laramie and as a member of the lower house of the Wyoming legislature.

Arnold's own description of his prior ventures in the law point to their irrelevance for purposes of the demanding Washington, D.C. practice in which he and Fortas had decided to embark. In his own autobiography, Arnold recounts his pursuit of the legal profession in Chicago in terms both poignant and amusing -- again invoking his unsurpassed gift for poetic expression.

In his words:

> After a brief period as an employee of a large firm which paid me the munificent salary of ten dollars a week, I decided that I could improve my station in life by forming a firm of my own. And thus the great but short-lived firm of O'Brian, Waite & Arnold was born.

My cash resources were so low that I was forced to live in a cubicle at the local YMCA in Ravenswood, from which I would take the elevated every morning to my office. The rules of the YMCA forbade smoking in the building. The commanding secretary had a nose like a bird dog and could detect cigar smoke through closed doors. For that reason, I was constantly in trouble. My impressions of the YMCA I expressed at the time in the following poem:

HOME OFF THE RANGE

I do not smoke, I do not chew,
I never drink a single thing,
And so when'er I'm feeling blue
(And generally, I find I do),
I lift my plaintive voice and sing:

Oh, I live in the wonderful Y.M.C.A.
And my comrades are faithful and true,
I eschew the narcotic,
and shun the erotic,
As every respectable young man should do.
And hereby take warning,
I pray night and morning,
And the cuss words I use, they are mighty damn few
(An occasional "hell" and a "goddam" or two,
Is just about all the cussing I do).
And this regeneration, I'm happy to say,
Is due to the wonderful Y.M.C.A.[25]

From his Laramie practice, Arnold learned that the economics of the time precluded a successful small town career in the law. He concluded:

As the years went by it became increasingly apparent that the West and the South were becoming afflicted with an economic blight known as absentee ownership. In the period of the 1920's the antitrust laws were, in practical effect, suspended. It was a period of rapid growth of nation-wide industrial combinations. These great enterprises would use their control over a product local enterprises had to have to force the latter to sell out at a distress price. The motion-picture industry is as good an example as any. The major distributors controlled the vast majority of feature films. They would supply them only on such terms as would bankrupt a local theater, after which the major company would buy the theater at its own price.

* * *

A practicing small-town lawyer could easily sense what was happening. The local motion-picture theater was about to be taken over by Fox. The local plaster mill was being purchased by Celotex. The local oil refinery was being absorbed by Standard Oil of Indiana. There went three of the big local clients. Divorce cases and collections grew to be the major source of revenue for the local lawyer.[26]

On the other hand, Arnold, Fortas and Porter had certain advantages. Each was exceptionally intelligent. Joseph Rauh, a top-flight lawyer and all-out, lifetime New Dealer who spent his life representing liberal clauses was effusive in his praise of their abilities. Although he decried their decision to represent business interests, he characterized them as follows: "Of those attorneys who went 'to the other side,' Rauh considered Arnold and his colleagues the ablest. 'You had to go a hell of a distance to find three lawyers as good as those three guys.'"[27]

Two other considerations promoted the prospects of the new firm. Having lived on modest government incomes, the founding partners were not motivated by an avaricious anxiety to accumulate personal wealth. They had never been exposed to the scramble for compensation characteristic of "big time" firms where the division of income among the partners was geared to "rainmaking" -- *i.e.*, the fees paid by clients that each had brought to the firm.

Another virtue enjoyed by each of them was wisdom in the ways of the federal government. Their knowledge reflected hands-on involvement in its complex litigation problems. It also comprehended personal knowledge of the *modus operandi* of the administrative bodies created by the New Deal during the Great Depression, such as the Securities and Exchange Commission ("the SEC"), the Federal Communications Commission ("the FCC") and the National Labor Relations Board ("the NLRB"). They were also familiar with the emergency agencies designed to meet the special needs of World War II -- *e.g.*, the War Production Board, the War Labor Board and the Office of Price Administration. In short, they enjoyed enviable reputations for outstanding ability and expertise in the newly evolving aspects of the legal profession, although litigation soon proved to be their primary activity.

As previously indicated, shortly after its doors opened I had the good fortune to join Arnold & Fortas. On March 1, 1946, immediately following my discharge from the Navy, I met with Fortas at his invitation in the Arnold & Fortas office. He offered me a position as an associate with the firm. My compensation would be my very modest Navy pay, plus a bonus if the firm prospered, and half of any fees earned from clients I brought to the firm. Of course, I accepted, although I was not counting on any compensation beyond my Navy level. I then told Abe that thirty days of paid Navy leave were due me which I wanted to use for a vacation. He said it would be o.k.

Abe then introduced me to the firm's small staff. Besides Arnold, it included three associates and two secretaries. In welcoming me, Arnold declared: "There's only one rule around here. Everybody calls me 'Judge.'" He was kidding, of course, but from that time forward I always called him "Judge."

One of the associates was Walton Hamilton, a distinguished member of the Yale law faculty, who worked on a part-time basis. Hamilton was widely respected for his writings on law and economics. Another associate was Milton Freeman, a graduate of Columbia Law School and a former member of the legal staff at the Securities and Exchange Commission. The third was Reed Miller, a recent graduate of the University of West Virginia Law School, of which Arnold had been Dean from 1927-30, and who had been the only associate in the short-lived firm of Arnold & Wiprud. Hamilton died many years ago. Freeman is still a firm partner. Miller retired in October 1995. It seems odd in retrospect, but I never had occasion to work with any of them.

In justice to my wife, I've got to add this item. I've always suspected that she was instrumental in my association with Arnold & Fortas. Unlike Thurman, Abe had no major client when they formed the firm. Soon after my association, Abe told me that Tommy Corcoran had been representing Lever Bros. in its effort to obtain a larger allotment of fats and oils, then essential to soap making, and still under wartime controls. Tommy, whom I knew fairly well, was a real hard hitter. He used every possible contact to push his objective with the person in authority.

That didn't sit well with Clinton Anderson, then Secretary of Agriculture, the official in charge of fats and oil allotments. One day Anderson got so fed up with Corcoran that he told him to get out of his office and never come back. As Abe explained it to me, Tommy said he had a "dead ball" on Lever Bros. and asked whether Abe would take the matter on. Abe, of course, knew that my wife was Anderson's secretary. Right after I joined Arnold & Fortas, he asked me whether I could meet with Anderson to find out whether he would permit Abe to present the Lever problem. I acted on the request and told Abe that Anderson would be amenable to his pursuit of the matter. Thanks to Abe's talent for impressing strangers, Lever became a long-term and valuable client.

**11/43 The author, when
commissioned as Ensign, USNR, in WWII**

CHAPTER SIX

NAVAL SUPPORT

When the founding fathers were with us, any overt solicitation of clients was a "no no" -- undignified and, indeed, regarded as unethical. Today, that's an outmoded anachronism. The modern law firm has a Practice Development Unit. As the name indicates, its function is to enhance the firms coffers by attracting new clients -- the deeper the pockets, the better.

One method is the development of colorful brochures complete with flattering pictures of the firm's legal specialists, plus narrations of their skills in currently active areas of the law. These are circulated to every potential client with the slightest connection to any of the firm's lawyers. On occasion, a brochure will feature a single lawyer whose accomplishments are deemed germane to selected personnel in particular organizations.

Potential and existing clients are also invited to in-house seminars on subjects considered of particular interest to them. These are conducted by firm members with expertise in the field. At other times, particularly promising prospects are invited to join legal specialists at small dinner parties which offer the opportunity for more personal contacts.

Then there are newsletters featuring current legal developments. These are sent to selected existing and potential clients likely to be concerned with the subject matter. They include notable decisions or newly evolved governmental policy on "hot" legal topics. These may cover securities regulations, environmental controls, product liability development, food and drug initiatives, or any other subject.

A less formal method resulted in our representation of my favorite client -- The Kroger Co., now the nation's largest supermarket chain -- soon after I joined Arnold & Fortas. It's hard to overstate my respect for Kroger and my pride in servicing it for more than 40 years. Its association with our firm began in the spring of 1946. It continues to this day, when our younger colleagues are doing its work. In all, our records indicate that we have handled well over 300 significant matters for it.

This is how it happened. After four years of civilian service at other government agencies, I obtained an appointment as an officer in the United States Naval Reserve in November 1943. By a strange quirk of fate that led Kroger to our firm.

The story of my naval appointment, and how it brought me to Kroger's attention, is so off-the-wall that it bears telling. I had been called up early in the "WWII" draft -- in May 1941 -- well before Pearl Harbor -- although I had a middle high draft number and was married. The Chairman of my draft board was Harlan Wood, Post Commander of the District of Columbia Chapter of the American Legion. He immediately called up every eligible male subject to his authority. (Women could only serve as volunteer nurses in WWII.) Numbers and any other "book" considerations were meaningless to Harlan Wood. In his view Army service was the highest of all possible callings.

At the time, the physical examinations were thorough. Following my call-up, a dozen specialists must have examined me. The last one, an orthopedist, caught my back problem -- scoliosis, a lateral curvature of the spine. Although it had never troubled me, he disqualified me for that reason, classifying me 4F -- *i.e.*, unfit for service. In doing so, he said: "Sonny, you'll have to seek your fun elsewhere."

Although it didn't occur to me until many years later, Harlan Wood did me a favor. If I had been called up in regular order, I would surely have been inducted. After Pearl Harbor, the physicals were quickies, performed by a single doctor. The Army was taking anyone who could walk. A new classification, 1-B, was provided for inductees who were not physically qualified for combat duty. Many were assigned to non-combat posts in war zones all over the world. My rejection by the Army ultimately meant that I stayed in Washington and was available when Arnold, Fortas & Porter beckoned.

In the spring of 1943 -- while working in the Claims Division of the U.S. Department of Justice -- I got restless. Everybody my age was in uniform. Both of my younger brothers were in the Navy. Being of obvious draft age, I felt uncomfortably conspicuous in civilian dress. This led me to visit the Office of Naval Officer Procurement on G Street, N.W., Washington, D.C., to explore the possibility of obtaining a commission in the U.S. Naval Reserve. (The Reserve consisted of wartime inductees, as distinguished from career personnel).

I caught a young red-headed doctor -- a lieutenant in the Reserve. Explaining that I was classified 4F on account of my back, I asked whether he thought there was any chance that I might be accepted for a Reserve Commission. After looking me over, he said: "Well, you might get by."

This encouraged me to file a formal application. A little while later, I took an active duty physical examination, at the same G Street office. This time I ran into an old career Navy doctor. He thought the Navy was Valhalla. He disqualified me for every physical disability he could think of, from malocclusion to flat feet. His list of my physical disabilities covered a whole page.

The outcome really depressed me. My wife noticed it and mentioned my problem to her boss, Representative Clinton Anderson of New Mexico. An ex-newspaper man, he was one of the outstanding intellectuals ever to serve in Congress (later as Secretary of Agriculture and United States Senator). Anderson empathized with my disappointment. He had volunteered for service in World War I, but had been rejected because of an arrested case of TB. Anderson must have had clout with the defense establishment. A possible reason was his major role in the passage of an extension of the draft by a single vote in the House in the summer of 1941.

Whatever his connection, he called Rear Admiral Lewis Denfeld -- Chief of the Bureau of Naval Personnel -- told him of my desire to serve and explained my difficulty. Denfeld said: "Well, if you can get him a billet [*i.e.*, a position], I will get him into the Navy." Anderson spoke to a man named Jacob E. Davis, who later played a vital role in my legal career. (He was personally responsible for my subsequent retention by Kroger.)

Jake, as he was called, had been a member of the 77th Congress, 1941-1942, representing a southeastern Ohio district. He was first elected in the same year as Anderson, but had been narrowly defeated for reelection in November 1942. Jake then became a Special Assistant to James Forrestal, at the time Under Secretary of the Navy (and later its Secretary).

At a meeting in his office, Anderson introduced me to Jake (a Harvard Law School graduate, as I later learned). I took an instant liking to him. He was tall, ruggedly good-looking, with a lean athletic build, a commanding presence, a deep voice, a personable manner and a sense of humor. I guess I passed muster because Jake said he would find a spot for me. Although I didn't know it, he was then organizing the Navy's "Procurement Legal Division," which was stationed in Washington, D.C. Its designated function was to handle the huge volume of commercial work that the war thrust on the Navy. Such work was for beyond the capacity of the Navy's Office of the Judge Advocate General. A Wall Street lawyer, Struve Hensel, was appointed General Counsel of the Division. Davis was its ultimate supervisor in the Under Secretary's Office.

Nothing happened for three or four months, when I got a welcome telephone call. A woman's voice said: "Could you come over and meet with Admiral Denfeld this Saturday morning?" I said, of course. His office was at the Arlington Naval Annex, across the Potomac in Virginia.

At the appointed time, I was ushered into Denfeld's office. He was a very charming man -- later to become the Navy's CNO ("Chief of Naval Operations") and after the war a Republican candidate for the U.S. Senate from Massachusetts. He immediately put me at ease. After we had chatted for about 20 minutes, he indicated that the interview was over. As he escorted me to the door, he said: "I'll bet you're wondering why I sent for you." I replied: "Well, to tell the truth, I am, Admiral; I know you have more important things to do." He replied: "When I saw the physical report from G Street I wanted to see if you would come in on a wheelchair."

I still have a hard time believing that I spent 20 minutes alone with the man responsible for manning our warships all over the seven seas while the outcome of the greatest war in history still hung in the balance.

A while later, when I got my active duty order, I had waivers on all the recorded physical ailments, thanks to Admiral Denfeld. The doctor who oversaw my active duty physical looked at the waivers and said: "Who the hell are you anyhow, Knox's cousin?" Knox was Secretary of the Navy. That's how I got into the Navy. I served in its Procurement Legal Division from November 1943 until March 1946.

Davis and I became great friends. We played in the same weekly poker game. He pitched and I played shortstop on our unit's softball team, which won the Navy championship for the D.C. metropolitan area. Jake left the Navy to become Vice President of The Kroger Co. At the time I had no idea what it did. About six months later, I joined Arnold & Porter where I happily took permanent root, beginning March 1, 1946.

When I sent out the customary announcements, I included Jake just to let him know where I had landed. A week or two later my phone rang. When I picked up, a booming baritone voice -- unmistakably Jake's -- declared: "Normie, you're on Kroger time now" and outlined a legal problem involving OPA. That's how I learned that Kroger was a supermarket chain. Incidentally, I quickly got the desired relief. That was the beginning of a law firm-client relationship which still endures without any retainer agreement or any other document recording the terms of our working arrangement.

**2/46 The author, when honorably
discharged as Lieutenant, Senior Grade, in WWII**

Part II - How We Lived

The Historic Townhouse at 1229 19th Street, N.W. --
The Happiest Home of Arnold, Fortas & Porter

CHAPTER SEVEN

THE FOUNDERS' WORKSHOPS

When I joined Arnold & Fortas, it was located in the Bowen Building, 815 15th Street, N.W., in the same suite which Arnold & Wiprud had occupied. At the time, 15th Street was the heart of the professional and financial business district. It was lined with office buildings which housed virtually all of Washington's major law firms and brokerage houses.

The Arnold & Fortas space really squeezed the firm's staff, small as it was. It had no reception area; just a small lobby around which the lawyers' offices were spread. The two for Arnold and Fortas were of modest size. The others barely exceeded the space of a closet. We had no library. We did our research at outside libraries -- either at the Department of Justice or at the federal court building.

The two secretaries worked at desks in the confined lobby space. Marguerite O'Brien, Judge Arnold's secretary, was a refined, serious and soft-spoken woman. She somehow managed to keep all of Arnold's papers in perfect order and to take his dictation -- usually with a cigar in his mouth -- directly into a typewriter. Arnold saw no sense in taking dictation in shorthand and then transcribing it on a typewriter. His method can rightly be considered the forerunner of the modern word processor. I tried the same system with two or three secretaries without success. They were too inured to shorthand.

Our quarters in the Bowen Building were so cramped that there was no space for Paul Porter when he joined the firm. To make room for him, I moved one floor below to the office of Virginia Bowman, the

public stenographer most of us used. There I worked at an extra desk
so beat up that Good Will would have rejected it.

With a rapidly growing practice, we soon needed more lawyers.
Having no place to squeeze even one more body, we had to move. At
the time Gustave Ring, a leading developer, was constructing an office
building at the corner of 18th and M Streets, N.W., just off
Connecticut Avenue. That location was then regarded as too far out
for commercial use. Strange as it now seems, in 1948 there was no
business activity whatever in that part of town. There wasn't a single
respectable retail store on Connecticut Avenue. Nevertheless, we took
the *avant garde* step of renting space in what became the Ring
Building, while it was still under construction.

Our new space was luxurious compared to what we had left. We
had space for several more lawyers, a reception area, more capacity for
our secretaries, plus a room for our first support personnel. They were
the previously mentioned Dorothy Bailey, a gracious lady who served
as our Office Manager, and Evelyn Joyce, our first bookkeeper, a
husky woman with a no-nonsense personality. The icing on the cake
was the initiation of our law library, in the form of the U.S. Supreme
Court Reports and those of the federal trial and intermediate appellate
courts.

Here I must interject a digression from the evolution of our physical
facilities to discuss the employment of our next two lawyers. Their
addition comprises my most vivid recollection of what proved to be an
unexpectedly short stay in the Ring Building. They were two young
veterans who saw combat duty in World War II.

The first was Leonard A. ("Nik") Nikoloric, a torpedo boat
commander during the Great War. The other was G. Duane ("Bud")
Vieth. He was a radio man on a B-17 bomber who flew 28 missions
over Germany, including one on which his plane was shot down.
Luckily, he crashed in allied-held Belgium just outside the German
lines.

Nik was a Yale Law School graduate, sponsored by Professor Fred
Rodell, who was well known to Abe and Thurman. He was slender,
dark-skinned and good looking, with a fun-loving, free-wheeling
temperament. I quickly learned that, like me, Nik was a sports addict,
especially for horse-racing, on which he loved to gamble. As the only
two sports fans in the shop, we hit it off from the day he came aboard.

Oddly enough, Nik's affinity for horse racing led to the association
of Bud Vieth. It happened because Nik knew a bookie and I didn't.

One Saturday morning in 1949 I wanted to place a bet on a horse owned by the famed Calumet Farm, then the premier breeder of thoroughbreds, which also maintained the sports top racing stable. According to the press, it had an entry in a big race, with overnight odds of 20 to 1. Calumet's trainer was Ben Jones, the best in the business. I figured he wouldn't have entered the horse unless he thought it had a good chance. Knowing of Nik's contact with a bookie, I walked into his office to ask him to get my bet down. He was talking to a stranger. It was Bud, blond, young and good looking. Following Nik's introduction, we chatted for a while. I learned that he was a graduate of the Iowa Law School, where he had served as Editor-in-Chief of its law review. It took only a few moments to convince me that he was very bright, as well as naturally personable.

During our brief conversation, Bud described the purpose of his trip. He was on his way to New York to see Lou Carroll, a partner in Wendell Willkie's law firm. Carroll was an Iowa Law School graduate who annually hired a fellow alumnus. As Editor-in-Chief of the *Iowa Law Review*, Bud was that year's candidate. He had stopped by our office at Bob Hunt's suggestion. Hunt was Nik's classmate at Yale. After graduation he had joined the Iowa Law School faculty. He felt Bud was an outstanding talent and had persuaded him to meet with Nik.

I quickly concluded that we ought to make a pitch to have Bud join us. I told him that as a native New Yorker I disliked the city and thought that coming from Iowa, he would find it especially uncomfortable. I urged him to make no commitment to the Willkie firm until he talked to me on the following Monday. He agreed to do so.

The first thing Monday morning I told Abe of the exceptionally strong impression Bud had made on me. Although at first reluctant, he agreed to interview Bud, if I could arrange it. When Bud kept his promise to call me, I told him that Fortas would like to interview him for a post with our firm. It was arranged for the two to meet on the next day. Abe was equally impressed by Bud and offered him a job on the spot. Bud accepted. He soon became a Fortas favorite. To my great satisfaction, he not only vindicated my judgment of his ability, but became my close friend. He still is.

Before long we hired two more highly talented lawyers. They were George Bunn and Patricia Wald.

Bunn was about 6 ft., 3 in., lanky and laid-back. A quality lawyer, he worked principally with Paul on communication matters. George left the practice to teach law at the University of Wisconsin, where he rose to be dean of its law school. He later became a leading authority on disarmament issues.

Pat Wald was petite, cheerful, composed and brilliant. She had been an outstanding student at the Yale Law School at a time when relatively few women studied law. She had been a law clerk to Judge Jerome Frank on the Court of Appeals for the Second Circuit in New York. Abe Fortas had worked for Frank at the Agricultural Adjustment Agency. They were close friends.

Pat somehow made sense of an assignment for me, which involved analysis of the virtually unintelligible provisions of the Agricultural Adjustment Act relating to cottonseed oil. After invaluable service, she left us in 1952 to raise a family. Subsequently, she started a career in public service, capped by her appointment -- by President Carter -- as Judge of the United States Court of Appeals for the District of Columbia Court. She ultimately became Chief Judge of that Court and one of the most respected appellate judges in the country. Her portrait now adorns one of the classrooms at the Yale Law School.

Another Ring Building recruit, at Paul's instigation, was Harry Plotkin, a skilled lawyer from the staff of the Federal Communications Commission. He filled a need for specialized manpower to sustain Paul's growing communications practice. Harry eventually accomplished the impossible. Around 1955, he fell out with his sponsor, Paul Porter, and left our firm.

The unabated expansion of our practice soon forced another move, I believe in late 1952. This time we made a change which was radical and virtually unprecedented. I'm not sure whose idea it was, but the fathers decided to relocate in a lovely old, red brick townhouse, four stories in height. It occupied the southeast corner of the intersection at 19th and N Streets, N.W. The distance from the Ring Building was short. But there was a huge improvement in the quality and quantity of the space we were to occupy. Beyond that we found comfort in the thought that we had satisfied our space needs for all time to come. (How wrong we were. As time went on, we needed and added more and more space).

When we acquired it, the structure was used as a boarding house for what were known as "government girls", mainly secretaries, who worked for various government agencies. The building itself was completely sound, but required substantial renovations to make it suitable for occupancy by a law firm. Of course, our acquisition of the property compelled the seller to evict the boarders. When Judge Arnold learned of their identity, he observed: "Maybe we should have looked them over first."

Perhaps Abe Fortas was the source of the townhouse concept. At any rate, he asked me to prepare a mortgage payable to the owner of the building. To this day, it is the only one I have ever drafted. It was somewhat unique. The seller was a lady, interested solely in income from the property. She wanted no down payment, a highly desirable feature from our standpoint, since the purchase required no capital investment.

While the renovations were in progress, we accidentally learned of the building's history. It happened when a middle-aged stranger stopped by while Paul and Thurman were spending a little time observing the work in progress, while seated on a stack of building material. The stranger introduced himself as Pierce Butler and asked them what was going on. Paul answered that the building was under renovation to house a law firm named Arnold, Fortas & Porter.

Butler said he had lived in the house for many years while his father, the elder Pierce Butler, served as an Associate Justice on the Supreme Court. An extreme right wing member of the Court, his tenure occurred before and during the New Deal. Knowing this, either Paul or Thurman observed that Justice Butler must have turned over in his grave when he heard of the liberal firm planning to occupy his former residence. In the ensuing dialogue, Butler traced the fascinating history of the townhouse. Porter repeated the highlights to me.

Chauncey Depew, a famous New York lawyer, originally built the house as a wedding present for his niece, who, in fact, never married. It became the residence of Theodore Roosevelt while he served as assistant Secretary of the Navy. Pierce Butler, a Minnesotan, became its occupant upon his appointment to the Supreme Court.

As a true Irishman, Butler had an appetite for good liquor. It happened that the house was adjacent to the British Chancery. This proved a great convenience for Butler who lived at 1229 during the prohibition era. He had no problem in obtaining adequate supplies of his favorite drink through the Chancery. Nevertheless, as a loyal son of Erin, he delighted in disposing of the empties on the Chancery's manicured lawn.

Strangely enough, Justice Butler and Justice Oliver Wendell Holmes were close friends, although their philosophies differed widely on many judicial issues. Holmes frequently dined with the Butlers. The dining room at 1229 was on the second floor. One evening, after finishing an after dinner liqueur, Justice Holmes stumbled on the staircase on his way to the exit. This led Justice Butler to advise Pierce, Jr.: "We'd best put in a lift or the Justice may not come to dinner with us any more." This resulted in the installation of an elevator which afforded access to all four floors of the building. Following Butler's retirement, the building became the Dutch Chancery. When the Dutch moved out, it became a boarding house until we succeeded to its ownership.

The firm's days at 1229 may well have been the happiest in the firm's entire history. When the renovations were complete, we finally had space for everyone. All but the ground floor was served by the original and very beautiful circular stairway, plus the elevator installed by Justice Butler.

The ground floor was divided into two distinct sections. On the left of the entrance were the supply and duplicating facilities, plus a room for Harry, our all-around handyman, a ladies restroom and the boiler room. On the right side, there was additional living space. It included a small semi-kitchen equipped as a bar room, always well stocked with an ample supply of liquid refreshments. There were also two large rooms. One was used for miscellaneous purposes, including firm lunches held every Monday and occasional meetings. The other was known as the "Garden Room" because it was just inside a small open garden, situated on the outer wall of the south side of the building.

The Garden Room became a gathering place for the lawyers at the end of the work day. Judge Arnold and Paul Porter were usually on hand at about 6:15 to indulge in a libation and watch the television news. Their relaxed presence and insightful observations regularly attracted all members of the firm whose work permitted them to attend.

At the head of a short stairway to the first floor, we had our first true reception area. There we placed our first full-time receptionist, who doubled as our office telephone operator. She occupied a perfect position to welcome all visitors. There were seating areas on both sides of her desk and switchboard.

All three upper stories provided a number of good-sized offices. Arnold and Fortas were ensconced on opposite ends of the first floor. Arnold's space was really a suite. In front of his office, there was a large round room occupied by Marguerite O'Brien and two other secretaries. This might have been the original living room. Beyond it was Judge Arnold's office. It had previously served as a greenhouse. All three of its outside walls were made of glass. At the center of the ceiling there was a lighting fixture covered by a green globe. When this came to Porter's notice, he suggested that Arnold inscribe it with the words: "Ninth Precinct". The expanse of glass in Thurman's office made it frigid on cold winter days. I have a recollection of the Judge occasionally sitting at his desk in an overcoat.

Abe's office was on the N Street corner of the first floor. There was a smaller office adjacent to Abe's, which Bud Vieth accepted. Paul's office was directly above Abe's on the second floor and of the same size. In the middle of that floor, another larger room -- facing N Street -- served as our first real library -- a huge advantage in comparison with our previous quarters. Beyond the library, also looking out on N Street, there were two additional offices, each quite comfortable. Several additional offices were located on each of the two upper floors.

My first office at 1229 was located on the N Street corner of the fourth floor. It had only one drawback. Because there was no insulation, the roof was so close that the office could not be adequately heated on extra cold winter days or sufficiently cooled on extremely hot summer days, even with the use of two convectors.

My mind still retains a vignette of a steamy Sunday night in August when three of us worked in that office until midnight. The heat was almost unbearable. Besides myself, there were Judge Arnold and a young associate named Abe Krash. We were laboring on a brief which presented several knotty problems.

A University of Chicago law graduate, Krash was a scholarly, perceptive and articulate young lawyer. He hailed originally from Cheyenne, Wyoming, where he wrote sports for the *Wyoming Eagle*, a newspaper owned by an old friend of Judge Arnold's, Tracy McCracken. Krash soon became one of the firm's real stars, both in counseling and litigation.[1]

The job on that August night involved editing the first draft of a brief, which I had prepared, in response to a dangerous appeal from a substantial antitrust verdict won by Judge Arnold in Denver, Colorado. We were troubled by a number of difficult issues, particularly a serious question about the credibility of our client's principal witness. (The case is subsequently discussed in CHAPTER ELEVEN).

As the clock approached midnight, Judge Arnold was perspiring so profusely that Abe and I became concerned about his well-being. At that point, we exchanged knowing glances and I said: "Judge I think we've got this pretty well under control. Why don't you get on home while Abe and I wrap the thing up." After we persuaded him to leave, we kept working for another couple of hours before we were satisfied that we had a worthy product. As we left the office, Abe said: "Gee whiz, Norm, don't we ever get anything but oxygen tent cases?" I said: "Abe, that's our bread and butter. You might as well get used to it."

My most amusing memory of the 1229 townhouse is the day a glamorous film star called on Thurman. I don't remember her name. Our receptionist quickly buzzed the news to every woman in the office. In a flash they were all stationed on the staircase waiting for the lady to appear. So were some of the guys. After awhile, Thurman escorted the beautiful celebrity to her waiting limousine. As he stepped back into the office, he glanced at the staff assembled on the staircase and said: "I regret to state that I have reached the stage in life when I cannot afford to take yes for an answer."

Besides enhancing our comfort, the move to the 1229 townhouse led me to an unexpected revelation about Judge Arnold's sensibilities. As previously mentioned, the Judge's appearance was invariably rumpled, suggesting a total indifference to his apparel. Burn marks on his suits and shirts from the ashes of his cigars were virtually his trademark. He once noted with glee that the ashes did not cause his new shirts to burn up. He explained: "It's made of nylon, a new synthetic fabric; the ashes just make these little round holes." It was a natural assumption, therefore, that his clothing expenses were minimal. In contrast, I was always clothes conscious. So I wasn't prepared for what happened when I paid a call on Carlton's, a men's shop located in the Ring Building from which we had moved to 1229 six months earlier.

On greeting the proprietor -- Iz Semsker -- I said: "Hi, Iz, do you miss us?" He answered: "Man, I sure do, especially the Judge." I replied rather incredulously: "The Judge! You've got to be kidding." "No," said Iz, "he was our best customer." Still unconvinced, I asked for proof.

Iz was up to the task. "You know," he said, "I once sold the Judge three identical hats on the same day." "You're putting me on!" I exclaimed. "No," he insisted, "it's the absolute truth. He came in one morning about 9:30 and asked for a new hat because he had to attend some ceremony at the courthouse, for which his secretary, Marguerite O'Brien, said a hat would be in order.   At about 11:30, he returned and asked for another hat.   He explained that he had left the first one at the courthouse and had to attend an important luncheon engagement.   At 2:30, he came back and asked for a third one.   I said: What do you want with a third one, you already bought two? He told me: I know, but I forgot the second one at lunch, and I'm ashamed to tell my secretary that I lost two in one day."

Iz added, "The Judge was also my best tie customer.   On many days, he would come in after lunch, cut off his tie with a scissors and buy another one."   To those who knew, loved him, and frequently dined with him, the stains on the Judge's ties were a familiar and customary symbol of his persona.   But, none of us had any idea that he felt that fresh ties were *de riguer*.

CHAPTER EIGHT

THE MANAGEMENT

Abe took over the management of the firm from the very start. Neither Thurman nor Paul had any interest in that phase of the practice. Nor did it interest anyone else as long as Abe was in charge. All of us just assumed that his skills would ensure that things would be properly done. Actually, looking back over a history of fifty years with the firm, I think the surviving veterans of its early days now realize that its financial affairs were very simple. They consisted largely of overseeing the firm's expenditures, paying and signing checks for the firm's bills, including rent, the salaries of its personnel -- lawyers and staff -- plus filing occasional tax, social security and business license forms.

As I recall it, Fortas first handled these chores with the assistance of Marguerite O'Brien, Judge Arnold's secretary, and later hired a full-time bookkeeper. We also had an all-around handyman and one messenger. That was the entire supporting staff for some time. Later, we added an office manager -- the previously mentioned Dorothy Bailey.

No one felt intimidated by Abe's control of the firm's business affairs. Once Abe asked me to sign a note for a $500 loan from the firm. It didn't bother me. But when Thurman heard of it -- probably through Marguerite -- he was upset. He immediately sent for it and tore it up in my presence. He said, "It's your money," referring to the upcoming Christmas bonuses. However, Abe wasn't rigid about our fees. On one occasion, I raised his quotation in the presence of a client. It didn't bother him. Actually, I think Abe was something of a softie when it came to billing. I remember instances when he readily yielded to a client's protest about our charges.

Activities to develop clients were unknown. While they served with the firm, I don't recall that Arnold or Fortas ever once attended a Bar Association meeting. I doubt that they had much use for any professional organizations. It's my belief they thought the time could be better spent on the firm's affairs. Porter sometimes attended sessions of the Federal Communications Bar Association. I think he occasionally served as toastmaster at its annual dinners.

Abe once told me he deliberately tried to keep the firm understaffed because he thought it was more productive that way. While the founders were with us, I can remember only one case to which the firm assigned more than two lawyers. More often than not, the younger lawyers were pretty much responsible for handling a matter, subject only to the oversight of a more senior colleague. The full-time assistance of one associate was a luxury. We worked long, hard hours but enjoyed every minute of it. Remember, in those days paralegals, law clerks and legal assistants were unknown. The lawyers' work included the tedious aspects of the practice, notably document searches, sometimes in rundown out-of-town locations. We didn't mind. Building a law practice was an exciting venture. When the phone rang, you hoped it wasn't your wife or a social call.

There were no committees. Our meetings were few and far between. The only ones conducted with any regularity were those held at year-end, originally by the name partners, and later by all partners, including those with lesser equities in the firm. Their purpose was to decide on promotions to partnership status plus bonuses for all other lawyers. These were invariably generous and based solely on meritorious contribution to the quality and productivity of the firm's professional performance. When it came to monetary awards, the firm was a true meritocracy.

That this was not standard practice among major law firms was vividly brought home to me at our annual meeting in 1960. It was the first one attended by Carol Agger, Abe's wife. She had joined our firm, following substantial years of practice at the Washington outposts of two leading New York firms. After that meeting, she expressed amazement at the good cheer and harmony which had prevailed. She added that "at the other firms" where she had worked -- Lord, Day & Lord and Paul, Weiss, Wharton & Garrison -- partners would fight like tigers over decimal points when it came to compensation.

In justice to Abe, I think I should mention the circumstances which brought Carol to our firm.   Abe had nothing whatever to do with it. Arnold, Fortas & Porter originally had no tax lawyers.   Whenever we were presented with a matter involving tax considerations it was our custom to bring in a consultant from Carol's firm.

What precipitated her association with our firm was an unhappy experience I had with a treasured client, Nelson Poynter, publisher of the *St. Petersburg Times.* He was a client of Judge Arnold.   We had regularly performed substantial labor relations work for his newspaper, described in the succeeding CHAPTER TWENTY-ONE.   I was very active in the representation.   In the process, he and I had become close friends.   One day he asked to see me on a family matter which involved important tax elements.   As a matter of course, I brought in a lawyer from Carol's firm.   I don't remember who it was.

During a lengthy discussion of the problem, the tax attorney did most of the talking and recommended a solution.   The tax lawyer then left.   Poynter immediately expressed outrage at the presence of the outside lawyer.   He vehemently declared that he had retained Arnold, Fortas & Porter and no one else.   With that, he brusquely strode out of the office, without saying another word.   I sensed that Poynter was breaking his relationship with us for good.   That proved to be the reality.   He never called on us again.

I promptly reported the incident to Abe and suggested a need for our own tax lawyers, noting the growing proportion of our matters with significant tax implications.   Abe replied that he would never compete with Carol.   I asked whether he would object if I spoke to Carol.   He said I was free to talk to anyone, but would have no part in any discussions with Carol or anyone in her firm.

She was then practicing law with the Washington office of Paul, Weiss, Wharton & Garrison.   It was probably the nation's leading tax firm, headquartered in New York.   The head and shining star of the firm was Randolph Paul, who had chosen to locate in Washington.   By good fortune, I had worked with him.   He was a truly modest and likeable man, especially admirable, considering his towering stature in the tax field.   He was universally recognized as the nation's leading authority on tax law.

Besides his eminence as a practicing lawyer, Paul was the principal author of a six volume treatise on the subject of income taxes.[1]   For many years it was the indispensable source of guidance in the field and the bulwark of virtually every course on taxation taught in the nation's law schools.

Immediately after my discussion with Abe, I talked to Milt Freeman, suggesting that we immediately get in touch with Carol to see if she would be interested in joining our firm along with her Washington colleagues. Randolph Paul had recently died. I don't know whether his death influenced her thinking, but she proved willing to join us. In any event, Milt and I met with her and her major remaining Washington partner, Louis Eisenstein. Paul told me Eisenstein possessed the best tax mind he had ever encountered. We quickly worked out a mutually agreeable arrangement. Soon afterward, the Washington office of Paul, Weiss joined forces with us. Carol turned out to be a real trooper who proved a perfect fit for our shop. Sadly, Eisenstein died in the mid-1960's as the result of a brain cancer. It was a major loss for our firm.

**Carol Agger at work as head
of the Firm's Tax Department**

CHAPTER NINE

LIFE WITH THE FATHERS

It was a junior lawyer's delight to work with Judge Arnold. If anything went wrong, it was Arnold's fault. If something went well, the junior man got the credit. It wasn't an affectation -- just his normal way.

Arnold's generosity of spirit was not limited to exchanges among lawyers within the office. He was no less liberal with his compliments to his colleagues in the presence of clients. By way of example, the Judge had been retained by the owner of a British company called Scophany. It had lost a Supreme Court case which held that it could be sued in the United States under the Sherman Antitrust Act for restraint of trade and monopoly in the manufacture of television equipment.[1] Our job was to develop a proposal by which Scophany could work out a satisfactory settlement with the Antitrust Division of the Justice Department. Arnold handed the task to me.

When I came up with a suggestion, he approved it and called in the client's president. The Judge then outlined our recommendation. The client was elated. He congratulated Arnold for a wonderful idea. The Judge replied: "Oh, don't give me any credit. Thank Norman. It was his idea. I never would have thought of it in a million years." It was a real thrill, hearing such an accolade from the most creative legal mind I'd ever known.

Arnold's wit was a source of continuous delight. One of his all-time classics was the following memorandum, circulated among all lawyers and staff members of the firm about the physical disarray of our offices:

MEMORANDUM: Partners, Associates, and
                         Staff of Arnold, Fortas and
                         Porter and their Heirs and
                         Assigns forever.

FROM: Thurman Arnold

The Department of Health and Sanitation of the District of Columbia is about to indict the firm of Arnold, Fortas and Porter for conditions of chaos, disorder, and general litter in their offices which the Department alleges are a menace to health and safety and an affront to the aesthetic sensibilities of the entire population of the District, which the last census shows to be nearly a million people.

The Committee on Un-American Activities has informed me that the office looks like the kind of an office in which Communists congregate and multiply.

For these reasons I have given Miss Dorothy Bailey the responsibility of raising sufficient hell with everyone from the partners up, to the end that the papers, gadgets, files, books, briefcases and other flotsam and jetsam which are now scattered around the place from hell to breakfast shall be removed and the semblance of order restored and continuously maintained during the balance of this year of our Lord, 1951.

More specifically, Dorothy Bailey is directed to remove the files which Paul A. Porter has placed on the floor of the library. She is directed to inform Paul A. Porter that the reason we put shelves in the library was to keep things off the floor, an idea which might automatically occur to a more reflective mind. She is further directed to inform Walton Hamilton that the disreputable looking file which he keeps on the floor of the large room must be removed to a less conspicuous site, preferably in his own office although he may keep it in the men's room if he finds it more convenient.

The so-called Conference Room is to be rearranged according to more adequate aesthetic principles. In this connection I offer the strong suggestion that the couch is a singularly inappropriate piece of equipment for any purposes for which the said conference room is intended to be used.

No one seems to remember to close cabinet doors. It will lighten Miss Bailey's task greatly if anyone who opens them will immediately thereafter close them again. This technique may be difficult at first, but, like riding a bicycle, once acquired, it is never lost. It is also a very beneficial exercise which I hope may tend to reduce the weight of some of the heavier members of our little group. The same observation holds for books left on the library table. Replacing them after use creates better circulation of the blood and improves one's metabolism.

The partners, associates, and staff may have access at all reasonable times to my own office so that they can observe how a well-kept office looks.

Yours for a better life
in the future

Thurman Arnold

I hardly need add that Thurman's office was far from a clean-desk model. An assortment of papers, briefs and mail were usually piled one foot high on his desk, in no discernible organization. At least once a week he would dump a barely lit cigar, on which he had chewed for sometime, into a half-filled wastebasket from which heavy smoke would soon pour through the halls, until the fire was extinguished.

For some reason, Laura Kalman felt impelled to detract from the firm's image as a place where "[t]he morale of the entire office is exceedingly high."[2] This led her to cast Fortas as a tyrant who bullied his younger colleagues at every turn. However, after doing the damage, she seems to soften that portrayal. In my opinion she just never could get a valid reading of Fortas.

In her negative vein, she began:

> Arnold, Fortas & Porter seemed superficially very different from the average conservative Wall Street firm. Outsiders saw it as a warm and convivial place, with weekly luncheons to which all associates and partners were invited and nightly cocktail hours in the firm's Garden Room, where Arnold and Porter held forth . . .

*   *   *

> Appearances, however, contrasted with reality. Fortas controlled the firm. . . .[3]

As already indicated, she then denigrated Abe, almost exclusively through anonymous sources which I suspect were unduly sensitive, younger members of the firm. Later, however, she saluted the firm's *"esprit de corps."* In that focus she suggested that Abe's demeanor may have been an act designed to offset the sense of comfort radiating from Thurman and Paul, by reminding the staff that the practice of law was serious business. In her words:

> . . . Arnold and Porter created an esprit de corps. Arnold, as one lawyer said, was "marvelously warm," the sort of person who would tell everyone that a document an associate had written for him was the best piece produced in the firm in the past five years. "Next week [Arnold would praise] something else," the underling recalled, but "you would go home and tell your wife because you would walk on air. You would glow . . . because he made you feel so good. He had a wonderful ability to encourage you and inspire you. Porter too was inspirational and encouraging. As long as Arnold and Porter encouraged associates so frequently, Fortas might have reasoned, he did not need to do so and perhaps should be that much harder on them. "He felt that someone in a law firm had to be the mean guy, the tough guy, the heavy," a colleague recalled.[4]

I don't buy Kalman's assessment of Abe's persona. Admittedly, he was not by nature a "hail fellow well met." But I think she misses a point which her research should have readily disclosed and I've already discussed. His intensely reserved attitude was a product of his elevation to high positions at a very young age.

The idea that Abe was mysterious is a recurrent theme in Kalman's work. At one point she is curiously moved to observe:

> Even his choice of law partners seemed puzzling. Arnold, Fortas, and Porter shared a love of humor. Beyond that, they could not have been more different.[5]

This observation makes no sense to me. For one thing, I can't understand the implication that law partners should be products of the same cookie cutter. For another, the choice of his partners certainly wasn't "puzzling" to Abe. His knowledge of Arnold traced to their concurrent service in three different environments. They were colleagues on the Yale Law School faculty. They worked on at least one common project at the Agricultural Adjustment Administration.

Both were involved with investigations relating to the passage of securities legislation and the establishment of the Securities and Exchange Commission. Porter had also served at the AAA and was a well-known New Dealer with a common affinity for liberal principles.[6]

Talk about being puzzled: I just don't get her conclusion that Abe "shared a love of humor" with Thurman and Paul. Humor was ingrained in them, but superficial in him. Nor do I grasp this peculiar observation:

> . . . Fortas retained the playfulness that had characterized him as a young New Dealer. His jokes were strained but Fortas never stopped trying to match the humorousness of Arnold and Porter.[7]

This doesn't accord with my recollection. I don't recall that Abe ever told even a single joke in or out of the office. He rarely tried to say anything funny. The idea that he "strained" to match wits with his partners is way off the mark. Abe was much too smart to be a distant also-ran to his super-humorous partners.

I worked with Abe on many occasions and sometimes traveled with him. On occasion, we shared a room when engaged in an out-of-town matter. I never found his manner imperious or uncivil, although it was seldom companionable. We generally spoke man to man on the legal issues jointly occupying us at any particular time.

By way of illustration: although I sensed his feeling that my ownership interest in a horse racing stable encroached on my time for office business, he never criticized me for it. In fact the horses took me from the office every Friday from Memorial Day through Labor Day. I compensated for that by coming to the office at about 5:30 a.m. four days a week during those intervals, but I never mentioned it to Abe. On one occasion while we were Cincinnati on Federated business, he referred to a phone call he had taken from one of my co-owners, advising that our horse had won an important race. End of conversation.

In my experience, which included a fair number of joint projects with Abe, I always felt free to express my thoughts whether we were conferring with a client or with representatives of the opposition. I spoke with the same candor in their presence as I would with my colleagues in the office.

The significance of Abe's recognition of his juniors' "First Amendment" rights dawned on me early in the practice. At the time,

I had been retained by Kroger to represent it in a novel case -- the first brought under Section 8 of the Clayton Act. That provision prohibits interlocking directorates among competing corporations.[8] In other words, it outlawed simultaneous service on the boards of companies in competition with each other.

The case was brought in the U.S. District Court for the Southern District of New York. A man named Hancock was the individual defendant. He sat on a number of corporate boards, including Kroger's. The interlocked, competing corporations -- among them Kroger -- were named as defendants. I brought Fortas into the case and worked on the matter with him. It was then in a preliminary phase. He immediately advised Kroger to drop Hancock from its Board. Kroger got the job done, which ultimately helped to establish a successful defense.

The key defendant, Hancock, and the other corporations, were represented by Eustace Seligman of Sullivan & Cromwell, the epitome of a "white shoe" Wall Street law firm. Seligman was one of its major partners and one of the very few Jews occupying such a position.

We won in the trial court on a theory advocated by Abe.[9] The Supreme Court agreed to review the case. Seligman was disappointed that he had to split the oral argument with Abe. He came down to meet with us the day before the argument, accompanied by two colleagues, both at least ten years my senior. As we discussed strategy for the argument, Abe and I expressed our thoughts. I was speaking just as freely as Fortas. When we got through, Seligman, who had those two lawyers in tow -- said "Humph, my technicians tell me, etc." He was a real stuffed shirt. Neither one of the other two lawyers ever opened his mouth. We also won the case in the Supreme Court -- again, in my opinion, thanks largely to Abe's strategy and argument.[10]

Paul's typical conversations at the office were usually characterized by colorful comments. If he heard that something untrue was being spread about the firm, he wouldn't just say it's a lie. Instead he'd suggest that the tale bearer be told to stop telling lies about us or we'd start telling the truth about him. When groping for the answer to a legal problem, he might observe: "I'm like the blind dog in the meathouse. I can smell it, but I can't see it."

Paul was a daily tonic for just about everything that could have ailed us at Arnold, Fortas & Porter. His presence contributed in large measure to our well-deserved reputation as a congenial fun-loving

LIFE WITH THE FATHERS   99

organization. Following Abe's elevation to the Court, a writer for *The Washingtonian* magazine had this to say:

> Arnold & Porter (Abe Fortas' old firm), has an off-beat, youthful, racy personality that makes stuffy people nervous, but all things considered, it probably has more quality per square inch than any other firm. It is also the most likable. Lawyers speak happily of it, almost as if they slept better at night knowing it was there. "There's not a dud in the lot," one lawyer said, his admiration untinged with envy.[11]

I've already mentioned the nightly happy hour in the Garden Room at 1229. I recall arriving a little early one evening. I had started to pour myself a drink when I noticed that the only other persons in the room were Judge Arnold and Bob Woodruff, CEO and major stockholder of Coca Cola. I started to back off, when Woodruff said: "Come on in, Norm, join the fun, have a drink."

Offhand, I remember that Marty Pendergast, Vice President and General Counsel of Lever Brothers, was another client who attended. George Leonard, Kroger's long-time Vice President and General Counsel was frequently on hand. So were Marty Riger and Jack Ratzkin, the top lawyers for Federated, and many others. What made so many of our clients' personnel feel at home with us traces back to what was known in the firm as the "lateral pass." I quote Kalman:

> . . . Fortas believed in what he called the "lateral pass." He convinced the client he could not function without Abe Fortas, and then he persuaded him he could not live without G. Duane Vieth, Norman Diamond, or someone else who became the client's caretaker.[12]

I fervently favor this formula. It enhances everyone's devotion to the firm. I'm absolutely convinced that it institutionalizes the firm's practice, for the benefit of the entire membership, present and future. Accordingly, I assigned many young partners and often associates to handle matters for me on their own, as soon as I thought they were ready. My only request was that they keep me informed about the progress of their assignments while so engaged.

The practice paid dividends. Kroger dealt with a number of law firms besides our own. Leonard told me on several occasions that the senior partners at all law firms were top-notch professionals. He emphasized that what distinguished Arnold & Porter was the superb quality of its talent, all the way from its senior to its most junior lawyers.

There was lots of socializing during the years when the three founding fathers were active. There were luncheons every Monday for all lawyers in the room adjoining the Garden Room of our townhouse offices. A formal dinner dance for all lawyers and their spouses or special friends was a regular feature of the year. So was a Memorial Day picnic. Every summer Arnold held an outdoor party for the legal staff at his beautiful estate just outside Alexandria.

The staff shared the conviviality of Arnold, Fortas and Porter. The administrative staff, secretaries, handyman, messengers were all part of the family. There was no hierarchy.

Perhaps the cheerful spirit which permeated the firm during the active times of the name partners is best exemplified by the carefree mood of the annual, sit-down Christmas dinner parties. These were attended by lawyers and staff. There were skits by the younger lawyers -- usually the associates -- invariably hilarious takeoffs on anyone and everything around the firm, including all partners.

The regular highlight of the event was the eagerly awaited windup speech by Thurman Arnold -- always a mixture of nonsense and wildly imaginary events. In 1965, Thurman was introduced by Abe Fortas, on his return to share our Christmas Party, following his appointment to the Supreme Court that same year. Fortunately, the events of that dinner were recorded since Thurman always spoke without a text. We never knew what he'd say in the next sentence.

Abe began by spoofing Thurman's Ivy League education -- including his participation at Princeton in a course called "How to Mature Cigars and Make Women Feel Younger." He then delivered the following heartfelt tribute to Arnold:

> "I love him very, very much, and I'm sure you all love him. There is no man that I have ever known that I admire as much as I do Thurman, or from whom I have learned as much as I have from him. I've learned so much about what life is and what the obligations of a man are, and what it is to be a man, and what it is to cope with fear, and what it is to fulfill a man's destiny, from Thurman Arnold,"

Then Arnold spoke:

Mr. Justice Fortas, and ladies and gentlemen comprising that great eleemosynary institution known today as Arnold & Porter. I am grateful for the historical research that Abe Fortas has dedicated to my career. Everything he said is about 20% accurate. The only quarrel I have with him is his understatement of my qualifications at the end of his speech. Mr. Justice, as an alumnus of this firm, we are grateful to welcome you back to this party. We have a feeling of awe and reverence that you're standing on the highest pinnacle known to the law, your black robe flopping in the wind.

No other court in the history of civilized jurisprudence since the days of Hammurabi has done so much for helpless minorities. You have made the lives of Don Traughton and destitute criminals happiest. I'm not unaware of the fact that many earnest and holy men have advised me that the Court is solely responsible for the present increase in crime. I say that is very true. But it is a small price to pay for the encouragement of these men who roam the streets, snatching pocketbooks and earning a very inferior living. And the second greatest achievement of your Court, and I am sincere about this, is the relief of schools from the responsibility of writing prayers. Here, I applaud, but I want to call the Court's attention respectfully and deferentially to the danger of these decisions in a problem which I don't think the Court quite realizes, and that is the devaluation of the dollar.

I do not think it is the drain of gold that is causing the fears of devaluation. I think that Europeans who are selling the dollar short are afraid that these religious decisions will ultimately result in the removal from the dollar of the phrase "In God We Trust." Now, if those decisions are escalated -- I do not criticize, of course -- but if those decisions are escalated, God may get sore. And if He does, and He goes on the side of the Communists, and a couple of more decisions like that may cause him to do so, the dollar will go to hell.

And so I respectfully remind the Justice, and ask him to convey my message to his colleagues, that he must not cross the Yalu River with respect to disrespect to God. I do not say he's gone too far now, but the same dangers that face us in the escalation of the recent War, face us in the war of the United States Supreme Court against religion. And finally, I commend the Court for having the most greatest and most solid reputation of any Court in the civilized world since the days of Hammurabi for complete unpredictability. The result, the happiest and the most prosperous bar in the world. There is only one fly in this judicial ointment and that is the worries and the fevers and the frets that now plague the firm of Arnold & Porter since Abe has gone. Abe was the goose that laid the golden egg. He was the captain and the scrambling quarterback of this firm, throwing passes in all directions and every one of them found a receiver.

Now, as I look forth on this sea of upturned faces, I am compelled to observe that there are more than about 25 people whom we've had to retain in order to do the work that Abe did all by himself.

I do not criticize the distinguished lawyers who took the risk of joining this firm. They are men of the greatest courage and dedication. I consider them comparable to the soldiers in Vietnam. They are trying to preserve American democracy. You gentlemen who come with us are fighting to preserve and fighting for the survival of Arnold & Porter. But on the other hand, the problems of caring for and feeding the rapidly growing firm -- ah, families, of these men who have joined us at this great risk, are bleeding us white. Their ideas of what are required to live on a scale which they consider necessary are extravagant.

And so, the firm of Arnold & Fortas -- Arnold & Porter -- is today loaded below the plimsoll line. We cannot carry on our projects any more than the United States can carry on its projects because of this enormous expense for the people who replaced Abe Fortas. Arnold, Fortas & Porter -- Arnold & Porter, I should say -- is at present in the situation of a sinking ship in shallow water and sinking mighty fast.

I have hope here, and I -- things sustain me in these dark days -- I think that the American public is beginning to realize that our contribution to the public weal and to the judicial establishment in giving Abe Fortas to the Supreme Court is greater than the contribution of any other organization in the United States, except perhaps the NAACP. And it is my belief, and I am informed, that there is going to be a nationwide drive to raise funds for Arnold & Porter to replace Abe Fortas. Next spring, you will see the slogan all over the United States -- "Give until it hurts. Arnold & Porter need shirts."

And I am informed that the next Congress, in recognition of our gift of Abe Fortas to the public sector, has provided for his affairs so as to give us a perpetual subsidy. So, I think we will survive and you gentlemen who have taken the risk and have joined this firm will probably be remunerated far more than you are entitled.

Next, for a more cheerful note, Paul Porter always leaves for Christmas. But he never fails to give us a message to be read at the dinner. The wit and wisdom of these messages -- you people have attended several dinners -- is notorious.

This time, Paul Porter spent, before leaving, the entire morning in writing out his message, which I am about to read, but I think that I should inform you that this is the wittiest, the most succinct and the best message that he has yet given this firm in his absence. I will read it now.

"Memo to Judge Arnold from Paul Porter. This is to remind you that you agreed to deliver a message on my behalf to the dearly beloved who are assembled in the Christmas party. My message is as follows: "Merry Christmas." You know, for originality, you can't beat that. My prediction is that phrase, which was coined just before Paul Porter left, will be on every Christmas card sent in the United States next year.

When Abe Fortas joined the firm, he was horrified. He said, "This firm has been grinding down the hired help, making them buy their own typewriters. I will not put up with it. You must remember that the sole purpose of this firm is to feed and clothe and make happy the stenographers and the associates. The profits of the members of this firm are nothing. Our purpose is to make our associates happy. And that has been the policy of this firm ever since Abe Fortas took over control and captured this sinking ship and got it afloat again, and the policy's paid back. It has paid off in great degree, and I was very much moved to what happened this year.

This year, we gave the most extravagant and undeserved bonuses to the associates in the history of civilized law. And as they came in, I told them that Vic Kramer [a firm partner] had agreed to stabilize the situation. I said, "If you don't think you've got enough, you can go to Vic Kramer, and he will write his personal check and give you what you think you ought to have." I said, "On the other hand, if you think you've got too much, you go to Vic Kramer and turn your check in to him." I thought Vic was undergoing a risk there, but he wasn't. The last reports I have are that, of the income and outgo, he has made $15,000 which is a great tribute to the associates of this firm, and I think from now on, we'll let them set their own bonuses.

Well, we're getting to my reminiscences, and I want you to evaluate them by two standards. First, as loyal members of this firm, you should believe implicitly in everything I say. Second, you should recognize that I am an old man, and most of the things that I remember best never really happened.

With those standards, you can easily, being antitrust lawyers, come to an equitable result, and I want to tell you who it was and this may be of interest to the ambitious young man who wants to succeed in the law. How it was that I came to be a partner in this worldwide eleemosynary institution known as Arnold & Porter. I was a student at the Harvard Law School, and my roommate and I decided there wasn't much sense in practicing law. It was too hard work, and so we thought of another career. We both were fond of cigars, and we thought perhaps the profession of aging cigars would be one that would appeal to people of our sophisticated taste. Now, the profession of aging cigars is not a difficult one. You store cigars of the best Havana types in humidors. You then sit down and take them out, one by one, and smoke them to see if they are aging properly and if they are not aging properly, there isn't a god damn thing you can do about it. Such a profession is obviously superior to the drudgery of practicing law.

But there were certain obstacles in our path. One is that, if we adopted that profession, we couldn't marry because no respectable woman will marry a man who intends to spend his life sitting around in the house smoking cigars. And there was a real problem because it happened that we were both so attracted to women that they fought for our attentions and we thought we might succumb.

And so we decided that we would retire to the top of some snowy peak in the Rocky Mountains where there were no women and there was a difficulty there because if we picked a peak so steep that the women couldn't climb up, we couldn't climb up there either. Well, in any event, we picked Medicine Bow Peak in the Rocky Mountains near Laramie, and we decided to build a castle up there. The living room of that castle would be 100 feet long and 50 feet wide, and because we never intended to go down from the castle, we needed religious instruction and we needed something to quench our throat and we needed music.

So, on the 100 foot side of the castle we designed a bar where there would be ten bartenders and at the far short end of that living room, we designed six pulpits, which would be occupied by six preachers of different denominations. At the other end of the hall, we designed a great pipe organ that could peal forth religious music and on the other side were the humidors filled with cigars that we intended to age.

Now, as for the women problem because we -- the mountain was not steep enough to prevent any women from climbing it. We designed the following solution: we had a trusty seneschal -- I hope you understand that word -- who would stand at the gate and as each woman climbed the mountain to reach us, the trusty seneschal would put her in a grease slide protected on each side and she would go shooting down 4,000 feet to the plains below. And if she did it again, he would do the same thing again and we hoped eventually she might get discouraged.

Well, picture the scene as we envisioned it on a Sunday morning. At 11 o'clock, my roommate and I would wake up. We would press button number one and the six preachers would start preaching all at once, shouting to drown each other out and we would press button number two and the great organ would peal forth and we would press button number three and all the bartenders would start mixing drinks and the rule was that all drinks mixed in the room must be drunk, and outside would be this inspiring sight, a long line of women, beautiful women, climbing this 4,000 foot slope. As each reached the top, she would be put in the slide by the trusty seneschal and descend to the plains below. And the organ would be pealing, and the preachers would be preaching, and the bartenders would be mixing drinks, and the women would be going up and sliding down below. Can you imagine a career of aging cigars more attractive than that and, of course, we didn't want to practice law and had we achieved that dream, I would never be the head or the tutelary divinity or a part of Arnold & Porter.

But there was one difficulty. That profession required financing, so we adopted a plan to finance it. Major Lee Higginson, who was an avaricious man, was a great banker in Boston. He later fell for Kreuger, the match king, and we decided to go to him and say, "Major Higginson, we will bet you $500,000 that on the 8th day of June in the time of a full moon over the Charles River in Cambridge, we can make the moon do a figure eight." Well, of course, being an avaricious man, he would certainly bet on such a sure thing as that, and we expected him to take us up without even examining our financial qualifications to pay the bet, and it seemed pretty simple, and then the evening of the -- the scientists who scoff at us and say we couldn't do it -- and we would scoff back and the matter would get international publicity and then on the evening on the 8th of June or whatever date it was on the full moon --

Whatever the date was of the full moon there would be this assemblage on the banks of the Charles for Norey Pearson; my roommate and I would be in frock coats and silk hats. We would have the Nobel prize winners and the eminent astronomers on this platform with us. Lee Higginson would be there. There would be a number of bright Swedes just to add color, because I always believe that bright Swedes add color to everything. The moment would approach to do a count down. Ten seconds. Nine seconds, and so on until the exact second came when the moon would do the figure eight and then we would make the moon do it. Unfortunately, we never devised a method of making that moon do the figure eight. Otherwise, that perfect scheme which we, in our secret correspondence designated as El Schemo, was defeated by this little technicality, which we later designated as El Rubbo. Well, no one -- today, I doubt if in the age of miracles, Major Higginson would have taken the bet but remember that was in the year 40 B.C. I mean by B.C., before commuters. Well, the scheme didn't work. We gave it up. I became a practitioner of law and that is how I got to be a partner in the firm of Arnold & Porter.

And now, I end my reminiscences. I say that I am dreaming of a small firm just like the firm I used to know, where stenographers were cheery and nobody got weary until the god damn thing began to grow. And I close with the benediction which I have always closed with for the past 20 years. That is the benediction of the Benevolent and Protective Order of Elks, which I joined in nineteen hundred and twenty because it was the only place you could get a drink in Laramie, and I'm giving away a secret of that order and I hope you will keep it confidential but we have adopted this secret ritual of the Order of Elks as our own ritual and so will you repeat after me as I say this benediction: And now --

AUDIENCE: And now --

ARNOLD: The mystic hour of eleven approaches --

AUDIENCE: The mystic hour of eleven approaches --

ARNOLD: And the great heart of elkdom --

AUDIENCE: And the great heart of elkdom --

ARNOLD: Throbs and beats --

AUDIENCE: Throbs and beats --

ARNOLD: As we say the toast --

AUDIENCE: As we say the toast --

ARNOLD: To our absent brothers --

AUDIENCE: To our absent brothers. (applause)

I'm certain that Arnold, as usual, delivered his speech extemporaneously.[13] Abe's reference to the course at Princeton on "How to Mature Cigars and Make Women Feel Younger" doubtlessly stimulated Arnold's imagination.

The sense of fun that pervaded the office did not merely keep us amused. It promoted the firm's productivity and the excellence of its legal work. To me our way of life proved that the best results are truly achieved by those who take their work, but not themselves, seriously.

Arnold proved that he was aware of that fundamental truth by his inscription to me in my copy of his autobiography which reads:

"To Norman Diamond

From the greatest lawyer in the United States to his only conceivable competitor

Thurman Arnold

If I hadn't learned the lesson before, I surely did from that inscription.[14]

**The author is surprised on his 75th birthday
by a brief office party arranged by his secretary**

Part III - What We Did

CHAPTER TEN

FROM NEW YORK TO NEW YORK

Immediately after signing on with Arnold, Fortas & Porter, I left for my folks' place in New York. After a fine dinner, drowsiness beckoned me to an early bedtime. The next morning a long distance call awakened me from a sound sleep. Marguerite O'Brien, whom I had informed of my whereabouts, told me Judge Arnold was eager to see me right away. "Sure," I said, stimulated by a sense of duty to my first private employer. I caught the next train to Washington and arrived in Judge Arnold's office at 3:00 p.m, on a Thursday afternoon. As soon as he saw me, the Judge said, "Glad you're here! We've got to leave for New York at once." I never let on where I had been.

We took the New York overnight that same evening -- boardable after 10:00 p.m., departure at 2:00 a.m. and debarkation by 7:00 a.m. Just after 7:00 a.m. Friday morning, I looked for Judge Arnold on the station platform. He was nowhere to be seen. Vaguely recalling an intimation that he had planned to stay at the Roosevelt Hotel for the weekend, I made my way to its dining room. There sat the Judge in the middle of a hearty repast. He glanced at me and casually said: "Sit down and have some breakfast." The Gods were smiling when I found him. He hadn't told me where we were going or who we were to see.

After breakfast, we hailed a cab to meet the client. It was Samuel Goldwyn Productions Inc., an independent motion picture producer. More specifically, we met with the Executive Vice President of the organization, James "Jim" Mulvey. As a rabid Brooklyn Dodger fan, I recognized the name. He had married one of the daughters of the McKeever Brothers. Along with Charles Ebbets, they were the original owners of the Dodgers -- then a religion with every kid raised in Brooklyn.

At that time films would open in a downtown first-run house and then move to second, third and fourth run theatres. The first run was by far the most profitable. Goldwyn's difficulty was that all of the nation's first-run houses were either owned or contractually controlled by the five largest motion picture producers. They monopolized them for their own films, plus those of the three other largest film producers. Mulvey's question was whether an action for triple damages could be successfully prosecuted against any of the five producer/exhibitors -- for antitrust violations -- because of their refusal to provide first-run theatres for Goldwyn films.

At that time a government antitrust suit was pending against those eight producers.[1] The case had been filed by Arnold while he headed the Antitrust Division of the U.S. Department of Justice. Its principal aim was to force the producers to divest either their film exhibition businesses or their film production enterprises. This would restore competition within the motion picture industry. In either event, the financial incentive for preferences would evaporate. There would be no advantage in reciprocal back-scratching. No final decision had yet been rendered in the government's case at the time of our meeting with Mulvey.

After some general conversation, Judge Arnold left, advising Mulvey that I would get all the details. We would then submit the firm's opinion. As soon as Judge Arnold left, Mulvey said to me: "Let's take the afternoon off. It's Friday. We'll get started first thing Monday morning." Imbued with dedication on my first assignment in the practice, I solemnly stated: "Mr. Mulvey, we've got lots of work to do; we'd better get started this afternoon." He answered, "Let's go to lunch."

We then repaired to Toots Shor's, a bistro frequented by numerous figures from the sports and entertainment worlds. Toots was a real New York character; a large, heavy-set man with a ruddy complexion, genial manner and a hearty voice. If you made his inner circle, he was apt to greet you as a "crumb bum."

As soon as he had introduced me to Toots, Mulvey was spotted by Ford Frick, then a prominent sports writer, soon to become President of the National League and later Commissioner of Baseball. After greetings were exchanged, a round of martinis was ordered. I was able to join in, thanks to my Navy training.

FROM NEW YORK TO NEW YORK

Mulvey soon greeted a succession of other sports celebrities. A round of martinis was mandatory with each introduction. I was pretty well smashed by the time Mulvey and I sat down to lunch. He ordered yet another martini for the two of us. By this time the whole room was spinning around me. I was barely conscious. I somehow managed to order chicken curry when another martini arrived. I couldn't face it. Realizing that I was about to pass out, I staggered to my feet, mumbled to Mr. Mulvey that I needed to prepare for our afternoon session and left the table.

The next thing I remember, a nice lady -- Mr. Mulvey's secretary -- was tapping my shoulder and saying, "it's 5:00 o'clock, time to go home." I awakened with a start, looked around, and realized that I had been sleeping on a window seat in Mr. Mulvey's office. I immediately asked: "Where's Mr. Mulvey?" "Oh," she answered, "he never came back from lunch."

Mulvey's strategy had worked. To this day, I have no recollection of anything that occurred between the time I left the restaurant and the 5:00 p.m. wake-up tap from Mulvey's secretary. I've often wondered how I managed to find my way back to his office.

Beginning on Monday morning, I worked with Mulvey for ten days in a manner never repeated with any other client. He carried on his regular business affairs throughout. When those affairs permitted, he described in great detail Goldwyn's futile efforts to gain first-run exhibitions and adequate compensation for its films, meanwhile answering my intermittent questions.

Upon our completion and transmittal of a thorough opinion letter, the Judge sent it to Mulvey, along with a short letter advising that our fee was $10,000.00. This elicited a pained protest from Samuel Goldwyn -- Yogi Berra's only rival in the history of malapropropion anecdotes. Goldwyn nevertheless paid the fee.

He later used our opinion as the basis of a treble damage action under the Sherman Antitrust Act, but employed California attorneys for the litigation. The defendants were Twentieth Century Fox Films and various of its theatrical agencies and affiliates. Goldwyn won a judgment for $300,000.00 in damages, plus a $100,000.00 attorneys' fee.[2]

I told Abe about the Mulvey episode when I got back to the office. He said: "Well, you've just learned a lesson. You need a cast-iron stomach to practice law."

CHAPTER ELEVEN

THE BURMA THEATRE

In 1952, Judge Arnold brought an antitrust action for treble damages in the United States District Court for the State of Colorado on behalf of Cinema Amusements, Inc. It owned The Broadway, an independent downtown theatre located in Denver, Colorado. The charge was that the defendants had conspired to deprive The Broadway of first-run films, although it was eminently qualified for that status. By that time the government had won its suit against the five major producer/exhibitors, for monopolizing both the filming and theatre exhibition of motion pictures.[1] The defendants in the Denver suit were three of them. Notwithstanding a near disaster during the trial, described below, the jury returned a substantial judgment -- $300,000 plus attorney fees -- for our client.[2]

As usual, the preparation largely comprised "pre-trial discovery." Its purpose is to prevent trial by "ambush" -- i.e., the introduction of surprise evidence. The process involves the pre-trial elicitation from the opposition or third parties of evidence related to the issues in the case or information likely to uncover such evidence. There are three basic methods by which this may be accomplished. One is oral or written examination of any knowledgeable individual, usually represented by counsel, who is noticed for an oral or written "deposition." Another is by written "interrogatories" to the opponent which must be answered under oath. The third is by a motion for the production of described documents in possession of the opposition. Pertinent documents in the possession of a person other than a party are obtainable by subpoena.

In the typical fashion of the firm's early days, Judge Arnold never enjoyed the assistance of more than one associate. In the *Cinema Amusements* case, he was initially assisted by the newly hired Yale Law graduate named Leonard Nikoloric -- "Nik" to all of us. He had the responsibility of conducting our discovery. In doing so, he embarked on a marathon series of oral depositions. When he arrived at the appointed time and place for the first one, he found four representatives of a Wall Street law firm representing the defendants. The junior among them had been a law school classmate of Nik's. Time went by without presentation of the witness. After about twenty minutes, Nik asked: "What's holding us up." His classmate said: "We're waiting for your partners." Nik answered: "There aren't any, I'm it, let's go."

Later on, following the completion of discovery, but before trial, Nik announced that he was leaving the firm to practice law in Portland, Oregon with C. Girard ("Jebby") Davidson, a close friend of Fortas and his colleague at Interior. We all assumed Nik had surrendered to the belief that there was "gold in them thar hills."

To replace Nik we hired Bill McGovern, previously mentioned in CHAPTER TWO. He was one of my law school classmates. The son of a Bridgeport, Connecticut cop, the shamrock itself couldn't have been more Irish. Loaded with personality, he was good-natured, good-looking and blessed with a marvelous wit -- an ideal addition to the firm. Professionally, Bill had top notch antitrust credentials, with a special courtroom skill. He had served with distinction in Arnold's Antitrust Division.

In addition, Bill had a special gift that distinguished him from anyone else I have ever met. That was a flair for original profanity, freely used and for some mysterious reason acceptable in any company -- all-male or mixed. It found expression when he took Nik's place in the Cinema Amusements case.

Before consulting Nik about his progress in the matter, Bill undertook a thorough review of all of prior activity in the litigation. He found himself puzzled by the contents of the numerous depositions taken by Nik. This prompted the following conversation between Bill and Nik, which I've never forgotten. Here is a verbatim quotation, as Bill told it to me:

> Bill: Nik, just what did you think you were accomplishing by taking all those depositions?

Nik: Well, I figured if I kept shooting from the hip long
       enough, sooner or later I'd hit them in a vital spot.

Bill: You sure did. You hit them right in the ass hole
       and got a fart in your face.

Not long afterward the case went to trial in Denver before Judge
Knous, a former Governor of Colorado, and the customary jury of 12.
Judge Arnold personally carried the laboring oar for the plaintiff.

Unhappily, in the course of the trial, the credibility of a major
witness for our client was badly damaged on cross-examination. He
was John Wolfberg, a prominent member of the family that owned the
plaintiff. On direct examination, he had testified in great detail --
including the exact place and date -- about a crucial discussion with a
representative of one of the defendants. In it there was a stark admission that the defendants were blacklisting The Broadway.

Cross-examination elicited the fact that at the time of the "blacklist"
conversation specified by Wolfberg, he was in the U.S. Army during
World War II, serving in the Burma theatre. That was the take-off
point from which supplies were flown by the "Flying Tigers,"
operating under General Clair Chennault, to the Chinese Nationalist
forces, headed by Chiang Kai-Shek. After that, defense counsel made
merry with the "Burma Theatre" at every opportunity. They not only
overplayed the point -- as the jury's verdict indicated -- they had
reckoned without Arnold's wit. In his closing speech to the jury, he
turned the parody around. "Now," he asserted, "we've been hearing
a lot of talk in this case about the 'Burma Theatre.' Well, I suppose
the defendants owned that one too."

Following the jury verdict in our favor, the defendants appealed to
the U.S. Court of Appeals for the 10th Circuit. Judge Arnold and I
shared the argument to sustain the verdict (which was upheld).[2]

The argument went well, inspiring confidence that we would prevail.
At any rate, even if prematurely, we had a victory dinner that night
with the client's family. At the conclusion of the dinner, Judge Arnold
invited me to drive over the mountains with him to Laramie the next
morning. I politely declined, knowing of his well-earned reputation as
a haphazard driver. I excused myself on the ground that the Jewish
holidays were about to begin and I was needed at home as soon as
possible.

I can't close out this chapter without recounting one of the most awkward, embarrassing moments of my life. It involved Supreme Court Justice Byron White. As a young man, he was our Denver counsel in the *Cinema Amusements* case. If my memory is accurate, at one time we hoped he would join our firm. But, of course, he went on to greater things, ultimately as an Associate Justice of the Supreme Court of the United States. In any event, we continued an acquaintanceship in Washington.

One of the things I learned about Justice White was his really droll and subtle sense of humor. He'd say something that would slip by you for a moment or so before you got the drift and started laughing.

The incident in question occurred during a Redskins game. Through my good friend and partner, Bud Vieth, I had access to two tickets for all home Redskin games. However, none of my family was particularly interested in football. Consequently, I sometimes had to search for someone to use the extra ticket. It was often Barbara Whitbred, the sister-in-law of my partner and close friend, Murray Bring. Possessed of outstanding talent, he had served two terms as clerk for Chief Justice Warren, while Justice White was on the Court.

Barbara was an RN and a very attractive young lady. She was a rabid football fan, who would happily join our game-day group, using my second ticket. On one occasion, when she was along, the usher noticed that I had mistakenly brought the tickets for the following week. He suggested that I could get passes for that day's game by explaining the situation at the box office. It meant a bit of a walk. Barbara volunteered to accompany me. On the way, we encountered Justice White. As I greeted him and started to introduce Barbara, I suddenly realized that he had recently met my wife and had now caught me in the company of a very pretty young woman.

This flustered me to the point that I couldn't remember Barbara's name as I tried to introduce her. For a moment I stood there absolutely paralyzed. Meanwhile the Justice was obviously amused by my discomfort and just stood by, stone-faced. I finally blurted out: "Justice White, may I present Murray Bring's sister-in-law." This must have been stimulated by the fatuous hope that he would remember that Murray had clerked with the Chief Justice and therefore would not regard Barbara as a stranger to me. Embarrassment surely clouds the mind.

Murray was not only a colleague at Arnold, Fortas & Porter. We remain close friends, even though he has now served for some years as a principal executive of Philip Morris, still a major firm client. Among his other functions, he is the General Counsel of the Company. Murray is not only a superb lawyer, he is one of the few I ever knew who is a "clean desk" man. Adjacent to my always cluttered quarters, his immaculate office afflicted me with an inferiority complex. Hard as I try, I just can't maintain an orderly office. The problem is that Murray's example haunts me with the knowledge that it's possible to do so.

Evelyn Walsh McLean
Wearing The Hope Diamond

CHAPTER TWELVE

THE QUEEN OF DIAMONDS

Evalyn Walsh McLean was Washington's leading hostess throughout the times of the Great Depression and World War II. But she is probably best remembered as the owner of the Hope Diamond. Her father was Thomas Walsh, who had made a killing from his mining interests during the Colorado gold strike. She lived in a magnificent mansion called "Friendship," encompassing an entire square block in the fashionable Georgetown section of Washington.

Mrs. McLean was the wife of John R. (Ned) McLean, the publisher of *The Washington Post*, then of modest circulation and suffering financial problems. Ned McLean had been a member in good standing of President Harding's famous or infamous inner circle which included Albert Fall, Secretary of the Interior and William Daugherty, Attorney General.[1]

An intimate friend of Judge and Mrs. Arnold -- perhaps because of a Colorado/Wyoming rapport, she was also the Judge's client. Nevertheless, it was Abe Fortas who arranged to have me handle the legal affairs of her estate after her death. I never knew why. I had not had anything to do with Mrs. McLean's affairs. I had no background in probate, estate or trust law, nor anything related to estate and inheritance tax obligations. I'm sure this was the first estate the office ever handled. Anyway, Fortas said do it, so I did. Starting from scratch, I began with the petition for the admission of the will to probate and the issuance of "Letters Testamentary" to Judge Arnold.

An insightful description of Mrs. McLean and her way of life appears in a Chapter devoted to her in Arnold's autobiography. They are pretty well summed up by the following excerpts:

> Though Evalyn loved to entertain on a lavish scale, she had little regard for the Social Register. She was always in revolt against people

121

whom she regarded as smug or conventional. When I knew her, only a few of her intimate friends were wealthy. She had little interest in organized charity; her generosity was toward individuals whom she knew and thought she could help.

*   *   *

When I came to Washington, Evalyn's weekly dinners at her home, "Friendship," were an established institution. Sometimes they would be for as few as one hundred people. Other times there might be three hundred. She developed a great liking for the New Dealers. This was somewhat of an amorphous group. At the top were the Brain Trusters. Following them there was a larger group known as "eggheads." Then at the bottom there was a vast army, known as the bureaucrats, devoted to the senseless harassment of American business. By and large they were the most interesting group of people that had ever come to Washington, and Evalyn loved to meet and talk with them.

She was equally fond of conservatives and industrialists and prominent politicians. At one of her large dinners you could find General William S. Knudsen, who had left his position as president of General Motors to work for the government; Leon Henderson, Clare Booth Luce, Walter Lippmann, and Walter Winchell; members of the Supreme Court; Martin Dies, head of the UnAmerican Activities Committee of the House of Representatives; Lord and Lady Halifax, Joseph Hergesheimer and other authors, and a goodly scattering of motion-picture actors. She managed to have on her list the most colorful cross section, all shades of opinion from reactionary to radical. If some government official had been attacked by a Senator, she took particular pleasure in seating them at the same table at her next dinner.

*   *   *

Evalyn was famous for her jewels which included a pear-shaped diamond called "The Star of the East" and the Hope Diamond. She loved to load her arms with priceless bracelets, but there was something irresistible and original about the way she did it. At every move she sparkled like the Milky Way . . . .[2]

As Arnold goes on to relate, she died unexpectedly on Saturday afternoon, April 26, 1947. These were the circumstances as he describes it:

I remember the afternoon she died. Father Edmund A. Walsh, her favorite priest, who was vice president of Georgetown University, was there. Also present were Frank Murphy, Associate Justice of the Supreme Court of the United States, Cissy Patterson, owner of the *Washington Times-Herald,* Frank Waldrop, managing editor of that paper, Mrs. Arnold, and myself. Her death was sudden, and none of her family could get there in time.[3]

Because she died on a Saturday, an immediate problem was created by the need to insure the safekeeping of her jewelry -- believed to be worth over $1 million -- which was loosely scattered around her bedroom. It was now the property of her estate. The co-executors appointed in her will were Judge Arnold and Justice Frank Murphy. (Murphy later renounced the appointment, leaving Arnold as sole executor).

Arnold and Waldrop gathered the jewels and put them in a shoebox. They then tried to find a suitable place to hold them over the weekend. There was no way to gain access to a bank vault because all had been set on time locks and would not reopen until Monday. None of the jewelry stores would accept the responsibility because of insurance implications. Waldrop then hit upon the idea of calling upon one of Hoover's assistants at the FBI, Edward A. Tamm (later a federal judge). Tamm got telephone clearance from the FBI Director, J. Edgar Hoover, to keep the jewels in the FBI vault until a permanent repository was available.[4] Subsequently, Arnold retrieved the jewels and placed them in a safe deposit box at National Savings & Trust Company.

As fiduciaries, we had to take greater precautions in caring for the jewels than Mrs. McLean ever did. To her they were just playthings. According to Arnold, she had never insured them and cavalierly wore them in public even if unescorted. When he asked about the consequent risks of loss and robbery, she answered: "That's the fun of having them."

Arnold, Murphy and two other notable friends of Mrs. McLean's were designated as co-trustees of a testamentary trust established by the will, to which she left the greater part of her estate, including the jewels and "Friendship." The other two were Father Walsh and Monsignor Fulton J. Sheen. Although still relatively young, the Monsignor was already a renowned prelate and missionary. Among others, he had converted Clare Booth Luce and Heywood Broun to Catholicism. Like Justice Murphy, Father Walsh soon renounced.

Judge Arnold therefore became sole executor to administer the estate, in accordance with probate law of the District of Columbia, and also was co-trustee, along with Monsignor Sheen, to carry out the terms of the trust. Because Arnold was acting in both capacities, James Rogers of Hogan & Hartson -- a prominent Washington law firm -- was retained to act as independent co-counsel to the trustees.

In reviewing the files of the estate for the purpose of this volume, I was astounded by the intricacy of the matter, both as a matter of law and of fact. For one thing, the laws of the District of Columbia regarding probate were both inadequate and cumbersome. There was no unified probate code, nor was there a probate court. Judges of the United States District Court for the District of Columbia -- a federal court -- rotated as probate judges. Under that system, none of them could, or ever did, acquire expertise in probate matters.

For guidance on the numerous blanks in the law, it was essential to call the Register of Wills, Theodore Cogswell. In fact, many probate requirements of the District of Columbia were maintained only in his mind.

In such circumstances, administration of the McLean estate and the trust was tedious and complicated. The executor had to file a list of every asset and liability of the estate. Every asset had to be valued by official appraisers employed by the Register of Wills. Petitions had to be filed with the court to obtain an order stating its consent to transfer a legacy, to sell an asset or pay a debt. It was also necessary to file proof of service of required notices of all such matters to beneficiaries, debtors and creditors of the estate.

The appraised value of the estate's personal property totalled $705,307.55.[5] This was exclusive of "Friendship." When Mrs. McLean's estate was administered, the treatment of real property was quixotic. It could pass by will, but was not part of the estate subject to probate.

It was essential to file annual accounts. These had to separately describe every asset, together with its appraised value, plus explanations of each distribution and disbursement. This was no small chore. The first account submitted by Judge Arnold was 18 pages long. It listed assets of $1,177,488.50 -- including those in Maine and Colorado -- and distributions and disbursements of $231,057.84. This left a net estate of $946,431.26 (exclusive of "Friendship"). I prepared that account and had it reviewed by an accountant. He didn't change a line and charged a substantial fee.[6]

I dispensed with the accountant when I prepared the "Second & Final Account." It was 24 pages in length. My particular recollection of that process is that my initial itemization of the assets and disbursements was 1¢ out of balance. After a couple of hours, I found the source of the discrepancy. That was a matter of personal pride, considering my limited mathematical skills. The final "Gross Personal Estate" amounted to $1,119,440.84.[7]

The system was not significantly changed until December 28, 1994. Mayor Kelly then signed the D.C. Probate Reform Act as "one of her last acts in office."[8] The *Legal Times* provided the following description of the previous probate requirements in the District of Columbia:

> Under D.C.'s current system, which processes about 2,500 estates a year, the average case takes 12 months to 18 months to complete because of regulations that require mounds of paperwork, audits by court staff, and costly legal services just to execute routine procedures. Two probate judges oversee the cases, with the help of about 75 employees from the court's probate division.[9]

But for me the drudgery of the process was offset by two factors. One was the opportunity to work closely with the two remarkable men responsible for the affairs of the estate -- Judge Arnold and Monsignor Sheen. The other consisted of fascinating sidelights provided by Mrs. McLean's jewelry collection, notably the Hope Diamond and the Star of the East.

Mrs. McLean's survivors included her two sons and seven grandchildren, all of whom were minors. At least one was an infant -- Mamie Spears Reynolds -- the child of her deceased daughter, Evalyn Washington McLean and Senator Robert R. Reynolds of North Carolina. Along with Mrs. McLean's two adult sons -- John R. and Edward McLean -- Mamie was an heir at law and next of kin, since her mother had died. Appointment of a guardian *ad litem* for her was therefore necessary. The issuance of letters testamentary, authorizing administration of the estate, had to await his report.

The nature and location of Mrs. McLean's personal property in itself created time-consuming problems, from both legal and factual standpoints. Her papers in Washington were in total disarray and situated in at least two other locations besides her residence. Each had to be carefully examined because items of value, particularly old -- really old -- stock certificates were intermingled with antiquated bills, correspondence, advertisements, magazines, etc. Legal complications were occasioned by the property she owned in Maine and Colorado, which necessitated separate administrations, called "ancillary" in legal terminology.

The biggest headache of all was caused by the large collection of porcelain and other bric-a-brac stacked on scores of shelves at "Friendship." According to what I was told at the time, probably by one of the household staff, most represented gifts from all sorts of people Mrs. McLean had befriended and who had been told of her fancy for porcelain. Those items were part of the residual estate, along with all her other tangible property, aside from the jewelry. Each item had to be separately appraised. As a result, the official appraisal comprised 103 typewritten pages.

The whole collection had to be sold. The question was how. We didn't want hundreds, maybe thousands, of people wandering through Friendship, for an undetermined time, to gawk and perhaps purchase one or two items. For many reasons, Mrs. McLean was truly a public celebrity. As Arnold's book notes, among her many acts of generosity -- widely publicized -- she provided food for some of the war veterans known as the "Bonus Army," who had descended on Washington during the Great Depression, seeking government help from Congress during the Hoover Administration.[10] Camped in rickety leantos on the Capitol Grounds, they were dispersed on President Hoover's order by General MacArthur who oversaw the operation on horseback. (My wife, Luna, then 17, was an eyewitness, as an employee of the Federal Emergency Relief Administration.)

Mrs. McLean had also been involved in a widely publicized effort to find the kidnapped Lindbergh baby. One Gaston Means said that with $100,000 in cash he would be able to do so. She therefore temporarily pawned the Hope Diamond to obtain the money, which she delivered to Means. Of course, he was a fraud.[11] (I have a personal recollection of press and radio reports of Means' intervention).

As of the time it happened, the Lindbergh kidnapping was probably the subject of the widest coverage in the history of American journalism. It may still rank second only to the O.J. Simpson case in terms of media attention.

To get back to the nitty gritty of administering the estate: We quickly realized that a public auction was the only solution to disposition of the hodgepodge of personal property other than the jewelry.   But there was a practical problem: the normal method of delivering the sale items to the premises of an auction house would be inordinately expensive, considering the huge volume and low intrinsic value of the articles to be sold.   The possibility of holding the auction on site at "Friendship" then percolated.   The idea was checked with Mr. Mitchell Samuels, of French & Company, a New York art dealer. According to my file memorandum of February 8, 1948, he reported that "the bulk of the property was not of any outstanding value."   He thought the most valuable were "two genuine Dresden china birds worth possibly a couple of thousand dollars apiece."   As I recorded his comments, he heartily endorsed the idea of an on-site auction at "Friendship":

He felt that the executor could realize a maximum return for the property by holding an auction on the premises in the Spring, probably during the cherry blossom festival.   He said that the best way to insure maximum return would be to print a catalog and give it wide circulation. He estimated that the cost of such catalog would be about $8,000 and that it would take a couple of months to put it together.   He said he knew a man who was a fully qualified person to perform such a job.

So far as the suitability of Friendship for an auction was concerned, he said that he never had seen a more desirable setting in any auction house in the whole country; that the surroundings would contribute substantially, in his judgment, to the prices that could be obtained.

As far as auctioneers were concerned, he said that it would be hard to get anyone better than Parke-Bernet, although they were quite high priced.

With such encouragement, we quickly obtained authority to sell a "miscellaneous lot of Mrs. McLean's household effects" -- appraised at $85,387.90 -- "at public auction to the highest bidder or at private sale at not less than the appraised value thereof."[12]   Before long we learned that the auction preliminaries involved some headaches.

After a careful search, Meredith Galleries, a second tier New York firm, was chosen as best in terms of competence and cost.   While it was setting up the sale items, I received a call from *Life Magazine* seeking access to "Friendship." I refused as emphatically as I could. The call troubled me. I remembered how *Life* had tricked Thomas E. Dewey.

The magazine had asked him to pose for a full page photograph while sitting at his desk -- perhaps when he was first elected Governor in 1940, or maybe after he won the Republican presidential nomination in 1944. A short man, Dewey sat on two telephone books to present a more imposing image. While one photographer went through the charade of shooting him head-on, another sneaked a side picture showing the phone books -- which *Life* prominently printed.

With that episode in mind, I called the chief auctioneer and warned him not to allow access to "Friendship" to any outsiders, particularly from *Life Magazine*. It did no good. The next issue of *Life* included a full page photo of two kids jumping up and down on Mrs. McLean's deathbed. They were the children of one of the auction house's employees. One of the pretty young women often used by *Life* as photographers had somehow maneuvered her way into "Friendship" and shot the shameful photo. Naturally, Mrs. McLean's sons raised cain with the Judge and me, in person. We were acutely embarrassed and apologetic. I hope it helped a little when I explained how *Life* had mousetrapped Dewey, a very sophisticated man, not to mention his highly intelligent staff.

A more serious problem arose on the Thursday afternoon preceding the scheduled start of the auction on the following Saturday. The auctioneer called in a panic. He had just been notified that the license prerequisite to the conduct of a public auction had been withdrawn by the Board of Commissioners. Comprised of three members appointed by the President, that Board then governed the District of Columbia. (Home Rule was not in force until 1975.) It was apparent that the local auctioneers had been at work. The asserted reason was that only local D.C. houses were eligible for the necessary license.

Unable to reach anyone who could resolve the problem that afternoon, I hustled over to the library of the Bar Association of the District of Columbia, located at the federal courthouse. It was open until midnight. I frantically researched the matter for hours -- almost until closing time -- and finally came up with a useful precedent. It was a case holding that an out-of-town fortune teller was entitled to a D.C. license.

The next morning, armed with that case, I raced over to the office of a personal friend -- Charles Stofberg, Secretary of the Board of

Commissioners. The license was promptly issued. I don't know what we would have done but for the happenstance that Charlie was a good friend.

The auction was held from May 8 to May 15, 1948. It was a success. The proceeds exceeded the appraised value by $71,389.95.[13]

Because of the trust, the jewels could not be included in the auction. *In toto*, they were appraised at $591,107.50, of which the Hope's value was $176,920 -- a bit less than its 1912 purchase price of $180,000 -- and the Star's value was $185,000. Their combined value comprised more than one-half of the appraisal of all of the Estate's jewelry.[14]

The trustees were confronted with an off-beat problem because of the trust's provision concerning the disposition of her jewels. It stated:

(a) I request my trustees to put my jewelry away in safekeeping until after all the following of my grandchildren reach the age of twenty-five years:

> John R. McLean
> Evalyn Walsh McLean [grandaughter]
> Mamie Spears Reynolds
> Emily McLean
> Edward B. McLean II

at which time my jewelry shall be distributed with the rest of my property as provided below.

Mamie Spears Reynolds was less than five years old when the will was admitted to probate. Consequently, the prescribed distribution in kind involved retention of the jewelry for more than twenty years. That was wholly impractical considering the personal property tax then in force in the District of Columbia. The tax on the jewelry exceeded $12,000 in 1947. This meant an ultimate tax of at least $240,000 before the time for distribution -- assuming that the tax rate remained stable. The trustees accordingly decided to petition the Court for authority to sell the jewels. The petition was granted.[15]

Between the time the Estate took possession and the date of its ultimate sale, the Hope created quite a sideshow. When Cartier sold the piece to Mr. and Mrs. Edward B. McLean for $180,000 on January 28, 1912, this was its description:

1-Head ornament composed of oval shaped links all in brilliants containing in the center the "Hope Diamond", weighing 44½¢ Price agreed following terms of contract signed February 1, 1912.

The Star of the East was nowhere described. But we were advised that it was a flawless blue-white diamond, pear-shaped and weighing more than 93 carats. Mrs. McLean wore the Hope and the Star as pendants.

The Hope carried a mystique: a popular belief -- never shared by Mrs. McLean -- that it was afflicted by a curse insuring that tragedy would befall its owner. The firm's files contain a somewhat tattered newsprint article, dated November 24, 1916, on which the headlines read:

LINKS THE HOPE DIAMOND WITH HOUSE OF HAPSBURG

Death of Aged Emperor Francis Joseph Recalls a Strange Superstition Which Is Traced to the Looting of a Burmese Temple and Now Told by the London Express.

The lead sentence of the article states:

An extraordinary narrative, linking the misfortunes of the House of Hapsburg with the tragic history of the Hope Diamond and linking both to the looting of a temple in Burma, acquire special interest by reason of the death of the Austrian Emperor.

The report cited as its source "a soldier on active service" who informed the Express that it had been told to him in Ceylon by a "Buddhist priest . . . of high repute . . . [who] assured me that every word of his narrative was strictly and absolutely true." As told by the priest, "a member of the house of Hapsburg, one Count Hermann," and others looted the "priceless [treasure of] the great temple of Rama and Sita" and in the process "slaughtered the priests and all the guardians of the temple". According to the priest, the finest of the stolen gems "formed the eyes of the golden statute of Rama. One (to be known later as the "Blue Hope Diamond") was appropriated by Count Hermann." The priest further reported that "Rama called down upon the thieves the vengeance of all the gods," with the result that more than fifty owners of the stolen treasures -- described as "persons of high degree" lost their lives by violent means. The priest concluded:

> . . . with their death the curse came to an end, but in the case of the House of Hapsburg, it goes on forever.

The *Express* next identifies numerous members of the "royal families" who fell victim to the curse, including the following Hapsburgs:

> The Crown Prince Rudolf was another owner who died by unnatural means; the Empress of Austria was killed in Geneva; the Archduke Johann ("John Orth") was drowned at sea; the Archduke Francis Ferdinand and his wife were assassinated in Sarajevo; Maximillian was shot in Mexico and his wife lost her reason.

According to this account, it could be reasoned that the curse of the Hope was responsible for Ferdinand's assassination at Sarajevo and therefore the ensuing tragedy of World War I.

There was as much interest in the Hope Diamond on this side of the Atlantic. Under date of May 16, 1947, Drew Pearson -- the famous columnist -- received a letter from one John F. Lindsay advising that he had been told "how to cast the curse from the so-called 'Hope Diamond.'" As it happened, the Pearson and Arnold families were close -- they became in-laws when Pearson's daughter married Arnold's younger son. The letter was soon in Arnold's hands. In pertinent part, it read:

> In the latter part of 1917 and the first part of 1918 I spent [time] in Karashi Sadar India. During those few months that I spend (sic) there, I gave aid and comfort to two very old natives, and for my help to them, they compensated me by telling me how to cast the curse from that so-called "Hope" diamond.

*   *   *

> I trust you will send this letter to the one that would be mostly interested, and I assure you that I am the only living person in the United States that has this power, to fulfill my claim.

Yours very truly

John F. Lindsay
321 N. Pilgrim Street
Stockton, Calif.

P.S. -- I assure you, Mr. Pearson, that the above mentioned diamond certainly has a peculiar influence over the owners and double so as long as owned by a woman.

Karachi-Sadar

Perhaps out of an excess of caution, we did not accept his offer. On the other hand, would the Hope retain its exotic mystique without the spell of the curse?

The topper during our custody of the Hope was a telegram from Columbia Pictures, dated June 9, 1947, asking to borrow it for a single day's shoot in an upcoming film -- "It Had To Be You" -- starring Ginger Rogers. She would wear it "only in a wedding sequence." In reply, Arnold wired that the gem had not yet been appraised and that $1,000,000 of insurance coverage would be needed. A follow-up telegram from Columbia of June 10, 1947 outlined its proposal in detail, offering a higher per diem than Miss Rogers was earning. The offer was ultimately rejected because Mrs. McLean's sons disapproved of the transaction.

The last jewelry episode preceding the Estate's sale of the collection was a letter of March 12, 1948 from the Gemological Institute of America. It somehow reached Judge Arnold despite the following laughable address:

Mr. Arnold Truman
Executor, Evalyn Walsh McLean Estate
Court of Appeals
Washington, D.C.

The Post Office Department of that day was evidently more efficient than the present day semi-private Postal Service. The letter recited that the Institute was preparing a revised copy "of our book *Famous Diamonds*" and that its 1945 edition stated that the Hope "was purchased in 1911 by Edward B. McLean for $300,000." To avoid printing anything "not authoritative," Arnold was requested to provide "the present state of the Hope."

The letter also requested information concerning the Star of the East, citing various rumors:

> In an Associated Press story mention is also made of another stone in the estate of Mrs. McLean, the Star of the East, which is given a higher valuation than the Hope although the story does not mention the weight of this diamond. May we also have some information on this? It has been rumored that the Star of the East is the same as the Star of Este - weight 26.26 metric carats -- which was once owned by Archduke Ferdinand of Austria-Este. Can you tell me if this is true?

My response stated that the Hope was in Arnold's safekeeping and that the Star of the East weighed 93 plus carats.

The entire collection ultimately was sold to Harry Winston, the famous New York dealer, for $611,500. He was a tiny man -- maybe 5 ft. 1" in height -- cheerful, a great salesman and an even better promoter. His interest in the collection centered on the Hope and the Star of the East. He used famous jewels solely for publicity purposes. His real business was selling 1/4 carat engagement rings and the like to volume customers, such as Sears Roebuck. Unlike other famous jewelry houses, *e.g.*, Tiffany and Cartier, who tried to "cherrypick" the best of the lot, Winston wanted all or none of it.

Winston's offer proved best for the estate. He made a big deal out of mailing the collection to his home base in New York via Parcel Post. It was a front page story, complete with photograph -- maybe the best promo in Post Office history. Winston then got reams of copy by giving the Hope to the Smithsonian, where it remains on display to this day.

Winston had a far better sense of the Hope's fame than I. A recent issue of a prominent newsmagazine, observing the Smithsonian's 150th anniversary, had this to say:[16]

> Number of visitors per year: **More than 25 million**; most popular exhibits: **Hope Diamond, Spirit of St. Louis, first ladies' gowns**

On September 18, 1996, the Washington Post reported that the Hope is the world's leader among museum exhibits, surpassing the Mona Lisa (p. B3).

Winston had real hard luck with the Star of the East. I ran into him some years after the estate closed and asked what he had done with it. He said "I sold it to King Farouk just before he was deposed. I never got a dime for it."

A real bonus of my connection with the Mclean Estate was the opportunity to become friendly with Monsignor Sheen. He played an active role in the affairs of the trust. The Monsignor was an arresting, dramatic figure. He was slight in stature, extremely handsome and very charismatic. His sparkling blue eyes were unusually deep-set, which he attributed to a childhood siege of tuberculosis in his birthplace, located in the Southern Illinois coal country. When looking into them, his eyes were the most gripping and compelling I have ever witnessed.

Time out for a moment: after the McLean Estate was settled, the Monsignor became the star of a weekly television show on the old Dumont network -- Channel 5 in Washington, D.C. -- in the early fifties. It had a religious motif -- which today's conservatives would have appreciated. However, it attracted a wide secular audience because of Sheen's tremendous personality, even though it played head-on against one of the legendary shows of early television -- Milton Berle's Texaco show. When the Monsignor swept on stage in his flowing robe, he appeared to be an actor of extraordinary talent -- which in fact he was. Never having been a fan of "Uncle Miltie", I was a regular member of the Monsignor's audience.

As you have doubtless recognized, I was an ardent admirer of the Monsignor. For some reason, we developed a close personal rapport. We often spoke about all sorts of things except matters of religion. Despite his genuine missionary zeal, previously noted, he never tried to convert me.

Among his other personable qualities, Monsignor Sheen had a quick wit and an appealing sense of humor. It was on display when we undertook to sell "Friendship", the major asset of the trust estate, other than the jewelry.

Under the trust established by Mrs. McLean's will, Senator Robert R. Reynolds of North Carolina -- her son-in-law -- was to have the use of "Friendship" or the income from the proceeds of its sale, during his lifetime. By a letter of October 3, 1947, he turned down his option to live at "Friendship", while preserving his right to the income. A sale was therefore necessary. This necessitated a conference to agree on the asking price. Judge Arnold and I attended, along with the

Monsignor and Jim Rogers, outside co-counsel to the trust. At the start of a discussion about the asking price, Rogers said: "Let's ask $300,000 and hope and pray." Before anyone else could comment, the Monsignor observed, "You mean 'prey' -- 'P-R-E-Y' -- don't you?"

By today's standards, that price for the property would be less than a peppercorn. But at the time, in the late forties, $300,000 was a big number. (About the same time, I brought a fair-sized Tudor-style home in Chevy Chase, Maryland for $25,000).

As it happened, we got the asking price, but not from any of the prominent Washington real estate brokers we had solicited. Two unknowns showed up with the cash and quickly closed the deal. They divided the property in two. One took the part fronting on Wisconsin Avenue, which had commercial zoning. The other, the balance of the property with residential zoning. Both made sizable profits. Naturally, as soon as word of the sale spread, every broker in town tried to get us to reopen the bidding.

My friendship with the Monsignor resulted in an unexpected sequel. During the administration of Mrs. McLean's estate, my wife Luna, was secretary to Clinton Anderson, then Secretary of Agriculture in President Truman's cabinet. The secretaries to all of the cabinet members comprised an informal group -- known as the "cabinet girls". They occasionally socialized together. All but my wife were Roman Catholic. As the only married woman in the group, my wife held more than her share of their gatherings at our home.

The Monsignor had recently published a best selling book entitled *Peace of Soul*.[17] He had given me a copy with a rather flattering inscription. It was noticed by one of the secretaries when she picked up the book in our library. "Oh," she asked, "does Norman know Monsignor Sheen?" Luna replied: "They're very close friends." One of the other women exclaimed: "God, how I'd love to meet him." Luna needed no more urging. "Well," she said, "I'll have him to dinner and you're all invited."

When the last of the group had left, I said to Luna: "Now you've really dug yourself a hole. Didn't you read the newspaper story the other day quoting the Monsignor's statement that he never accepted dinner invitations? Don't expect me to carry the ball." She didn't. A few days later she casually remarked, "The Monsignor will be here for dinner the Saturday after next. I've invited all the girls, Secretary Anderson, and some people from the Hill" (where Secretary Anderson had served in the House for two terms). It turned into a smash. All the cabinet women arrived a little early. The Monsignor, driving his own Cadillac, came precisely on schedule 15 minutes later. I was on the lookout, opened his car door and escorted him into the house. The arrival of the Pope couldn't have caused more excitement. It was one great party.

As I walked the Monsignor to his car, some three hours later, I said: "Well, you really made a liar out of me. I told Luna about the newspaper item that said you never accepted dinner invitations" and asked: "What made you come?" "Well, he said, "Luna has such a charming telephone voice, I just had to meet her."

Luna Diamond charming a telephone listener

CHAPTER THIRTEEN

THE LOYALTY LUNACY

Soon after the end of World War II, the nation was swept by anti-Communist hysteria. There were intensifying accusations from the House Un-American Activities Committee that the government was riddled with Communists and Communist sympathizers. The principal focus was the State Department.

The Republicans then controlled the Congress. Under the leadership of the Committee's post-War Chairman, J. Parnell Thomas, the claim was widely circulated for political purposes.

The issue soon began to excite widespread public interest.[1] Before long, the executive branch of the government was intimidated to the point that on March 21, 1947 President Truman issued Executive Order No. 9835. This established official boards in every government agency, to investigate the loyalty of all federal employees.[2] The President quickly asked for an appropriation of $11 million to fund the loyalty program.

I've already noted Arnold's perceptive prophecy that this "steal the ball" strategy would backfire. Truman himself ultimately so conceded. David McCullough first quotes Clark Clifford to the effect that there was no real concern "about a real loyalty problem" but that the program was a political necessity.[3] McCullough then refers to Truman's concession that the program had been a "bad mistake" stating:

> Writing in his memoirs years later, well after the pernicious influence of the Loyalty Program had become all too clear, Truman could say

only in lame defense that it had started out to be as fair as possible "under the climate of opinion that then existed." In private conversation with friends, however, he would concede it had been a bad mistake. "Yes, it was terrible," he said.[4]

With the institution of the loyalty program, employees from all echelons of government were rapidly summoned before departmental loyalty boards to prove their loyalty -- with their jobs at risk and under procedures devoid of any semblance of due process. Charges were vague and frequently involved long past activities and associations. Informants were unsworn and unidentified by the loyalty boards who nevertheless accepted their "testimony." There was no opportunity to confront and cross-examine them. In her book on Fortas, Laura Kalman records the anti-communist madness of the period and, in part, the role of our firm in defending its victims, including several of its most prominent targets.[5]

Before too long, Senator Joseph McCarthy of Wisconsin had captured the leadership of the red-baiting crazies. Initially his wild charges grabbed headlines from the right wing press. Later the whole media joined the inquisition. He used his post as Chairman of the Senate Committee on Government Operations to provide the nation's television cameras with a daily dose of his ruthless inquisitions of hapless witnesses. As previously noted, his brutal tactics soon led to coinage of a new word --"McCARTHYISM."

The mania engendered by McCarthyism is inconceivable even in today's politically polarized society. It cowed the Supreme Court into a frightened silence on fundamental constitutional principles. Reporters representing respectable publications, as well as tabloids, elevated McCarthy to the status of a celebrity. It sickened me to see them chase him through the Capitol's corridors like hounds after a fox. I can't recall any other time when I felt concern about what I said in the presence of strangers.

Owen Lattimore was probably the most abused victim of McCarthyism. The Senator had characterized Lattimore as "a top Russian espionage agent [and] had promised his charges of Communism in government would stand or fall on the credibility of his case against Lattimore"[6] He was surely McCarthy's most publicized target. As a result, he was subjected to two public hearings by Congressional committees and two criminal prosecutions by the United States Attorney for the District of Columbia. We represented him in all four.

Lattimore's ordeal began with a hearing before a subcommittee of the Senate Committee on Foreign Relations. It was followed by another before the Internal Security Subcommittee of the Senate's Judiciary Committee. Fortas represented Lattimore in both of them. The first was chaired by Senator Millard Tydings of Maryland. It was sensibly conducted and exonerated Lattimore.[7]

The result did not suit Senator Pat McCarran, Chairman of the Senate's Internal Security Subcommittee. In July 1951, he reopened public hearings after extensively examining Lattimore in executive session. Following lengthy sessions devoted exclusively to witnesses adverse to him, Lattimore was subjected to a grueling cross-examination which lasted twelve days. Arnold described it as "the longest Congressional interrogation of one man in Congressional history"[8] He further perceived that the questions were "not asked in order to obtain information, but for the purpose of entrapment [and said that he] had never before seen an investigation conducted with third-degree methods"[9] But the termination of the McCarran hearings did not end Lattimore's ordeal.

The nomination of James P. McGranery as Attorney General was then pending before the Judiciary Committee. As the price of confirmation, McCarran exacted a promise that Lattimore would be prosecuted for perjured testimony. McGranery kept his word.[10]

Soon after McGranery's confirmation, the United States Attorney for the District of Columbia, Leo Rover, obtained a multiple count grand jury indictment against Lattimore. Arnold then took over Lattimore's defense.

There were seven counts, but only the first was significant. It charged that Lattimore had perjured himself by denying that he had "followed the Communist line." Judge Luther Youngdahl, a former Republican governor of Minnesota, granted Arnold's motion to dismiss. He agreed that count one of the indictment alleged no acts demonstrating perjury, but only speculative accusations that Lattimore's thought processes were unlawful, a ruling upheld on appeal.[11]

Although the dismissal of the crucial first count had been affirmed, Rover did not seek Supreme Court review. Instead, he filed a second indictment on October 7, 1954. This time there were only two counts, essentially no different from the first count of the original indictment. One charged that Lattimore had perjured himself by testifying "that he was not a follower of the Communist Line." The other alleged that he falsely "testified he had never been a 'promoter of Communist interests.'"[12]

In an astonishing move, Rover additionally filed an "Affidavit of Bias and Prejudice." This asserted that Judge Youngdahl was disqualified to hear the second case because the dismissal of the first indictment demonstrated his bias against the government. If such an affidavit is well-founded, the court must step down.

But the affidavit filed against Judge Youngdahl was utterly out of order. As a matter of law, it was incontrovertible then, and is now, that a judge cannot be disqualified for rulings made in his judicial capacity. Rather, a cognizable affidavit of "Bias and Prejudice" must be grounded solely on extraneous matters -- for example, a judge's -- or his family's -- ownership of stock in a corporate party or a blood relationship to an individual party.

Judge Arnold and I met personally with Attorney General Herbert Brownell to discuss the motion. We noted that the affidavit was virtually unprecedented, only the second such document ever filed by the United States to that date; and further, that the basis of the affidavit was totally out of bounds. Brownell's sole response was: "I have the fullest confidence in the United States Attorney."

Arnold accordingly filed an opposition to the affidavit of the United States Attorney. He also filed a motion to dismiss the second indictment on the grounds that it violated Lattimore's constitutional rights under the First and Sixth Amendments. These were essentially the same points that led to dismissal of the controlling first count of the earlier indictment.

The issue of the Judge's right to sit took priority. Judge Youngdahl met the bias and prejudice issue head-on. He struck the government's affidavit "as scandalous" and refused to disqualify himself.[13] In a brief opinion, he noted the holding of a leading Supreme Court precedent "that the bias or prejudice which can be urged against a judge must be based on something other than rulings in the case. (*Berger v. United States*, 255 U. S. 22, 31)."[14]

During his presentation on the merits, Rover sarcastically referred to the briefs for Lattimore as unintelligible to an ordinary man -- representing mystical Harvard language. He then said something to the effect that he had been raised in the school of hard knocks, had studied at a local law school and spoke plain, everyday language. When Arnold rose to speak, he put Rover in his place. I vividly remember his words: "I do not propose to waste the Court's time by debating Mr. Rover's legal education or his lack of it."

After denying the government's motion that he disqualify himself, the motion to dismiss the second indictment was considered by Judge Youngdahl. He dismissed both counts, relying principally upon the Court of Appeals' decision which sustained dismissal of the vital first count of the prior indictment. He ruled:

> In upholding the dismissal of the first count in the prior indictment Judge Prettyman, speaking for the Court of Appeals, had aptly stated:
>
> > "Not only is it a basic rule that criminal statutes must have an ascertainable standard of guilt or they fall for vagueness, but it is equally well established that an indictment must charge an offense with such reasonable certainty that the accused can make his defense. The cases on the point are myriad, as reference to any authority quickly reveals."
>
> Testing the two counts against this principle, the Court is satisfied that they fail to meet the prescribed standard of definiteness and so must fall for vagueness."[15]

In *Fair Fights and Foul*, Arnold explained the defendant's dilemma in confronting such amorphous charges. Addressing the first indictment, Arnold explained:

> . . . when Lattimore made the statement for which he was prosecuted in Count I, it was a statement of his belief that he had never done or said anything in the interest of what he conceived to be Communism. The charge was that he lied about that belief. What were these Communist interests? Did the United States promote Communism when it aided Russia? Did President Roosevelt promote Communist interests when he furnished Lend-Lease to Russia? Did General George C. Marshall promote Communist interests when he criticized Chiang Kai-Shek's government? Was Wendell Willkie a promoter of or a sympathizer with Communist interests because of passages in his book, *One World?* Since Tito was a Communist and his interests were of necessity also Communist interests was the government of the United States a promoter of Communism and a sympathizer with Communist interests when by both legislative and executive action it came to the aid of Tito? [16]

Concerning the second indictment, alleging that "during the period 1935-1950 Lattimore had been a follower of the Communist line," and that Lattimore had lied under oath when he denied this, Arnold stated:

> . . . The government had gone through every one of Lattimore's voluminous writings since the year 1935 to extract, out of context, any statement that might conceivably indicate that Lattimore agreed with any Communist country. There were four periods covered. The first was from 1935 to 1941, when a debate was going on about the active intervention of the United States against German, Italian, and Japanese aggression. Lattimore, along with Roosevelt, Chiang Kai-Shek, and Churchill, was willing to accept Russian collaboration. His position was used to indicate that he had been a sympathizer and promoter of Communism. The second period was from 1941 to 1945, a period of cordiality among Allies. During that period the United States gave support to French, Italian, and Yugoslav Communist partisans and resistance groups. During the third period, 1945 to 1946, the United States was co-operating with Russia in trying to solve the problems of world peace. Late in 1945, General Eisenhower, after a trip to Moscow during which he had reviewed a Red Square parade from atop Lenin's tomb, told a House committee that "nothing guides Russian policy so much as a desire for friendship with the United States."

> The fourth period, after 1945, reviewed Lattimore's views on the victory of Communists in China. He had pointed out the strength of the movement. One of the quotations used by the prosecution to show that he was a promoter of Communist interests was the following: "My own opinion is that now and for a long time to come the Chinese Communists will have great defensive strength if attacked, but little offensive strength beyond their own frontier." Later events showed the accuracy of this statement. Yet the government attempted to smear Lattimore by putting this citation under the heading "Chinese Communists are not a menace to China or the world" to make it appear that the statement promoted Communist interests. Thus the Department of Justice of the United States sought to convict Lattimore of perjury because of his opinions and writings since 1935, with nearly all of which most sensible men now agree. A more blatant invasion of the right of free speech has never occurred in our history.[17]

There was an informative sidelight to Arnold's loyalty labors. During the McCarthy onslaught -- and particularly the *Lattimore* case -- many of the liberals were backtracking despite the blatant impairment of civil liberties. Gressley noted:

As Arnold's life came to a close, he would increasingly voice cynicism, though not of the conservatives, for these he could understand. What disturbed him far more than the people who looked under their beds every night for agile Communists were the "pseudo-liberals" who hid under their beds. With clarity and a touch of "bitters," Arnold expressed his thoughts to Ernest Angell in 1968.

I recall the Dorothy Bailey case, which this firm defended and lost, where a career was ruined on evidence which was not disclosed to the accused; the Fort Monmouth spy case, where scientists were discharged on secret evidence, which this firm defended and finally won, but not until the careers of twenty-six scientists had been irretrievably damaged. In those days noisy people like Dr. Spock and Chaplain Coffin were entirely silent. It was impossible to raise among college professors a fund to defend Lattimore. Arthur Schlesinger [Jr.], who was accused of being soft on Communism on the floor of Congress, was sufficiently frightened to prove his virtue by writing a column attacking Lattimore."[18]

In an earlier letter dated October 29, 1954, Arnold advised Herbert Monte Levy that "he wanted the American Civil Liberties Union to stay out of the [Lattimore] case." His letter was more than adamant and is worth repeating:

Washington, D.C. Oct. 29, 1954

Dear Mr. Levy:

Apparently I have not made my position clear to you in connection with the American Civil Liberties Union's participation in the Lattimore case. In the first full paragraph on page 2 of your letter of October 28th, you state that your Committee considered whether American Civil Liberties Union could join in a motion to dismiss the new Lattimore indictment on First Amendment grounds, as amicus curiae.

I am a member of your national committee. I have in the past supported the American Civil Liberties Union. I don't want you in the Lattimore case. If the American Civil Liberties Union attempts to participate in the case as amicus curiae or otherwise, I will object strenuously. I repeat, I want the American Civil Liberties Union to stay out of this case.

I thought that the position that you took with respect to the first count of the old indictment, insisting that the correct procedure was to demand a bill of particulars in lieu of filing a motion to dismiss, was wrong and was an unwarranted attempt to interfere with the conduct of the case by Senator O'Mahoney and this office. I was confirmed in my opinion as to the strategy of the case by the District Judge and by eight judges to one in the Court of Appeals and by the Solicitor General, who refused to apply for certiorari. But whether we were right or wrong, in our judgment the threat that the American Civil Liberties Union might interfere was highly objectionable.

I have seen some of the letters that have emanated from American Civil Liberties Union's office about the Lattimore indictment. I don't like them.

Your present letter is a resumption of the kind of quibbling debate which ignores the fundamental legal and constitutional issues, and violates the fundamental civil liberties values that are concerned. I have no patience with your approach, and no time to devote to dealing with it.

If the American Civil Liberties Union management does not realize that the new indictment of Owen Lattimore is a fundamental assault upon civil liberties, it will certainly be beyond my capacity to demonstrate the point. Beyond this, the technical questions of law and the questions of legal procedure should, I suggest, be left to me, Abe Fortas, Paul Porter and our partners and associates -- and to Senator O'Mahoney when he returns to participate as co-counsel in the case.

At your request, I send you under separate cover a copy of our Motion to Dismiss. I have no doubt that you will disagree with it as you did with the Motion to Dismiss the old indictment, but I have no intention this time to engage in a debate with you. The only thing I want is for the American Civil Liberties Union to stay out of this case.[19]

There weren't many Edward R. Murrows to be found. Paul Porter was among the few who never wavered in his open dedication to civil liberties. During the McCarthy madness, Paul appeared on a talk show panel -- either on radio or TV, I don't remember which. One of the panelists was Morris Ernst, famed as a protagonist of civil liberties. Ernst had also begun to feel the pressure of the anti-Communist assault. The moderator asked each panelist about his reactions to the Congressional investigations and Truman's loyalty program. All panel members except Paul softened their responses, in effect conceding there might be some smoke beneath the fire. Not so Paul. He condemned the whole process as an outrage and said to Ernst: "You know, Morris, it's easy to be a fair weather friend of civil liberties."

While serving as secretary to Senator Clinton Anderson of New Mexico, my wife, Luna, probably provided McCarthy with the soundest advice he received during his reckless red-baiting delirium. He was a notoriously compulsive gambler, always ready for a game with anyone available -- a fact well known all over Capitol Hill. One day, while McCarthy was at the peak of his celebrity, he came by Anderson's office. Seeing him, Luna piped up:: "Senator, why don't you stop all this nonsense and go back to your old card-playing days?"

CHAPTER FOURTEEN

COURT FRIGHT

The bottom of the loyalty pits was plumbed in the Supreme Court case involving Dr. John Peters.[1] The Court there ducked the profound constitutional questions raised by the loyalty program. That evasion provided reason to believe that McCarthyism had also intimidated the nation's highest tribunal.

Peters was a member of the faculty of the Yale School of Medicine, specializing in nutrition and metabolism. He had served as a consultant to the Public Health Service "from four to ten days each year [doing] work which was not of a confidential nature and did not involve access to classified material"[2] The nominal appellee, Mrs. Oveta Culp Hobby was the first Secretary of the newly established Department of Health, Education and Welfare which had absorbed The Public Health Service.

The case reached the Supreme Court on review of a ruling by an overall Loyalty Review Board that there was a reasonable doubt of Dr. Peters' loyalty. The Board had so ruled after pulling the matter up on its own motion for a "post-audit" of two decisions in Dr. Peters' favor by the agency loyalty board.[3] As the Supreme Court acknowledged, the Review Board's finding -- sustained by two lower courts -- was based solely on the secret, unsworn testimony of unidentified informants -- some unknown even to the administrative board -- none of whom was cross-examined.[4]

Arnold, Fortas & Porter challenged the ruling before the Supreme Court on the ground that the procedure violated Peters' constitutional right to confront the witnesses against him. A second-hand description of the procedure used against Peters would defy belief. Quotation of the Supreme Court's own description is therefore in order. After reciting the proceedings before the Agency Board -- resulting in Peters' exoneration -- the Court described the hearing before the Review Board. Having first noted that the "post-audit" was based on the Review Board's own Regulation 14,[5] the Court stated:

> . . . *Once again, as at the previous hearing, the only evidence adduced was presented by petitioner.* In his own testimony, petitioner denied membership in the Communist Party, discussed his political beliefs and his motives for engaging in the activities and associations which were the subject of the charges, and answered all questions put to him by the Board. In support of petitioner's testimony, five witnesses stated their long acquaintance with petitioner and their firm conviction of petitioner's loyalty. *In addition to this evidence, the record before the Board contained information supplied by informants whose identity was not disclosed to petitioner. The identity of one or more, but not all, of these informants was known to the Board. The information given by such informants had not been given under oath.* The record also contained the evidence adduced by petitioner at the previous hearing. On this record, the Board determined that "on all the evidence, there is a reasonable doubt as to Dr. Peters' loyalty to the Government of the United States."[6]

A record like that wouldn't support a parking ticket. But incomprehensibly, notwithstanding such flagrant violations of elementary principles of due process of law, the Court elected to rule for Peters on the trivial technicality that the regulation authorizing the post-audit review was unauthorized. In deciding the case on that narrow basis, the Court disregarded post-argument briefs -- submitted at its request -- in which counsel for both sides concluded that the constitutional issues required disposition. (They were our firm for Peters and Assistant Attorney General Warren Burger -- later Chief Justice of the Supreme Court -- for the government).

The Court's refusal to consider the constitutional questions had been presaged by Justice Frankfurter. When Justice Harlan asked Arnold whether the Review Board was empowered to issue the "post-audit" regulations, he answered affirmatively and added that he preferred to have the case decided on the constitutional issues. In response, to quote Kalman, Justice Frankfurter "barked":

The question is not what you would like to whittle it down to. The problem before this court is to decide all legal questions that arise on this record and to reach the Constitutional questions last, not first.[7]

As Arnold perceived, the decision settled nothing. It "left the badge of infamy around the neck of Dr. Peters."[8] Despite two opportunities to defend the nation's charter of freedom -- in the *Bailey* and *Peters* cases -- the Supreme Court had declined to do so.

A short time after the *Peters* decision was handed down, Frankfurter encountered Paul at a legal function. Apparently expecting to be complimented because Peters had won, Frankfurter asked: "Well, Paul, how did you like the *Peters* decision?" Paul replied: "I thought it was a monumental act of judicial cowardice."

Forty years passed before a court -- rising like a Phoenix from the ashes -- summoned the courage to award relief to a victim of the loyalty madness and condemn the evils of the McCarthy era. The startling impact of this resurrection drew a front page report on *The Washington Post* of March 8, 1996. These were its headlines and first three paragraphs:

> *'LOYAL TO HER FRIENDS,*
> *FAMILY AND COUNTRY*
> *McCarthy Era Victim*
> *Posthumously Cleared*
>
> *By Cindy Loose*
>
> Beatrice "Bibi" Braude won back her reputation yesterday, nearly nine years after her death and 43 years after she was fired in a spasm of anti-communist hysteria best known as the legacy of Sen. Joseph R. McCarthy.
>
> A judge in the U.S. Claims Court ruled that during what he called a "dark era in American history," Braude was accused unfairly of disloyalty, fired unjustly from the United States Information Agency and blacklisted as a security risk merely because of the "political beliefs of a few casual, social acquaintances."
>
> Braude's posthumous victory brings vindication not only for her but also for thousands of innocent Americans accused and blacklisted in the 1950s, said her pro bono attorney, Christopher Sipes, of Covington &

Burling. Yesterday's decision, he added, is an important page in the annals of U.S. history.

It would never have happened but for the dedication and skill of her *pro bono* lawyer, plus the learning, decency and sense of justice of Judge Roger B. Andewelt of the United States Court of Federal Claims.[9]

The case was heard pursuant to a private Act of Congress -- sponsored by Senators Moynihan and D'Amato -- referring it for decision to the Court of Federal Claims. These are excerpts from the Court's opinion:

> This congressional reference action harks back to a dark era in American history when Senator Joseph R. McCarthy was a powerful political force in this nation, when promising careers in the public and private sectors were arbitrarily cut short based on innuendo, unsubstantiated allegations, and irrational fears, and when blacklists prevented loyal American citizens from securing employment in jobs for which they were well qualified. . . . .

> In its post-trial brief, the defendant [the United States] describes the "McCarthy era" as follows: "There is no doubt that, during the years that have become known as the "McCarthy Era," there were individuals, both Government employees and otherwise, who were wrongfully accused and labelled by individuals in the Government as "communists" or "communist sympathizers." The lives and careers of some of these people were irrevocably damaged, and there was, and is, simply no excuse for the wrongs that were visited upon them. As a result, we must be ever vigilant to ensure that the Government never engages in this type of behavior again.

*   *   *

> . . . ("It is undisputed that there were many individuals who were blacklisted -- that is unable to pursue their livelihoods -- during the McCarthy era" . . .)[10]

These were the facts: Ms. Braude was a talented linguist employed by the federal government. Notwithstanding a loyalty clearance by the State Department, after ten years of government service, she was discharged in 1953 by the United States Information Agency ("USIA") on loyalty and security grounds. This happened one day after she was praised for her work and promised a raise. She was told, however, that the action was based on "budgetary reasons".[11] In fact, the Court found that the USIA had "blacklisted" her.[12]

As a result she spent many years in a futile effort to obtain employment at various federal agencies.[13] It was 1982 -- 29 years later -- before she finally obtained a government position at the CIA.[14] During that interval she had obtained a Ph.D and had served in a number of private occupations. Among them was a tenured associate professorship at the University of Massachusetts.[15]

Meantime, she had acquired her government records after passage of the Privacy Act of 1974.[16] These disclosed the truth: that she was dismissed on "loyalty and security grounds." In 1977 she sued in the United States Court of Claims for reinstatement and back pay, but her complaint was dismissed as out of time -- barred by the "Statute of Limitations."[17] She died in 1988.[18]

In 1993, the two New York Senators, at the behest of her relatives, secured the enactment of a private bill authorizing her Estate to sue for back pay.[19] Noting "Dr. Braude's excellent employment credentials," the Court ruled in favor of the Estate, because of the USIA's unlawful statements "that Dr. Braude was on the black list."[20] The Court then suggested that the parties negotiate a monetary settlement.[21] According to the *Post's* report, the family intends to donate the Estate's recovery to Hunter College.

This is not a case where it can be fittingly said: "better late than never". Rather, it is a classic instance of an event which merits characterization as "too little and too late". The Supreme Court in *Bailey* or *Peters* should long ago have delivered what Judge Andewalt declared at the start of his opinion in the *Braude* case.

Unhappily, other than Judge Youngdahl, the courts which sat during the McCarthy era deserve to be remembered only for their timidity. The appellate court in the *Monmouth* case acted only after McCarthy was censured by the Senate and had died of alcoholism.

Associate Justice Felix Frankfurter

CHAPTER FIFTEEN

THE INEFFABLE JUSTICE FRANKFURTER

Justice Felix Frankfurter's put-down of Arnold in the *Peters* case reflected two features of his career and persona. One was the evolution of his increasingly conservative attitude toward civil liberties, the other his peacock personality. The high point of his enthusiasm for civil liberties was his ardent opposition in the 1920's to the Sacco-Vanzetti murder prosecution, in which the defendants -- two Italian tradesmen -- were convicted and executed. Frankfurter, then a professor at the Harvard Law School was a leader of the numerous critics who believed that they were victimized solely because they were avowed anarchists. Gressley put it this way:

> . . . As Mr. Justice Holmes had championed legal restraint in the economic area, so Frankfurter advocated the same Holmesian position be extended to civil liberties cases. For his admirers who recalled Frankfurter's courageous stand in the Sacco-Vanzetti case, Frankfurter's civil libertarian view of the fifties not only did not make sense, it plainly mystified them.[1]

In Arnold's case, Frankfurter's vanity was compounded by a personal animosity between the two men. I suspect it originated in an incident of which I was the only witness. It happened following one of the annual *Yale Law Journal* banquets in New Haven, during an after-party at one of the campus fraternity houses. I noticed Arnold and Frankfurter in conversation and stopped to listen. Frankfurter was expounding the virtues of the casebook system for studying law, originated by Dean Langdell of the Harvard Law School. As already noted, casebooks consist of excerpts from actual appellate opinions on one particular branch of the law -- *e.g.*, Contracts, Criminal Law, etc. These were grouped into a single volume which purportedly covered all of the legal principles pertinent to the legal topic it addressed.

As I've said, Arnold had no use for the casebook system. He felt that most appellate judges never really connected with the events at the trial level, especially if they lacked experience as litigators, which was often true. As they conversed, I vividly recall his rejection of Frankfurter's view that the casebook system represented the fountainhead of wisdom for teaching legal principles. "Look," he said, "if you want to teach legal principles, nobody has ever beat the Hornbooks." (They are a series of text books narrating legal principles on virtually every area of the law, written without the quotation or citation of any judicial opinions). Frankfurter continued to carry on about how casebooks created legal discipline, because the students had to deduce the principles from the opinion extracts. Arnold replied: "Oh, mental muscle building, eh?", pumping his arms up and down over his head. Frankfurter turned purple and angrily stalked off.

Subsequently, I saw and read a good deal of Frankfurter's performances on the Supreme Court bench and heard many anecdotes about him. They occurred during the years 1942 to 1943, when I served in the Supreme Court Section of the Claims Division [now the General Civil Division] of the Department of Justice. Under the general supervision of the Solicitor General's office -- which controls all government appeals -- that section's function was to write the government's Supreme Court briefs in cases arising from a number of the federal administrative agencies.

In those days, opinions were handed down only on Monday mornings, before the Court heard oral arguments. Members of our section were usually there because one or more decisions in cases we had briefed might come down. Sometimes we would stay on if an especially interesting case was on the docket for argument that same day.

Frankfurter's pomposity and intellectual exhibitionism were on full public display after his appointment to the Supreme Court. During oral arguments, he habitually dominated the dialogue, seemingly at times for the sole purpose of displaying the superior depth of his knowledge of the issues raised by the cases before the Court. He would frequently seize on some obscure procedural point and press questions about it to the point of exhausting the allotted time of some hapless lawyer. The victim might be making a rare appearance before the Supreme Court and suffer utter frustration in his effort to present the argument for his client.

It's hard to exaggerate the overawed sensation felt by a neophyte Supreme Court lawyer, looking up from his lectern. He is facing nine black-robed justices seated in a row behind their elevated podium, all wearing their solemn "game" faces. I remember one instance when Sam Slade, a law school classmate of mine and a colleague in the same section of the Claims Division, was making his first argument before the Court. By nature he was exceptionally high-strung. As he tremulously began his argument, the Chief Justice remarked: "Counsel, will you please raise your voice; some of the members of the Court can't hear you." Sam was barely able to respond: "I will when I'm able to, sir."

Frankfurter's indifference to the feelings of the lawyers who appeared before the Court is hard to exaggerate. When I was at the Claims Division, Paul Freund, the recently deceased and deeply venerated Professor of Constitutional Law at Harvard, was a young star in the Solicitor General's office. Then, as later, his skills were unmatched. It was a treat to watch his advocacy before the Supreme Court. The Justices hung on his every word, often soliciting his views on the appropriate limits of the opinion to be written in a case he was arguing.

Above all, Paul was a kind and gentle human being, beloved by all who knew him, incapable of uttering an unkind word to or about anyone. Ultimately, he was chosen by the Court to be its historian. There was a widespread feeling among the bar, particularly members familiar with the Supreme Court, that Paul should have been appointed to it. Some feel that Frankfurter was responsible for Freund's failure to reach the Supreme Court. Frankfurter is alleged to have discouraged Freund from accepting an appointment by President Kennedy as Solicitor General of the Department of Justice. That post was in charge of all government judicial appeals including particularly all arguments before the Supreme Court. It is often a stepping stone to the Supreme Court. Freund reportedly declined the job. When an opening on the Court occurred, Kennedy nominated Byron White. If the story is true, I suspect that Frankfurter feared that Freund would outshine him.

One day, Paul and I left the Court together after Paul had argued a case named *Clearfield Trust Co. v. United States*, 318 U.S. 363 (1943).

His opponent had been subjected to one of Frankfurter's more unrestrained performances. His capacity to make a coherent argument was wrecked. As we walked to the Department, Paul observed: "I've often thought that the rules of the Court should be amended to allow one hour for argument by counsel for each side and one hour for Felix." (More recently, the rules were amended to allow only half an hour for each side).

Arnold was very much in tune with the idiosyncrasies of the members of the Court, and particularly those of Justice Frankfurter. In a private antitrust case before that august tribunal,[2] the Judge had been called in by a Tampa, Florida lawyer named Cody Fowler (later President of the American Bar Association). The substantive issue was whether the client -- Bruce's Juices -- had been victimized by illegal price discrimination and therefore could refuse to pay for goods purchased from the American Can Company.

In preparing for the argument, Arnold and Fowler decided that the one hour of argument available to them should be equally divided. Fowler, the trial counsel, would describe the facts and Arnold would argue the legal issues. The afternoon before the argument, Arnold told Fowler to beware of Justice Frankfurter's penchant for seizing on a minor procedural point and exhausting counsel's time by pursuing it *ad nauseum.*

Sure enough, when Fowler was about three minutes into his presentation, Frankfurter inquired about a procedural ruling during the trial, implying that it was erroneous. Fowler answered. Frankfurter pressed on. After two more questions along the same line, Fowler stated in his mellifluous southern drawl:

> Your honor, I've answered your questions the best way I know how. So I'd best get on with the rest of my argument. For some reason, time seems to fly by much faster on my side of the bench than on yours.

That ended Justice Frankfurter's interest in the *Bruce's Juices* argument. He didn't ask another question. Sad to relate, we lost the case on the ground that the proper remedy for price discrimination was the statutory action for treble damages. We didn't win them all.

In thinking of Frankfurter, I am reminded of a comment -- mentioned elsewhere in this volume -- when I asked one of Tom Dewey's lawyers whether another staff lawyer was "a smart guy." The response was: "Yeah, he's a smart guy, but he's not as smart as he thinks he is. Nobody could be that smart." In my opinion, that summed up Justice Frankfurter.

His limitations came to light during the Supreme Court argument of an admiralty case which I briefed for the United States -- incidentally my first such brief.[3] The issue was whether a lien could be enforced against a privately owned vessel for damages it had inflicted in a collision while previously in the service of the United States. Such a lien was admittedly unenforceable during its public service.

One of our principal precedents was a case called *The Western Maid*.[4] In an opinion by Justice Holmes, the Court there overruled a fifty year old precedent.[5] It had held that such a collision gave rise to a lien which was unenforceable while the vessel was serving the government, but was enforceable if it later became private property. In *The Western Maid*, Holmes rejected that view. His typically cryptic opinion stated:

> Legal obligations that exist but cannot be enforced are ghosts that are seen in the law but are elusive to the grasp.

The *Eglantine* was argued for the United States by Sidney Kaplan, head of the District Court Section of the Claims Division. He was a friendly, open-faced redhead of medium height, a native of Minneapolis. His brilliance as a lawyer verged on the incredible. He had finished second in his class at Harvard Law School, although his classmates affirmed that he rarely attended lectures. They said that he paid his way through by his poker-playing skill.

He could quote cases by report, volume and page from memory. With him at its head, the District Court section operated with just three other lawyers. The four of them oversaw all of the emergency litigation involving the United States during the first two years of World War II. Although they were under constant pressure, Sid always seemed to be perfectly relaxed. He was never too busy to discuss a problem with anyone in the Claims Division. After Sid left to join the Coast Guard as a Reserve Lieutenant Commander, and his assistants also entered service, the same section quickly ballooned to 32 lawyers.

When I submitted my draft of the *Eglantine* brief to Kaplan, he asked whether I had checked the English law. My negative response elicited the following comment: "You'd better check it and while

you're at it check the Australian law. If I know the English law, Felix
is bound to ask me about the Australian law."

While Kaplan argued the case, I sat beside the lectern. After about
three minutes, he cited *The Western Maid* as authority against the
plaintiffs' claims.   No sooner had he mentioned that case, than
Frankfurter took the occasion to show his knowledge of admiralty law,
stating: "Counsel, didn't *The Western Maid* create quite a stir among
the admiralty bar when it was handed down?" His implication was that
Holmes didn't know what he was doing in holding for the United States
despite the doctrine of the *Siren* case.   Quick as a flash, Sid replied:
"Yes, your honor and Mr. Justice Holmes was not unaware of that."
Sid simultaneously reached for a book at the base of the lectern. It was
Holmes-Pollock Letters.[6] Sid then read the following passage from a
Holmes letter of May 5, 1924, to Sir Frederick Pollock, a distinguished
Kings Counsel and long-time friend of Holmes:

> . . . As I said in *The Western Maid* (257 U.S. 419, 432), "there is no
> mystic overlaw to which even the United States must bow. In that case
> we held that a vessel, a military transport I believe, that had wrongly
> collided with another while belonging to the U.S. couldn't be sued after
> it was sold -- much to the wrath of some admiralty men -- *inter alia*
> Hough, a good old admiralty judge . . .

With that, Frankfurter turned white.   He had not only been
upstaged. He had been publicly humiliated by the exposure of his
unfamiliarity with a reference in the celebrated Holmes-Pollock
correspondence to a critical precedent in a case decided by the Supreme
Court. It may not be an overstatement to think that in Frankfurter's
mind, the incident demoted him from the Olympian heights of a judicial
deity to the level of a mere mortal jurist.

The recourse to the *Holmes-Pollock Letters* was purely a reflection
of Kaplan's extraordinary talent. It would never have occurred to me
to consider researching that potential resource.

In another Supreme court case,[7] Frankfurter also wound up on the
short end of dialogue, again with a Harvard Law school graduate,
Frederick Bermays Wiener. A nephew of Sigmund Freud, he was a
brilliant lawyer and reputedly Frankfurter's all-time favorite student.
Wiener was no less noted than Frankfurter for his intellectual egotism.

The case involved a suit by the target of a postal fraud order issued
by the Postmaster General. The recipient had sued the local postmaster

to enjoin implementation of the order. The Postmaster General had not been named as a defendant. The question was whether he was "an indispensable party," without whom the suit could not proceed.

During the argument Frankfurter and Wiener got into a discussion about the need to join the superior officer. Wiener's point was the practical one that the Department of Justice would be unduly burdened if any local postmaster could be sued to prevent effectuation of the numerous fraud orders outstanding at any given time. In the course of the argument, Frankfurter referred to his experience as a member of the staff of the United States Attorney for the Southern District of New York in 1906. He described how that office had handled what he deemed comparable problems without difficulty. He then asked Wiener: "Why can't such matters be handled that way today?" Wiener replied: "There must have been giants in those days."

In an opinion by Justice Douglas, the court ruled against Wiener. It held that since the relief sought was purely negative, it required no action by the Postmaster General. Hence, his presence was not essential to the action.

However irritating, Frankfurter's vanity proved an asset in another Supreme Court case I briefed for the United States while serving at the Claims Division.[8] It was a tough assignment. The major issue was the legality of an order of the United States Maritime Commission fixing minimum "demurrage" charges for vessels overstaying permissible "free time" for unloading their cargos at their destination ports. The order was prompted by the practice of the State of California and the City of Oakland to grant below-cost preferences to induce the use of their public terminals. This practice discriminated against competing private terminals. The problem was that Sections 17 and 18 of the Shipping Act of 1916 limited the Commission's "ratemaking power [to] common carriers by water."[9] As to other persons "who, like California and Oakland, are not common carriers by water," the Commission's authority was more limited, i.e.:

> "to 'establish, observe, and enforce just and reasonable regulations and practices relating to or connected with the receiving, handling, storing, or delivering of property.'"[10]

There is a routinely observed legal maxim which states in Latin: *expressio unios est exclusio alterius*. It literally means to express one is to exclude any other. In less cryptic terms, its sense is that the specification of a right or restriction applicable to only one of several subjects mentioned in a single legal document -- such as a contract or a statute -- precludes its application to the others.[11] Under this maxim, the statutory limitation of rate-making authority to water carriers would ordinarily prevent the application of such power over other subjects of the same legislation.

While brainstorming for a way to overcome this formidable barrier to the government's position in the *California* demurrage case, I recalled Justice Frankfurter's opinion in an earlier case interpreting the application of provisions of the National Labor Relations Act relating to the reinstatement of strikers.[12] In that case, the Board had held that the respondent's refusal to rehire certain union members had violated the anti-discrimination provisions of Section 8(3) of the National Labor Relations Act.[13]

The facts were that the great majority of the union members had gone on strike against Phelps Dodge. Two others had obtained equivalent employment elsewhere, instead of striking. They had nevertheless applied for employment by Phelps Dodge when the strike ended. The primary issue before the Court concerned the propriety of the provision of the Board's order directing employment of those two men.

The material provisions of the statute were Sections 2(3) and 10(c).[14] In relevant part Section 2(3) defined the term 'employee' as follows:

> The term 'employee' shall include any employee, and shall not be limited to the employees of a particular employer, unless the Act explicitly states otherwise, and shall include any individual whose work has ceased as a consequence of, or in connection with, any current labor dispute or because of any unfair labor practice, *and who has not obtained any other regular and substantially equivalent employment.*[15]

With regard to the remedy for unfair labor practices, Section 10(c) authorized the Board

> "to take such affirmative action, including reinstatement of *employees* with or without back pay, as will effectuate the *policies* of this Act."

The principal issue concerned the Board's conclusion that it had the "power to order employment in cases where the men discriminated against had obtained substantially equivalent employment"[16]

Frankfurter's opinion resolved that issue by focusing exclusively on the first part of Section 2(3) which stated that "employee shall not be limited to the employees of a particular employer," while ignoring the subsequent qualification in the same section which restricted the term to an individual "*who has not obtained any other regular and substantially equivalent employment.*" In a convoluted rationale, he wandered all over the statute and seized upon the generalized reference in Section 10(c) to the authority of the Board to take such remedial action, including reinstatement "as will effectuate the policies of this Act." On that premise, the opinion concluded:

> To deny the Board power to neutralize discrimination merely because workers have obtained compensatory employment would confine the "policies of this Act" to the correction of private injuries. The Board was not devised for such a limited function . . .[17]

Fishing for Frankfurter by quoting *Phelps Dodge* when I briefed *California v. United States* paid big dividends. He wrote the opinion in a 5-4 decision which held in our favor. *Phelps Dodge* was the first case on which his opinion relied.[18]

It would be hard to find any decisions which matched those two for judicial disregard or distortion of plain statutory language -- i.e., for engaging in the forbidden fruit of judicial legislation. So much for Frankfurter's self-proclaimed posture as the principal apostle of the necessity for judicial restraint -- i.e., the principle condemning the arrogation of legislative power by the courts.[19]

While critiquing that supposed judicial canon, let me address the notions, currently in vogue among some judicial scholars, of deducing "original intent" in construing the Constitution, and of "restraining" opinions to the narrowest possible ground -- as in the *Peters* case. Their essence is that constitutional interpretations must be resolved consonantly with the views of the authors of the document and that broad opinions constitute improper "judicial legislation." This is what the universally respected Associate Justice Robert H. Jackson -- hardly a liberal -- had to say about those shibboleths, while concurring in the decision condemning President Truman's seizure of the nation's steel mills during the Korean War as unconstitutional:

> A judge, like an executive adviser, may be surprised at the poverty of really useful and unambiguous authority applicable to concrete

problems of executive power as they actually present themselves. *Just what our forefathers did envision, or would have envisioned had they foreseen modern conditions, must be divined from materials almost as enigmatic as the dreams Joseph was called upon to interpret for Pharaoh.* A century and a half of partisan debate and scholarly speculation yields no net result but only supplies more or less apt quotations from respected sources on each side of any question. They largely cancel each other. *And court decisions are indecisive because of the judicial practice of dealing with the largest questions in the most narrow way.*[20]

In my opinion, unless they have access to H.G. Wells' time machine, members of the "original intent" and "judicial restraint" schools can aptly be described as judicial psychics and mystics. The real consequence of their pronouncements is to compound the already disturbing public cynicism about the rationality of our legal system and to foment excessive litigation.

CHAPTER SIXTEEN

THE DISCOUNTER

During the mid-fifties, a young and gutsy small business client plunged Arnold, Fortas & Porter into an all-out litigation war against the country's giant merchandisers. The client was an unsung New York retailer, Masters, Inc., the first membership retailer, founded in 1937, to sell consumer products at discount prices. It's hard to believe now, but the war was about the legality of off-price retailing.

At the time I met Steve Masters, so-called "fair trade" statutes in 44 of the 50 states authorized vendors of all trademarked consumer goods to require resellers to maintain contractually specified prices. Such statutes were reinforced by a federal statute known as the McGuire Act. That statute had two basic provisions. One legalized application of the state enactments to goods moving in interstate commerce. The other applied contractually specified prices to all resellers in a "fair trade" state with actual notice of them, whether or not they had contracted to observe them.[1]

The state statutes were exceptionally broad. A manufacturer could enforce his prices at wholesale and retail by entering into a single contract with a wholesaler and one with a retailer prescribing actual or minimum resale prices and requiring it to resell only to resellers who agreed to observe such prices. When just one such wholesale and one such retail contract had been negotiated, the manufacturer could bind all resellers in the state by publicizing the prescribed prices.

The "fair trade" system did not sit well with Steve Masters. Ignoring the fixed prices, Masters, Inc., soon did a land office business by selling "fair traded" products at sharply discounted prices through its large "membership" superstore in New York City. He had little difficulty in obtaining merchandise. Fair trade distributors who observed fixed prices in selling to other customers were glad to make "bootleg" cash sales to Masters at small mark-ups. Masters' resulting threat to their protected price structures was intolerable to the price-fixers who soon saddled it with numerous injunctions in the New York courts.

When it retained us, Masters was fighting for the right to sell such goods by mail at discount prices from the District of Columbia, which had no fair trade law, to consumers in states where such legislation was in force. For that purpose Masters had organized a subsidiary named Masters Mail Order Company of Washington, D.C., Inc. ("Masters Mail Order").

Just as interesting as the company's novel business venture was the personality of its president, Steve Masters, a first-generation American of Italian ancestry. Youthful, good-looking and athletic, soft-spoken and laconic, he was a creative merchandiser. The business had been founded and managed by his older brother Phil, regarded as a retailing genius. Each owned 50 percent of the corporate stock. When Phil suddenly died, Steve took over management of the business. Little was expected of him; his entrepreneurial talents were untested. He soon proved an aggressive merchant who built the business to unexpected stature. What brought him to our office -- specifically to Judge Arnold -- was a series of lawsuits to prevent the District of Columbia corporation from advertising or selling by mail at less than the fixed prices in "fair trade" jurisdictions.

Steve was an honest-to-God disciple of the capitalist competitive system, if ever there was one. To defend his economic principles, he willingly incurred substantial litigation fees and costs to fight off the legal attacks of numerous blue chip manufacturers.

The "fair traders" preached but did not practice the virtues of free and open competition. They were far more interested in establishing and protecting price-fixed markets wherever and whenever they could. As the litigation progressed, Steve Masters reminded me of a David battling a hydra-headed Goliath.

The result of the "fair trade" laws was to eliminate intrabrand price competition among retailers of a virtually endless list of consumer goods. These comprised small appliances: cameras, toasters, watches, hand irons, electric razors, vacuum cleaners, carpet sweepers, fountain pens, toys, records, etc. Indirectly, interbrand competitiveness was also softened. The justification was that such legislation merely permits

a manufacturer, whose trade-mark or brand name may represent a large advertising investment and a carefully nurtured good will, to prevent

retailers, over whom he would otherwise have little control, from
seriously impairing the value of that trade-mark and good will by
reselling his identified products at unreasonably low prices. [2]

That theory was pure and simple window-dressing. For example,
General Electric did not use "fair trade" contracts on its own "white"
appliances -- such as refrigerators and washing machines. Nor did any
automobile manufacturers or soft drink producers use such contracts.
The value of the trade marks on those goods suffered no impairment
from the lack of "fair trade" protection.

Price cutters were not only subject to injunctions prohibiting price
discounts which subjected them to contempt penalties for disobedience.
Another hazard was that newspapers in fair trade jurisdictions refused
to accept discount advertising. Among them were the *New York Times*
and *Daily News*. Both refused to accept the discount advertising of
Masters Mail Order Company.

As noted above, the state statutes were backed by a federal enabling
statute, known as the McGuire Act. The reason was that a prior
federal statute -- the Miller-Tydings Act -- had been held inapplicable
to merchants who had not contracted to observe the stipulated prices.[3]
Another case had ruled such statutes inapplicable to good shipped to
out-of-state buyers.[4] Both gaps were closed by the McGuire Act. The
result was a privately administered price control system which
guaranteed fat profits, from manufacturer to retailer, almost
everywhere in the U.S. Only six states and the District of Columbia
lacked fair trade laws.

A prominent New York lawyer -- Joseph Ruggieri -- brought Steve
Masters to Judge Arnold, who soon after passed the client to me. Our
first assignment for Masters was to appeal to the Supreme Court of the
United States for reversal of the New York decision upholding General
Electric's injunction against Masters.[5] The appeal was denied.[6]

But Steve Masters was not about to be confined in a fair trade box.
He saw an escape route via the District of Columbia, one of the very
few jurisdictions unburdened by a fair trade law -- doubtless to protect
the budgets of Congressional families. Steve quickly exploited this free
market refuge by opening Masters Mail Order Company of
Washington, D.C., Inc. He immediately began spreading the news in
"fair trade" states that discount prices were available by mail. To
quote a New York federal court which first outlawed such practices --

but was soon reversed -- Masters widely circulated handbills in New York which proclaimed:

> It's becoming a crime to offer bargains, Masters recently paid . . . a penalty of $1750 to G.E. for cutting fixed prices . . . Masters had continued to give its customers bargains despite court orders so that the discount house was found guilty and had to pay the penalty.
>
> Masters Mail Order Company of Washington, D.C., Inc. has been established in Washington, D.C. because it is a non-fair trade area. This means we are permitted from Washington, D.C. to offer you anywhere in the country sensational discounts on famous brands.[7]

However, if the price fixers could help it, Masters was not about to get away with the mail order challenge. The fair traders quickly launched another round of litigation -- this time against the D.C. mail order operation. This took the form of a coordinated attack by several fair traders in the federal courts of Maryland and New York, both noted for stringent enforcement of fair trade laws. Two cases were filed in each jurisdiction. Revere Camera Co. in Maryland and General Electric in New York filed suits for injunctions. They claimed that local fair trade barriers could not be penetrated either by advertising the availability of discount prices via mail orders to the District of Columbia or by fulfilling such mail orders. The other Maryland case was brought by Bissell Carpet Sweeper. It sought to restrain only the discount advertising, apparently reasoning that absent publicity, discount sales would be trifling. In the other New York case, Sunbeam Corporation moved for contempt penalties. It hypothesized that Masters' establishment of a subsidiary to conduct the Washington mail order business violated an injunction previously prohibiting the parent corporation from intrastate price cutting in New York.

Steve Masters was determined to fight each case to the bitter end. He never mentioned settlement or compromise. He paid his legal expenses on time and without question. Masters was fighting for principle and would not equivocate. He made that clear when I asked him why he had assumed the financial burden of such extensive and expensive litigation. His reply was a classic expression of the essence of capitalism: "It sticks in my craw that somebody should tell me the prices at which I 'gotta' sell merchandise that I already bought and paid for." That was it. Steve wasn't given to long speeches or heated denunciations.

Revere Camera brought the first case in Maryland, It prayed for an injunction that would prohibit Masters Mail Order from advertising or selling in Maryland below Revere's fair trade Maryland prices. It was heard by the United States District Court for Maryland, sitting in Baltimore, before Judge W. Calvin Chesnut. He was a retired Chief Judge of that Court, who had elected to exercise his prerogative to continue to sit as an active judge. He was well along in years, but still sharp of mind and tongue -- as competent a judge as any lawyer could hope for.

The argument before him proved a great learning experience for me. Less than a year earlier, Judge Chesnut had written the opinion in a case challenging interstate discount sales from a dealer in Maryland to one in Delaware, both governed by fair trade laws. It was the first test of the meaning of the McGuire Act. In support of a ruling that the sale was subject to the Maryland fair trade law, Judge Chesnut had delivered a comprehensive and learned opinion. He had exhaustively reviewed the McGuire Act and its interaction with state laws in permitting fair trade prices to apply to goods moving in interstate commerce.[8]

Against that background, I opened my argument by stating, "May it please the court: This case involves the effect of two statutes with which your honor is of course, familiar -- the Maryland Fair Trade Act and the McGuire Act -- upon mail order sales from the District of Columbia which has no fair trade law, to residents of Maryland in which there is such a law". Judge Chesnut immediately admonished me: "Young man, don't assume that I am familiar with anything. Tell me exactly what those statutes say."

Like a good student, I carefully parsed them out. I next noted that our case involved a different issue from the one decided by Judge Chesnut in the previous Maryland/Delaware context -- namely, deliveries from the District of Columbia, a jurisdiction without a price-fixing law, into Maryland, a state in which there was one. I argued that the McGuire Act merely allowed each of the various states freedom of decision regarding the enactment of fair trade laws, but gave none the right to impose its will on states which had no such laws.

In other words, merchants in states and the District of Columbia, which had not enacted "fair trade" laws were free to advertise and sell within such states or *from* such states at prices of their own choosing. The judge readily perceived the distinction and denied Revere's application for a preliminary injunction, while also denying our motion to dismiss, but without prejudice to its renewal.[9] The plaintiff then dropped the case. That left Masters one up and three to go.

Next in line was the demand of *Bissell Carpet Sweeper* for an injunction addressed solely to advertising in Maryland that discount prices on fair-traded items were available by mail order from the District of Columbia. Nothing was said about interstate discount sales. The legal theory was that while the Maryland law did not inhibit off-price sales from the District of Columbia, Maryland's ban on cut-rate advertising was a separable feature of its fair trade law which barred such promotion within the state. The pragmatic idea was that without such promotion, there would be few mail orders. We argued that the Maryland law against cut-price advertising could not be cut loose from its moorings, namely, sales by Maryland vendors. Our point was that the components of the act -- including both the ban against the cut price advertising and sales -- constituted a unified whole, addressed solely to transactions originating *within* the state's borders.

The *Bissell* case came up before another cracker-jack federal judge in the Baltimore federal court. He was Dorsey Watkins, a former professor of law at Johns Hopkins University, then newly appointed to the bench. He was also a perfect fit for W.S. Gilbert's "judicial humorist" category. Masters won again. Judge Watkins ruled that the various provisions of the Maryland law comprised an integrated whole -- that each of its provisions had the same focus and could sensibly be interpreted to relate only to sales and advertising by a Maryland vendor. He reasoned that to endorse Bissell's view of the extraterritorial reach of Maryland's advertising ban -- by detachment from sales in Maryland -- would logically mean that the same external reach should be allowed for the Maryland prohibition against discount sales. If so, he wrote -- with tongue in cheek -- the Maryland statute would govern a foreign sale in which

> "the only contract was entered into in New York, the only advertising was in Cairo, Egypt (in the native tongue) and the advertisement offered the commodity for sale only in Gussage Cow Down, Dorsetshire."[10]

Judge Watkins accordingly decided that all facets of the Maryland law were restricted to transactions originating in Maryland and that discount advertisements in Maryland by D.C. merchants for goods to be sent through the mails could be permissibly circulated within Maryland.

Unlike Revere, Bissell elected to appeal. The case was argued before a three-judge panel of the United States Court of Appeals for the Fourth Circuit. It proved to be quite an experience. The panel included two venerable and venerated members of that court -- Chief Judge John J. Parker and Associate Judge Morris Soper -- plus Walter Hoffman, a newly appointed, and then quite young, federal district judge from Norfolk. In legal jargon, he was sitting temporarily -- "by designation" -- as an appellate judge. Each side was allowed the customary thirty minutes for argument.

Both Parker and Soper were widely admired for their scholarship and acumen. Hoffman was a complete unknown. During the argument for *Bissell* -- presented first as the losing party below -- Judge Soper asked only one question. It persuaded me that he was on our side. Judge Hoffman was silent. The Chief Judge seemed strongly in favor of Bissell.

Now it was my turn at bat. I had barely uttered the customary salutation -- "May it please the Court" -- when Judge Parker began bombarding me with hostile questions. After I had strained to answer as best I could for about ten minutes, I said something which moved Judge Parker to say: "That's the first thing you've said that makes any sense to me." I haven't the faintest recollection of what evoked that comment. I vividly recall my reply: "Thank you, Your Honor; that completes my argument." It was my finest moment as an oral advocate; one I was never destined to repeat -- being normally infected with the lawyer's typical illusion that every second of time for argument must be consumed, lest some pearl of wisdom be left unsaid. Whatever the effect of my bob-tailed presentation, the court unanimously sustained Judge Watkins' decision for Masters.[11] Round two also belonged to Masters.

To digress once again: As this was originally written, Chief Judge Parker's name rang nostalgically in an important current context -- the Senate's rejection of Judge Robert H. Bork's nomination to the Supreme Court. In 1930, when Judge Parker had been nominated to the Supreme Court, the same thing had happened to him -- by a mere two votes compared with the 14-vote margin against Judge Bork. At the time Parker was likewise a sitting judge of a United States Court of Appeals. Unlike Judge Bork, however, Judge Parker remained on the bench and served with distinction -- amid a growing consensus that he had unjustly been denied confirmation -- until he retired in the late 1950's. It was also Judge Parker -- when he became Chief Judge of the Fourth Circuit -- who initiated the gracious practice of having the members of the Court descend from the bench after each argument, to introduce themselves personally to counsel in the case.

Now back to the Masters case: So far, so good. Masters was now two up with two innings to play. But it didn't win them all, at least not in the federal trial courts. Both New York cases were heard by the federal court in New York City -- the United States District Court for the Southern District of New York. The first, brought by General Electric against the D.C. mail order operation, sang the same refrain as Revere had in Maryland -- that New York's fair trade law was violated both by the advertising in New York and mail orders dispatched from the District of Columbia to New York residents at discount prices. There was one embellishment -- the presence of the parent company in New York City.

The Judge in the *General Electric* case, Alexander Bicks, was newly appointed. To say that he was equivocal in deciding our case is an understatement. Several months after hearing the original argument, he called a conference in chambers in which attorneys for both sides were asked to participate. The Judge opened the conference by pointing to two paper documents -- one on each side of his desk. He said both represented an opinion in the case -- one deciding for the plaintiff and the other for the defendant. At his invitation, some short dialogue ensued between opposing counsel. That ended the conference.

Sometime later, during the month of December, I received a call from the Judge's clerk. He told me the Judge desired to hold a further conference at 4:00 p.m., December 31. I responded that I could not attend because my wife was looking forward to a New Year's Eve ball. I added that if need be, I would suffer a contempt citation from the court, rather than risk a petition for divorce from my wife. Evidently the Judge reconsidered, for I heard nothing more about that conference.

Eventually, Judge Bicks issued an injunction against mail order dealings from D.C. to New York customers. He considered himself bound by a decision of the highest court of New York State, which had ruled that the New York fair trade law applied "to out-of-state mail-order sales by a New York retailer."[12] Such sales, of course, were made in New York, which had a fair trade law, while we were defending sales originating in the District of Columbia, which did not.

We appealed to the United States Court of Appeals for the Second Circuit.

The appeal was heard before the customary three-judge panel. It was headed by Chief Judge Charles Clark -- former Dean of the Yale Law School -- and, as already noted, a friend of Thurman Arnold. The other two members were Judge Jerome Frank and Judge Edwin Lumbard. I was up first, as the loser below. Edgar Barton, a well-known fair trade expert -- and a partner in White & Case, an esteemed New York law firm -- argued for General Electric. After the argument, I left the court in Steve's company. He said: "We'll never win this case." I asked, "Why?" He replied: "General Electric can buy off any court in the land." I answered: "We might win this case, and we might lose it. But I'll guarantee one thing, Steve, if we lose, it won't be because GE bought the court." Looking back, I suspect he had felt all along that the main event would be fought in New York and had pretty much resigned himself to ultimate defeat when we lost the GE case at the trial court level.

About six months later, the appellate court decided in our favor.[13] Following that, fair trade started to unravel. A lengthy article on the first page of *The New York Times* Business Section of May 26, 1957, told of an advertising campaign planned by "Stephen Masters." It carried the following lead and stated in part:

MASTERS READIES NEW BLOW AT G.E.

"The discount house chief seeks to increase volume for his Washington company to end General Electric price-fixing of small appliances and to smash fair trade."

Steve's determined digging was now reaching paydirt. But the press -- at least in New York -- was still recalcitrant about accepting ads of his Washington mail order business. So, we applied some antitrust pressure, including a not so gentle hint of a possible action for treble damages under the Sherman Antitrust Law. That got the job done. On June 24, 1957, the following item appeared at page 34 of *The New York Times*:

MASTERS BREAK

"The Sunday News yesterday became the first New York newspaper to carry an advertisement for the Masters Mail Order Company of Washington, D.C. The full-page advertisement offered "fair-traded" General Electric Company appliances at discount prices. Other newspapers in the city had declined to carry advertisements placed by the discount houses."

General Electric fought on to the bitter end. It filed a petition for certiorari, seeking review by the United States Supreme Court of the Second Circuit ruling. Before long, on October 13, 1957 -- soon after the Court reconvened after the summer recess -- I got word that the petition had been denied.[14]

I immediately called Steve and told him the good news. He said, "I just heard." I asked "How?" He replied: "I just got off the phone with the Vice President at Bridgeport" [GE's small appliance manufacturing division]. "Really, Steve," I queried, "what did he want?" Steve replied: "He wanted to know how much merchandise I wanted." "What did you tell him, Steve?" Steve casually said: "I told him go f__k yourself." His voice was, as always, matter of fact; no exultation. That was all he had to say. As we hung up, I mused about the satisfaction Steve must have felt in winning the war, at long last.

There was an anticlimax. Sunbeam pressed its contempt case in the federal court for the Southern District of New York. It claimed that the D.C. mail order operation had violated a preexisting injunction against the parent New York company. That matter was heard by Judge Edward Weinfeld. He was perhaps as renowned for his judicial competence as any other member of the New York federal bench in its entire history. Since the matter was brought on by a motion to cite Masters for contempt, it had to be heard on "motions day" -- at that time just one day a week. By tradition, a single jurist, serving as motions judge, had to clear the entire docket, no matter what. This involved the disposition of literally hundreds of motions in a single day. It was some job. To get it done, most judges scanned the attorneys' papers as they heard argument, trying to play the issues by ear.

Judge Weinfeld was different. He somehow always managed to read in advance, and thoroughly, all papers on the motions he was to hear. He put what he called "long motions" at the end of the calendar. Sunbeam's motion for contempt was so categorized. We did not get on until well past 7:00 p.m. During my presentation, Judge Weinfeld said; "I would love to find a way to rule against you, but I can't." He didn't.[15]

The repercussions of the Masters mail order cases were widespread. Steve Masters had blown Gabriel's Horn for fair trade. It became a dead letter. While the *General Electric* case was pending, the Antitrust Division of the Department of Justice adopted the Masters position in a friend of the court brief, filed on behalf of a Missouri mail order house which had followed Masters' D.C. model. Not many years later, the McGuire Act was repealed. The age of the modern retail discounter was about to dawn.

Finally, I can't help recording one memorable vignette in the Masters litigation. It concerns my mother. In the previously mentioned *New York Times* report of June 24, 1957 -- entitled "MASTERS READIES NEW BLOW AT G.E." -- there was a reference to me:

> Norman Diamond, partner in the Washington law firm of Arnold, Fortas and Porter, which has defended similar suits against Masters Mail Order, said his client will fight the General Electric action in the Supreme Court 'if and when it comes up.'

I was unaware of this article. To my recollection, this was the first press mention of any of the Masters cases. Anyway, at the rate we were working in those early days of the firm, weekends were scarcely distinguishable from weekdays. It was hard to squeeze time for the Sunday Washington papers -- then the *Star* and the *Post* -- let alone the voluminous Sunday *Times*.

But mother gallantly came to the rescue -- phoning to read me *The Times'* reference to my legal achievement -- while bursting with a Jewish mother's pride. Mom was no devotee of *The Times* Business Section, but it wasn't hard to guess her source. It was surely Dad, who was self-educated by his assiduous daily study of every line deemed fit to print by that copious publication. But he never mentioned the item to me. I'm sure that in his perspective, all I had done was what a lawyer did to earn his keep. He was right. But some ways of earning it are more rewarding than others. This was certainly how I felt about the Masters litigation.

Unhappily, Steve was only permitted a glimpse of the promised land. He never got to play a major league role on the level, free market playing field he had created. His plan to expand Masters on a grand scale by issuing stock to the public was blocked by his sister-in-law. She was the legatee of the 50% of the stock owned by her deceased husband -- Steve's older brother, Phil. On the advice of her counsel, she voted against a public issue. Even more sadly, Steve died early -- in the prime of life. Although he never knew it, Steve truly founded off-price selling -- today's predominant retailing method -- of which Wal-Mart is currently the major exponent.

It is not farfetched to analyze Steve's accomplishments in the elimination of fixed-price retailing to the effect of government deregulation of business. Besides Wal-Mart, a host of other off-price retailers emerged in Masters' wake -- exemplified by such enterprises as Korvette, K-Mart, Loehmann's, the Burlington Coat Factory, Today's Man, T.J. Maxx, etc. It wasn't long before many traditional and esteemed department stores were in big trouble: Federated, Macy's, B. Altman, Woodward & Lothrop, Wanamaker's and others were in the bankruptcy courts or out of business.

The effect was comparable to the result of the deregulation of the airline industry when the Civil Aeronautics Board was abolished. The emergence of such low price carriers as Laker Airways, Southwest Airlines and Valu Jet drastically reduced the price level of air travel and forced a drastic restructuring of the industry. Such giants as Eastern Airlines, Pan American and Braniff were destroyed. Others were forced to reorganize in the bankruptcy courts, including such major carriers as TWA and United.

Just one final note on the Masters litigation: Let me speak briefly to the current furor about alleged overcharges by law firms. Among other things there are complaints about excessive pre-trial proceedings known as "discovery", padding hours and other forms of overbilling on the part of the legal profession. Every one of the *Masters Mail Order* cases was decided without a minute devoted to pre-trial discovery, the preparation of affidavits, let alone a trial of the issues. Not a single witness ever testified. They were all decided on motions and briefs, plus court arguments of two hours or less.

CHAPTER SEVENTEEN

GILBERT & SULLIVAN TO THE RESCUE

It is almost axiomatic that as many cases are won by capitalizing on the opposition's mistakes as by the generation of an effective affirmative strategy. A striking example of that axiom emerged in a matter in which I successfully represented the Kroger Co. against a complaint filed by the Federal Trade Commission (the "FTC"). It alleged that Kroger -- one of the nation's leaders of supermarket chains -- had violated the anti-merger provisions of Section 7 of the Clayton Act.[1] That provision prohibits corporations from acquiring the stock or assets of another business when the consequence may be an anticompetitive or monopolistic impact which affects interstate commerce.

The complaint against Kroger was one of a series launched by the FTC in the Spring of 1959. It was filed April 1st of that year -- just five days after a similar filing against *National Tea Co.* Because of FTC blunders, that small time differential proved to be the decisive factor which enabled Kroger to prevail by successful motions to dismiss the complaint.

That was a source of immense satisfaction to the client and to us. The administrative agencies, such as the Federal Trade Commission, hold the high cards whenever they institute a proceeding.

The FTC is one of many administrative agencies -- among them, for example, the Securities and Exchange Commission and the Federal Communications Commission -- that are invested by Congress with regulatory powers. They are exercisable in particular areas of economic activity, such as securities markets or the broadcast industry, about which they are presumed to possess special expertise.

Such agencies differ from cabinet departments in that they are headed by multiple members -- ranging in number from three to seven -- rather than a cabinet secretary, who singly heads his or her department. The members of such agencies also differ from cabinet secretaries in other respects. They are appointed by the president -- one of them as chair -- subject to Senate confirmation, for fixed terms -- typically five to seven years -- while cabinet officers serve at the pleasure of the President and usually resign when there is a change in the party which captures the White House.

The FTC consists of five members. It has jurisdiction to enforce all of the antitrust laws, including the anti-merger statute[1] and the anti-price discrimination law.[2]

In addition, the FTC has broad general powers under a provision authorizing it to prevent "unfair methods of competition in or affecting interstate commerce."[3] By Supreme Court interpretation, that is a huge grant of regulatory authority. It comprehends the Sherman Antitrust Act's prohibition of restraints of trade -- such as price-fixing and boycotts -- and its proscription of monopolies.[4] It also covers "incipient" antitrust violations, namely practices which may develop into antitrust violations. That is a virtually unlimited power.[5]

Unlike the Department of Justice and state prosecutorial offices, those "expert" federal bodies are endowed with power to act as not only as prosecutor, but also as judge and jury. They bring the charges, try them and decide them. This means that in order to prevail, the target of an FTC complaint must persuade the agency to hold that its own complaint was erroneous.

However, that is not the only difficulty facing the respondent. If it loses before the agency and wishes to appeal to the courts, it is confronted by what is known as the "substantial evidence rule". The problem this presents is evident from the Supreme Court's declaration that the "substantial evidence" -- which dictates a denial of an appeal -- does not mean that the adverse ruling must be based on a preponderance of the evidence. To quote the Supreme Court's definition of "substantial evidence":

> . . . This is something less than the weight of the evidence, and the possibility of drawing two inconsistent conclusions from the evidence does not prevent an administrative agency's finding from being supported by substantial evidence. *Labor Board v. Nevada Consolidated Copper Corp.*, 316 U.S. 105, 106; *Keele Hair & Scalp Specialists, Inc. v. FTC*, 275 F.2d 18, 21.

Congress was very deliberate in adopting this standard of review. It frees the reviewing courts of the time-consuming and difficult task of weighing the evidence, it gives proper respect to the expertise of the administrative tribunal and it helps promote the uniform application of the statute . . .[6]

The background of the FTC's action against Kroger was that body's initiation of a series of proceedings to undo a number of acquisitions of other grocery businesses by various supermarket chains. Paul Rand Dixon was the newly appointed Chairman of the Commission when the complaints were filed. He was an alumnus of the Kefauver school of governmental histrionics, imbued with a belief that the government could do no wrong. When Kefauver chaired the Antitrust Subcommittee of the Senate Judiciary Committee, Dixon was its counsel. He was well aware of the Crime Committee's antics, described in the preceding CHAPTER TWO. He was a beefy ex-football player, undistinguished by his knowledge of legal principles. Like Kefauver, he was from Tennessee.

As already stated, the first complaint was issued against *National Tea Co.* on March 26, 1959; the second against Kroger five days later. The complaint against Kroger described the company, in part, as follows:

Respondent is engaged in the business of operating a chain of approximately 1,421 retail food stores in 20 States of the United States and sells a wide variety of merchandise, including a substantial number of items manufactured, processed and packaged under trademarks or brands owned or controlled by the respondent. The respondent owns or leases and operates bread and cracker bakeries, dairies, coffee roasting plants, and a general manufacturing plant for producing and packaging candies, salad dressing, preserves, gelatin pudding, peanut butter, spices, coffee, extracts, and other grocery items. The respondent operates egg exchanges. In addition thereto, respondent owns jointly with Westinghouse Electric & Manufacturing Company a patented process for tenderizing meat, known as "Tenderay Process." The respondent maintains the Kroger Food Foundation, a technical organization, which tests the quality of products it purchases, develops new products, offer technical services to all departments of the respondent, including a housewives' advisory service.

*   *   *

Respondent is one of the largest retail food chains in the United States and, as of December 28, 1957, ranked third in total sales volume among the food chains of this country. Respondent's net sales increased from approximately $258,000,000 in 1940 to $1,674,000,000 in 1957, an increase of approximately $1,400,000,000, or over 500 percent.[7]

As originally framed, the complaint identified more than 40 acquisitions by Kroger -- mainly retail grocery chains, but including a few wholesale grocers. All but five were acquired prior to 1950, when Section 7 was expanded to include the acquisition of another company's "assets" as well as its "stock" and to eliminate the prior restriction of prohibited acquisitions to those between competitors. Although the complaint charged that all of Kroger's acquisitions were illegal, the real focus was on the five acquired after 1950 -- from 1953 through 1958. All of them served markets in which Kroger had never before competed -- namely, Milwaukee, Houston, Shreveport, Dallas, East Texas, West Louisiana and Arkansas. Such acquisitions are known in antitrust parlance as "market extension mergers."

Subsequently, in 1963, Kroger entered the Los Angeles market by another market extension merger -- the acquisition of a local chain named Market Basket, which operated 56 supermarkets. Although I had generally advised Kroger that market extension mergers were legal, because of the pending complaint the company had expressly requested my opinion before acquiring Market Basket. I adhered to my previous advice. It was my judgment that ultimately -- if litigation ensued -- the acquisition would not tip the scales against Kroger, although it defied the Commission's declared position.

To my amazement, the complaint was followed by a seemingly interminable administrative war which consumed almost ten years. In the end the Commission was impelled to surrender by an order dismissing the charges against Kroger.[8] That left Kroger as the only winner among the retail grocery respondents in the FTC's campaign to halt mergers in the industry.

More specifically, the post-complaint history of the case against Kroger was a ten year exercise in bureaucratic ineptitude -- worthy of a comic opera. We took full advantage of the Commission's bloopers.

One of the critical events occurred on January 17, 1967 while the Kroger case was eight years old, but still unresolved. At that time the Commission promulgated a document entitled *Commission Enforcement Policy with Respect to Mergers in the Food Distribution Industries.*[9]

This set up the basis for a motion to dismiss the complaint on the ground that the case had been prejudged by the Commission -- an adjudicatory "no no."

In pertinent part the "*Enforcement Policy*," described as follows the Commission's initiation and the status of its anti-merger campaign:

> The structure of food retailing in the United States has undergone a number of very significant changes during the past decade and a half. Food distribution has become increasingly concentrated in both national and local markets. . . .
>
> . . . Much of the Commission's merger enforcement activity has been devoted to this sector of the economy. The Commission initiated its first legal action under amended Section 7 of the Clayton Act challenging mergers among grocery supermarket chains in early 1959. The first case challenged 13 acquisitions made from 1952-1958 by the National Tea Co., the fifth ranking grocery chain on a national basis. *The second case, against the Kroger Co., challenged 5 acquisitions made from 1955-1958 by that chain, the third ranking grocery chain in the country* . . .[10]

> *   *   *

> *Litigation has been terminated in all but one of the Commission's merger actions in food retailing.* The Commission's action against Grand Union was terminated June 10, 1965, when the Grand Union Co. signed a consent agreement which required the divestiture of certain acquired supermarkets and prohibited for a period of 10 years, without the prior approval of the Commission, the acquisition of competitors above a certain minimum size. The Commission issued its opinion and final order in the National Tea case on March 14, 1966. The case was not appealed. The final order in this matter prohibits National Tea from making any retail food store acquisitions for a period of 10 years without the prior approval of the of Federal Trade Commission. Consolidated Foods signed a consent agreement December 2, 1965, which required the divestiture of retail stores with combined sales in excess of $200 million and which prohibits Consolidated from acquiring without the prior approval of the Commission any grocery stores or dairy products stores.

> The Commission's case involving Winn-Dixie Stores, Inc., was settled with a consent agreement, September 1966, which prohibits

Winn-Dixie from acquiring without the prior approval of the Commission and retail food stores for a period of ten years.

The Commission's case involving the Kroger Company is still in the process of litigation. This complaint was recently amended challenging the Kroger Company's acquisition in 1963 of Market Basket, a Los Angeles based chain.

The Department of Justice case against Von's was decided in favor of the Government by the Supreme Court on May 31, 1966.[11]

* * *

Criteria Used to Identify Mergers Which Warrant Immediate Action

In view of the Commission's extensive legal activity in the area of food retailing and the probability that market forces will continue to create an environment conducive to mergers in the industry, it is appropriate that the Commission spell out as clearly as possible those mergers which the Commission's experience and knowledge suggest are most likely to have anticompetitive consequences. This is not to imply that the Commission has sufficient knowledge or foresight to draw with precision the legal boundaries around every prospective merger in food retailing. Conditions inevitably change with time and circumstances. On the other hand, businessmen contemplating mergers have a right to know whether particular mergers are likely to be challenged by the Commission and, perhaps, be forcibly undone after years of expensive litigation. *This is not to say that what is set forth below in any way represents prejudgment by the Commission concerning the way in which it will rule in particular litigated cases* . . . Mergers by companies with sales of $500 million or more are particularly significant. The ten or so retail companies of this size alone have accounted for about one-half of all retail mergers since 1948.

Thus the Commission has adopted the following enforcement criteria for evaluating acquisitions by large food retailers and wholesalers:

I. Mergers and acquisitions by retail food chains which result in combined annual food store sales in excess of $500 million annually raise sufficient questions regarding their legal status to warrant attention and consideration by the Commission under the statutes administered by it.[12]

*   *   *

It should not be inferred from the above criteria that all mergers by companies with combined sales of less than $500 million are unlikely to injure competition.   A threat to competition is posed whenever companies which are leaders in important metropolitan areas merge with direct competitors which are also leaders in the same market. *Similarly, market extension mergers may pose a threat to competition, particularly a series of mergers promising to create another industrial giant.* From the Commission's experience, however, it appears that market extension mergers involving companies with combined annual sales of less than $500 million generally do not pose a serious threat to competition except when they involve some competitive overlap.

These enforcement criteria are not to be construed as an expression of the views of the Commission or any individual Commissioner on the legality of any particular merger or acquisition . . .[13]

Implementation: To carry out this enforcement program expeditiously and uniformly, the Commission must know of prospective acquisitions and mergers in advance of their consummation. Every food retailer and wholesaler with annual sales in excess of $100 million will be required to notify the Commission at least 60 days prior to the consummation of any merger, acquisition or consolidation involving any food or wholesaler. The Commission will notify each year, so long as this enforcement program is in effect, the individual companies known to fall in this size class and will require each to file special reports with the Commission under the authority provided by Section 6 of the Federal Trade Commission Act.

This action by the Commission should not be interpreted to mean that grocery firms must request Commission approval prior to the consummation of any merger or acquisition.[14]

As will appear, the quoted document was a self-inflicted wound because it reflected in fact prejudgment of the Kroger matter, notwithstanding the Commission's pious declaration to the contrary.

The Commission's other crucial mistake in prosecuting the *Kroger* matter was an administrative blunder. That was the assignment to our case of the same Hearing Examiner -- Earl S. Kolb -- and the same lead attorney for the Commission -- Complaint Counsel John Walker -- as had been designated to try the *National Tea* complaint. The FTC's blooper was that the National Tea matter had been accorded undeviating hearing priority. This repeatedly forced Walker to delay proceedings in the *Kroger* case because of his duties in the other case. For example, following the specification of March 14, 1960 as the date for the initiation of the *Kroger* hearing, Walker moved for a continuance

> "to June 13, 1961 for the reason that counsel supporting the complaint, at the time now set for this hearing, will be engaged in the preparation for the hearing on the National Tea matter which will be held during April 1960."[15]

While the *Kroger* case remained in suspense, the *National Tea* litigation went forward. By an Initial Decision of April 5, 1963 Examiner Kolb dismissed the complaint in that matter. On June 13, 1963 a new Hearing Examiner, William K. Jackson was substituted to preside in the *Kroger* case in place of Kolb, but no new complaint counsel was designated in place of Walker.[16]

Consequently, on July 26, 1963, Walker was forced to move to postpone the *Kroger* hearings indefinitely, pending his "preparation and submission of a brief in the National Tea case"[17] Examiner Jackson responded by entering an order requiring Walker to show cause why the Kroger matter should not be "certified to the Commission for purposes of making a determination whether in the public interest the complaint should be dismissed." His order emphasized *"the fact that the complaint in this matter was filed April 1, 1959 and no proposed date for trial has been suggested."*[18] On October 7, 1963 Walker nevertheless moved to amend the complaint against Kroger by adding a challenge to its acquisition of the Market Basket stores in Los Angeles.[19]

Subsequently, under date of October 30, 1963, Examiner Jackson issued a *"Certification"* of the *Kroger* case to the Commission. It reviewed in detail the persistent procrastination which had prevented any progress in the conduct of the proceeding and concluded:

> In determining whether this matter should be certified to the Commission in its administrative capacity, the hearing examiner recognizes that in its present posture this matter raises the following questions bearing on the public interest: (1) the longevity of the case, (2) the necessity for amending the complaint, and (3) the fact that if the

complaint were to be amended there is a likely prospect evidentiary hearings would have to be deferred for additional time in which supplemental documentary or other evidence would have to be procured. Under these circumstances, the hearing examiner believes that these matters are not reasonably within his authority and competence and it is his duty to certify them to the Commission for determination in its administrative capacity. *In the Matter of Drug Research Corporation,* Docket No. 7179, October 3, 1963.[20]

After that, the *Kroger* matter remained in limbo for almost three years. During that interval, the Commission was silent on both significant pending matters: (i) the motion of October 7, 1963, to amend the complaint to include Market Basket; and (ii) the question of dismissal for excessive longevity in hearing the matter as propounded by the Examiner's Order to Show Cause of September 26, 1963 and his Certification of October 30, 1963.

The Commission's Rip Van Winkle interlude before attempting to hear the *Kroger* matter probably constituted an appropriate entry for the Guinness Book of World Records. Its slumber continued until the Commission issued its decision against *National Tea* on March 4, 1966. That reversed the Initial Decision which had dismissed the complaint and ruled against the respondent.[21]

Finally, four months later, Complaint Counsel reawakened the Kroger matter by filing a document requesting a ruling on its motion to amend the complaint and return of the matter to the Examiner for Completion of Proceeding.[22]

On August 10, 1966, more than seven years after the proceeding had begun, the Commission amended the Kroger complaint and returned the matter to the Hearing Examiner, with this farcical statement of purpose: "for expeditious completion of the proceedings."[23] No mention was made of Kroger's objection that an amendment would still further delay the matter because it would be followed by demands from the Commission's lawyers for additional information.

That is exactly what happened. Under date of November 23, 1966, a subpoena was issued to Kroger containing fifty "specifications," which demanded a massive turnover of documents.[24]

It will be recalled that the complaint alleged that Kroger operated 1421 retail food stores, exclusive of those later acquired in California. As to each such store, Specification 19 of that subpoena demanded this plethora of information and data:

(a)   the address including street, number, city, county and state;

(b)   the type of store according to the following classifications;

    1. grocery stores (SIC 541); ["Standard Industrial Classification"]
    2. other food stores which are not grocery stores (specify).

(c)   (1) the date opened;
      (2) if acquired, date of acquisition;
      (3) if closed, date of closing;

(d)   the total sales for the year 1963;

(e)   the profit or loss (or contribution) for the year 1963;

(f)   the average net markup percentage for the same 1963.

Those enormous demands were pressed notwithstanding the previous comment of the original Hearing Examiner concerning the similar specifications of an earlier subpoena,

> if we ever got into every store in the country, we are going to be here until long past the time I am going to retire. I know that.[25]

On December 30, 1966 Kroger filed two motions: one to quash the subpoena and the other to dismiss the complaint.[26] Aside from the oppressive breadth of the subpoena, the motions were based on the Commission's failure to comply with governing legislation and its own rule requiring timely conclusion of its proceedings. Specifically, we charged violation of the agency's duty to terminate the matter (i) with "reasonable dispatch," as required by Section 6(a) of the Administrative Procedure Act,[27] and (ii) "with all reasonable expedition' as prescribed by Rule 3.16(d) of its own Rules of Practice for Adjudicative Proceedings.

The motion to dismiss attributed responsibility for those derelictions to the Commission itself. It stressed the dual assignment of the same Commission personnel to try both the *Kroger* and *National Tea* matters and the decision to pursue the latter to conclusion before addressing the former. In this connection there was a detailed review of the of Complaint Counsel's repeated assertions of his need to attend to the necessities of the *National Tea* proceeding as justification for the numerous deferrals he requested in the *Kroger* matter. Time was the essence of the motion:

> . . . We know of no precedent in which a complaint has remained pending before the Commission for more than 7 1/2 years without one day of evidentiary hearings and, indeed, without any date yet scheduled for the initiation of such hearings.

*   *   *

> Extensive evidentiary hearings in *National Tea* began in June 1960 and were concluded in the fall of 1962. The Initial Decision was filed April 8, 1963. Oral argument before the Commission was originally heard on November 6, 1963. Reargument was heard on June 10, 1965. The Commission entered its final decision on March 4, 1966.

*   *   *

> A quick survey of available materials indicates that hearings have already been held in at least 14 merger cases in which the Commission issued its complaints *after* the complaint in this matter had issued. Initial Decisions have been entered in 13 of these cases. Final orders have been entered in 11 of them. A summary listing of the proceedings in those cases is attached as Appendix A.[28]

While these motions were pending, we received the above mentioned windfall by the promulgation of the *"Commission Enforcement Policy With Respect to Mergers in the Food Distribution Industry,"* on January 17, 1967.[29] This represented a pre-hearing adjudication that the Kroger complaint would be upheld, despite self-serving assertions that no prejudgment was intended. Among other things, it recited the commission's successful prosecution of complaints "in all but one of the Commission's merger actions in food retailing" and took pains to note that the "case involving the Kroger Company is still in the process of litigation."[30]

The *Enforcement Policy* was a radical departure in the practice of administrative agencies endowed with the power to act in the capacity of accuser -- exercising in effect a grand jury function -- plus the role of judge and jury as interpreter of the applicable law and adjudicator of the ultimate decision. On February 3, 1967, we accordingly filed a *Motion to Dismiss Complaint by Reason of Commission's*

Prejudgment of the Matter in Issue, etc. Among the several precedents we cited was *Texaco, Inc, v. FTC, 336 F.2d 754 (D.C. Cir. 1964)* in which the same incorrigible Chairman -- Paul Rand Dixon -- had referred to various statutory violations by respondents in cases then pending before the Commission. In *Texaco*, the Court of Appeals for the District of Columbia --- often described as the nation's second highest tribunal -- had unanimously disqualified the Chairman for participating in a decision against the respondents *Texaco, Inc.* (formerly Texas Company) and *B.F. Goodrich Co.*

More particularly, Texaco and Goodrich had been charged with violating Section 5 of the Federal Trade Commission Act -- which prohibits "unfair methods of competition in or affecting [interstate] commerce."[31] The alleged offense consisted of a contract by which Texaco agreed that its thousands of gasoline dealers would promote the sale of Goodrich products, in return for sales commissions. The Chairman had participated in the ultimate adjudication against Texaco -- over objection -- notwithstanding his previous speech "before the National Congress of Petroleum, Retailers, Inc., in Denver, Colorado on July 25, 1961, while the case was pending before the Examiner." During the speech Dixon had declared:

> We at the Commission are well aware of the practices which plague you and we have challenged their legality in many important cases.
>
> You know the practices -- price fixing, price discrimination, and overriding commissions on TBA. [Tires, batteries and accessories]
>
> You know the companies -- Atlantic, Texas, Pure, Shell, Sun, Standard of Indiana, American, Goodyear, Goodrich and Firestone.
>
> *   *   *
>
> Some of these cases are still pending before the Commission; some have been decided by the Commission and are in the courts on appeal. You may be sure that the Commission will continue and, to the extent that increased funds and efficiency permit, will increase its efforts to promote fair competition in your industry.[32]

This led the Court to reverse on the following rationale:

. . . In this case a disinterested reader of Chairman Dixon's speech could hardly fail to conclude that he had in some measure decided in advance that Texaco had violated the Act . . .

*   *   *

. . . We conclude that Chairman Dixon's participation in the hearing amounted in the circumstances to a denial of due process which invalidated the order under review . . .[33]

Our motion in the Kroger matter argued, among other things, that the prejudgment against Kroger in the *"Enforcement Policy"* was further demonstrated by Chairman Dixon's Congressional testimony, on February 10, 1966. In it he reviewed "antimerger projects now underway and certain to continue well into 1967," and expressly emphasized

. . . "food retailing, where FTC's *goal has been to halt acquisitions by the 20 or so largest chain stores* and to channel acquisitions in the industry to encourage growth of strong local and regional companies."[34]

Concerning the Commission's disclaimer of prejudgment in its *"Enforcement Policy,"* we referred to Judge Washington's separate opinion -- concurring in the Chairman's disqualification in the *Texaco* case. In it he stated that "[o]nce an adjudicator has taken a position apparently inconsistent with an ability to judge the facts fairly, subsequent protestation of open-mindedness cannot restore a presumption of impartiality."[35] This moved us to quote the Usher's admonition to the jurors in the Gilbert and Sullivan comic opera, *Trial by Jury*, an action for breach of promise of marriage:

> Now, Jurymen, hear my advice
> All kinds of vulgar prejudice
> I pray you set aside:
>
> With stern judicial frame of mind,
> From bias free of every kind,
> This trial must be tried.

> Oh, listen to the plaintiff's case:
> Observe the features of her face -
> The broken-hearted bride.
> Condole with her distress of mind:
> From bias free of every kind,
> This trial must be tried!
>
> And when amid the plaintiff's shrieks,
> The ruffianly defendant speaks -
> Upon the other side;
> What he may say you needn't mind -
> From bias free of every kind,
> This trial must be tried!

Following Complaint Counsel's answer to the prejudgment question, the Hearing Examiner issued another *"Certification."* This referred all pending motions to the Commission -- *i.e.*, Kroger's "oppressive subpoena," "lacks of reasonable dispatch," and "prejudgment" motions.[36]

After exhaustively reviewing the history of the proceeding the Certificate concluded:

GENERAL RECOMMENDATIONS

In view of the longevity of this case, the admitted need for additional information, and the prospects that this matter will not be ripe for hearings in the near future, the Hearing Examiner suggests that it might be fruitful to delay action on the three motions for 30 days to explore the possibilities of a settlement. In this connection, it should be noted that no such opportunity was afforded respondent prior to the August 10, 1966 amendment of the complaint. Furthermore, a consent order has been recently accepted by the Commission in *Matter of Winn-Dixie Stores*, Docket No. C-1110, September 14, 1966, which might form the basis for a settlement here. Finally, the Commission on January 17, 1967, announced its *"Enforcement Policy with Respect to Mergers in the Food Distribution Industries"* which referred to its prior actions in the *Winn-Dixie* and other food cases. By its announcement, the Commission spelled out *"its future enforcement policy in this important area."* Since respondent's most recent acquisition took place prior to these significant developments, settlement discussions would not appear to be inappropriate.[37]

The Examiner's Certification elicited an "ORDER OF REMAND" from the Commission to the Hearing Examiner for the purpose of exploring the possibilities of a settlement, [and directing him to] report to the Commission in thirty (30) days as to the status of such discussions.[38]

This was followed by the Examiner's "REPORT TO COMMISSION ON STATUS OF SETTLEMENT NEGOTIATIONS."[39] In it he advised that after his settlement conference with the parties on March 9, 1967, Complaint Counsel had proffered a Consent Order, which he simultaneously declared to be final and not subject to modification, by direction of his superiors. It required the divestiture of Market Basket and otherwise contained precisely the same terms ordained by the Commission to implement its decision sustaining the complaint against *National Tea*. Those terms imposed a ten year obligation to obtain the Commissioner's advance approval of any acquisition involving more than four food stores with combined annual sales exceeding $5 million and 5% of sales in any city or county of the United States. In the Examiner's words, we "flatly rejected complaint counsel's proposal as unacceptable" and saw no purpose in further negotiations in light of the "take-it-or-leave-it" ultimatum submitted with it.

Nevertheless, at the Examiner's request we made a Counter-proposal. This agreed that for ten years Kroger would not make any retail food or grocery store acquisitions without Commission approval except:

A.   acquisitions conforming to the four store, $5 million and 5% limitations of the Commission's settlement proposal; and

B.   food and grocery stores located more than 250 miles "from a then existing Kroger warehouse or other distribution facility that regularly furnishes distribution services to then existing Kroger stores."[40]

In other words Kroger rejected the proposed divestiture of the Market Basket stores and added an exception for market extension mergers from the advance approval requirement.

I was moved to make this offer by my conviction that Kroger's best interests would be served by adopting an accommodating stance, in contrast to Complaint Counsel's intransigence. Of course, in order to

make this offer we obtained clearance from Kroger.   The Examiner
then reported to the Commission:

> An examination of the two proposals shows that they contain
> fundamental differences.   In view of complaint counsel's inflexible
> position and the fact they have made no response to respondent's
> proposal, the hearing examiner is of the opinion that no useful purpose
> would be served in further discussions.

> Accordingly, the hearing examiner submits this report together with
> the attachments thereto as directed by the Commission's Order of
> Remand.[41]

Following that Report another offer of settlement was made by a
letter to me of July 8, 1968, from Peter Jeffrey, an attorney in the
Commission's Division of Mergers. It offered Kroger a consent order
based on the terms which the FTC had imposed upon Grand Union,
described as the nation's "10th ranking chain" in the *Enforcement
Policy* of January 17, 1967.   These were the same provisions as the
National Tea order, plus the requirement of 60 days' advance notice of
any merger, acquisition or consolidation within the industry on the part
of a food retailer or wholesaler with sales exceeding $100,000,000.
The latter provision was an obligation imposed on all firms within that
category by the Commission's Enforcement Policy.   Kroger did not
accept the offer.

Finally, the matter was brought to a conclusion by an ORDER
TERMINATING PROCEEDING, issued by the Commission on
October 31, 1968.   In pertinent part it read as follows:

> Upon review of this matter, the Commission has determined that the
> public interest does not warrant further proceedings. This determination
> is based on the longevity of the case, the fact that evidentiary hearings
> would have to be further delayed as a result of an additional acquisition
> challenged in the amended complaint, and the fact that the Commission
> has announced its enforcement policy with respect to mergers in the food
> distribution industries. In implementing this policy, the Commission is
> now requiring large food retailers, including respondent, to file special
> reports sixty days in advance of any merger activity in the food
> distribution industry. Accordingly, this proceeding will be terminated
> without adjudication.

Since this decision has been made by the Commission in the exercise of its administrative discretion, the motions certified by the examiner are moot.[42]

That was the final curtain on the ten-year epic composed and conducted by the Commission under Chairman Dixon's baton in the Kroger merger case. It was just one among many of his thoughtless abuses of the bureaucratic prerogatives of the Federal Trade Commission. It may be no exaggeration to suggest that his reckless exercise of the authority of his office contributed to the beginning of the distrust of government by Congress and the business community.

Joseph B. Hall, on the right, and Jacob E. Davis,
successive Kroger CEOs

CHAPTER EIGHTEEN

INDECENT EXPOSURE

Just as there are cases won by the oppositional mistakes, some succeed by creative legal strategy. One of those involved a case I initiated against the Federal Trade Commission ("FTC"). It's still a source of great personal satisfaction to me.

Viewed through a modern lens, it was perhaps my most exciting project for Kroger. It defeated an illegal effort to investigate its compliance with governing law. The attempt was made by the FTC under Chairman Dixon. It undertook to hold such an investigation in public while denying Kroger its right to representation by counsel, as guaranteed by the Constitution. Because of the split within our firm and among in-house lawyers for Kroger on the wisdom of my proposed strategy -- in which I prevailed -- the favorable outcome was especially gratifying.

In a word, the Commission made an unprecedented attempt to use the Congressional model for conducting investigative hearings by a body with prosecutorial and adjudicative power. Congress can enact laws but cannot enforce them. Consequently, in public Congressional investigations, counsel for a witness may lawfully be restricted in the exercise of his right of representation. The lawyer may whisper advice to his client off the record, but he may not otherwise participate in the proceeding. He cannot object on the record, cross-examine adverse witnesses, or present evidence on behalf of his client, no matter how unfairly, or even perjuriously, his client is attacked.

To emphasize the distinction: The FTC bears no resemblance to a Congressional Committee. It has the triple functions of investigation, prosecution and adjudication. It brings the charges, tries them and decides them. Consequently, its investigations, which can lead to prosecutions and penalties, differ markedly from those conducted by Congressional Committees which have no law enforcement consequences and are, therefore, free of various constraints, including the obligation to conduct prosecutorial investigations in private.

Nevertheless, Chairman Dixon, a Kefauver disciple, attempted to investigate Kroger and other supermarket companies in public while imposing the restraints on legal representation applicable in Congressional investigative proceedings. Dixon surely knew of the public excitement aroused by Kefauver's "Crime Committee," described by Judge Arnold in CHAPTER TWO.

Few of the vast audience that viewed the conduct of the Iran-Contra investigation will ever forget the "I'm not a potted plant" protest of Oliver North's counsel -- Brendan Sullivan of Williams & Connolly. That was his comment when the presiding officer, Senator Inouye, cut off his attempt to make an objection on the record. But at any Congressional Committee hearing, public or private, televised or not, every "defense" counsel is just that, even when representing a witness who is being victimized by hostile questions and accusatory testimony. All counsel can do is whisper advice to his client, off the record. That is almost always a direction to decline to answer on the ground that the 5th Amendment to the Constitution protects the witness from self-incrimination. On rare occasions, a refusal to answer may be advised because a question is deemed to be outside the bounds of the Committee's prescribed sphere of inquiry.

In contrast, regulatory investigations of illicit activities conducted by federal agencies, such as the FTC, are historically governed by the grand jury requirement of absolute secrecy.[1] When an executive of the target company is being questioned by FTC lawyers, no one is present apart from the company's attorneys and a court reporter transcribing the testimony. The presence of the target's attorneys is the sole deviation from the practice in grand jury inquests. But, as in Congressional hearings, they may only consult with their client off the record.

The effort to distort the traditional administrative practice occurred when Chairman Dixon decided to use his Kefauver training to teach the old FTC dog a new trick. His investigations of suspected violations of law would be conducted in *public* under the same rules as Congressional investigations -- *i.e.* without normal rights of counsel.

Kroger was among the targets in the first such investigation, by way of subpoenas issued to its CEO, Joseph B. Hall, and to the Company. They called for oral testimony and documentary evidence pertaining to milk pricing in the Indianapolis market area.[2] A Commission press release, dated February 28, 1962, announced that public hearings would commence in Indianapolis on March 13, 1962. It read in pertinent part:

FTC TO PROBE INDIANAPOLIS MILK PRICE WAR

The staff of the Federal Trade Commission will conduct a public investigational hearing to obtain facts on whether a milk price war now being waged in the Indianapolis, Ind., market area may be unlawful.

Ordered to testify and produce pertinent records are three national food chains -- National Tea Company, Chicago; Kroger Co., Cincinnati, and Marsh's Supermarket, Inc., Yorktown, Indiana -- and six supermarket concerns in the Indianapolis area.

FTC Chairman Paul Rand Dixon explained that the hearing was prompted by the need for speedy corrective action should the cause of the price war be found to violate the antitrust laws.

"We at the Commission," said Chairman Dixon, "are determined to make use of every tool our statutes provide to get at the facts while competitors are still alive and in business."

The decision to make the hearing a public one, he said, was based on the belief that the problem was of deep concern not only to the public but to other businessmen affected, and that their enlightenment on the facts as they are uncovered at the hearing could well produce additional information of value to the Commission's investigation.

The forthcoming hearing will commence March 13 for three weeks at the Indiana State Office Building, 100 North Senate Street, Indianapolis. Presiding will be William F. Lemke, Attorney in Charge of FTC's Chicago office. Attorney Alvin D. Edelson will conduct the questioning of witnesses.

*   *   *

Of course, as Kroger's senior official, responsible for its corporate policies and operations throughout the nation, Mr. Hall had no specific information about competitive activities in the Indianapolis milk market. Commission counsel so understood and agreed to accept a substitute Kroger official qualified to testify on the subject. We selected A.L. Shough, the head of Kroger's owned and operated Indianapolis dairy plant, to appear for Kroger.

Meantime my colleagues and I, along with Kroger's in-house lawyers, pondered the course to be pursued by the company in light of the FTC's newly adopted ground rules for the investigation. This was not simply an issue of legal principle. The scheduled public investigation, while Kroger's hands were tied, raised the specter of one-sided, hostile testimony, prejudicial to Kroger's image and its economic welfare in the Indianapolis market.

From the standpoint of legal principle, we were confident that Supreme Court precedent established that legislative grants of investigative power to administrative agencies are subject to the basic privacy restraints governing grand jury investigations. We decided that the appropriate response for Kroger would be to refuse to cooperate with the FTC's demands in public unless Kroger was accorded full recourse to representation by counsel, including cross-examination, the right to object to improper evidence and to present counter-evidence. Alternatively, Kroger would agree to respond in private under the Commissioner's prior practice, restricting the participation of counsel for investigative targets to off-the-record advice. If this proposal was refused, we would seek a court injunction against the public investigation procedure.

Mr. Shough, the Kroger witness, was scheduled to appear on March 15, 1962. On March 14, while I was in Indianapolis, we filed a motion with the Commission at its Washington Headquarters, *"For Relief With Respect to Hearing"* accompanied by a *"Memorandum in Support of Motion."* This was essential under a conventional doctrine requiring the exhaustion of administrative remedies before an agency action can be judicially challenged. In other words, agencies like the FTC must be afforded an opportunity to correct their mistakes before judicial relief may be sought.

My colleague, Dennis Lyons, prepared our papers under the stress of severe time pressure. His work was outstanding. The motion outlined the alternative conditions -- as above stated -- under which Kroger would comply with the Commission's demands. If neither was acceptable, it prayed that the outstanding subpoena "be quashed." Our legal memorandum emphasized the United States Supreme Court precedents analogizing administrative agency investigations to those of grand jury proceedings and therefore dictating their conduct in secrecy.[3]

The motion was summarily denied by the Commission over the dissent of the leading legal scholar among its five members -- Philip Elman. For many years, he had been a preeminent member of the Justice Department's Office of the Solicitor General which represents the federal government before the Supreme Court. His particular specialty in that capacity was antitrust law.

The Commission accordingly proceeded with the scheduled public investigation, as outlined in its press release. It turned out to be pretty heady stuff for a mundane agency like the FTC. No one but witnesses and their counsel, plus the assigned FTC lawyers, would have shown up had the proceeding been held at the Commissioner's Washington offices. But heralded by Commission press releases, the Indianapolis media whooped it up as a big league operation, including a live TV appearance by FTC counsel, Alvin Edelson. As a result -- much to my surprise -- when Mr. Shough and I arrived at the Indianapolis hearing room on March 15, 1962, it was packed with reporters and other media representatives, plus public onlookers.

That day's session opened with the interrogation of several officials of other chain grocers, starting with National Tea Company. Its counsel who had rejected our effort to persuade him to follow our intended course, merely protested that the public procedure was improper. Following noisy objections by their counsel, all other targets of the investigation likewise submitted to the unorthodox public process, as prescribed by the Commission.

Then it was Kroger's turn. Per our plan, Mr. Shough, head of Kroger's dairy operations, took the stand. He placed a voluminous pile of subpoenaed documents on a table in front of him. Before he was questioned, William F. Lemke, the presiding officer, issued the following admonition to Lemke and to me:

> All right, I will now read to the witness Section 10 [of the Federal Trade Commission Act 15 U.S.C. § 50]. I don't know whether you were here this morning, sir, when I read this at the beginning of the hearing, but I will read it to you again at this time. This section provides as follows:

That any person who shall neglect or refuse to attend and testify, or to answer any lawful inquiry, or to produce documentary evidence, if in his power to do so, in obedience to a subpoena or lawful requirement of the Commission, shall be guilty of an offense and upon conviction thereof by a court of competent jurisdiction shall be punished by a fine of not less than $1,000 nor more than $5,000, or by imprisonment for not more than one year, or by both such fine and imprisonment.

I also point out to counsel that the Commission has the right, for good cause shown, to suspend or disbar attorneys from practice before the Commission.

Counsel are herewith directed to confine their participation in this proceeding to accompanying and advising the witness.   If counsel persists in making objections and/or statements on the record, I shall find it necessary to call each such instance to the attention of the Commission for its consideration and whatever action it may deem appropriate.[4]

Those warnings were doubtless another Dixon innovation. They seemed out of character for Lemke, a mild soft-spoken man. I know of no counterpart in any of the many FTC proceedings -- investigative and adjudicative -- in which I have participated. In any case, they didn't work.

Mr. Shough answered the routine queries about his name, address and occupation.   But when Commission counsel asked his first substantive question, Mr. Shough testified that he respectfully declined to answer in accordance with the advice of counsel. After Lemke had acquiesced, Shough read the following prepared statement:

I have brought with me all of the subpoenaed records. I am here for the purpose of delivering those records and for the purpose of testifying in a lawful investigative proceeding. Counsel have advised me, and The Kroger Co., as well, that this investigation as presently conducted is not lawful. Accordingly, upon advice of counsel, I respectfully, for myself and The Kroger Co., decline to furnish documents or testimony in this public investigation.

However, I stand ready to testify and deliver the subpoenaed records when and if a lawful and proper investigation of this matter is undertaken by the Federal Trade Commission. *I stand ready to do so now, if the presiding attorney will insure that this investigation will henceforth proceed in private,* as required by the applicable statutes and rules and by the Constitution of the United States. *Or I will do so upon his assurance that Kroger will be accorded full representation by counsel -- including the right to cross-examine, to object to improper matters and testimony, and to present evidence -- if the investigation proceeds in public.*

I emphasize that the position of The Kroger Co. does not involve any challenge to the exercise of any of the investigatory powers of the Federal Trade Commission consistently with the procedures which the Commission is authorized to pursue by law. The Kroger Co. is willing to testify and produce the subpoenaed records in an investigation so conducted.[5]

The Commission elected not to seek judicial enforcement of its original subpoenas. In that event Kroger could have obtained a prompt judicial ruling on the validity of the novel public procedure. Instead, under date of April 24, 1967, the Commission issued broader subpoenas to Kroger's three principal executives: Messrs. Hall, Chairman; Davis, President; and Grieme, Treasurer.

The new subpoenas vastly expanded the territorial coverage and the detail of the original subpoenas to Mr. Hall and to The Kroger Co. Those had been limited to milk pricing "in the Indianapolis, Indiana market area." The newly issued subpoenas of April 24 covered all facets of "the distribution and sale" of any and all "*dairy products* in the Indianapolis, Indiana, *or any other trade area.*" The issuance of those subpoenas was announced by an FTC press release of April 27, 1962, which stated:

FTC SUBPOENAS TOP KROGER OFFICIALS
FOR NEW HEARING ON INDIANAPOLIS MILK WAR

The Federal Trade Commission has issued subpoenas requiring three top officials of Kroger Co., Cincinnati, Ohio, one of the nation's major grocery chains, to testify at a public investigational hearing on the company's pricing practices in the sale of milk in the Indianapolis, Ind., trade area. The hearing, to commence at 10 a.m. May 8 at the Indianapolis State Office building, continues the Commission's public investigation of milk pricing in that area, begun last March 13 and continued until March 28.

A Practice Almost Perfect

The subpoenas require testimony from Joseph B. Hall, chairman of Kroger's board of directors and its chief executive officer; and Jacob Erastus Davis, president of Kroger Co. The third subpoena requires testimony and the production of certain records by F.M. Grieme, treasurer of the company.

The subpoenas state that the investigation is for the purpose of determining whether any law administered by the FTC has been violated in connection with the "production, distribution and sale of *dairy products in the Indianapolis, Indiana, or any other trade area,"* and whether the public interest calls for remedial action by the Commission. The subpoenas state that a further purpose of the investigation is to determine whether the Commission "should report to the Congress concerning the need for additional remedial legislation" bearing on this pricing problem.

At the opening of the investigation in March, the Kroger Co.; National Tea Company, Chicago; and March's Supermarket, Inc., Yorktown, Ind.; and six Indianapolis area supermarkets were asked to provide the Commission with information on milk pricing practices in the area. *The Kroger Co. alone declined to give the information sought by the Commission, offering instead a statement presented by A.L. Shough, manager of Kroger's Indianapolis Division (sic,) stating in effect that the Commission had exceeded its statutory authority by making the investigational hearing open to the public and by denying the company's attorneys the same privileges afforded attorneys in adjudicatory proceedings.* The original subpoena demanding information from Kroger Co. had been addressed to Mr. Hall, who at the time of its issuance was president of Kroger Co. By agreement with Commission attorneys, Mr. Shough was permitted to substitute for Mr. Hall.[6]

*   *   *

The described subpoenas were served upon Kroger's general officers in spite of an introductory statement by Commission Counsel, Mr. Alvin Edelson, on the record, just before Mr. Shough's appearance on March 15, 1962. In it Edelson acknowledged that "we weren't interested in the testimony of Mr. Hall," and that "the information requested . . . is limited to the Indianapolis area." He then concluded:

The reason we weren't interested in the testimony of Mr. Hall is that quite usually in the course of big business, as we know it, the president of a large corporation is not familiar with the particular aspects of what is going on in the Indianapolis operations . . .

This is the policy usually followed. This is the policy that was followed with National Tea Co., and this is the way National Tea Co. replied, in perfect accord with me.

In respect to The Kroger Co. I planned the same thing, with the idea that the information requested, which is limited to the Indianapolis area and vicinity, would also be supplied by various experts responsible to Mr. Hall would could provide the information. *In that sense it was said that we were not really interested in the information of Mr. Hall.*[7]

The Commission's press release of April 27, 1967 consequently demonstrated on its face that the broadened subpoenas to Kroger's general officers were vindictively issued. They were an act of reprisal for Kroger's "lese majesty" in challenging Chairman Dixon's unprecedented recourse to the Congressional hearing analogue for the conduct of FTC investigations -- *i.e.*, in public and subject to similarly restricted rights of representation.

After consultation with Kroger, we determined to test the validity of its position in a judicial forum. As a preliminary matter, on April 30, 1960, we again moved the Commission to quash the subpoenas or, failing that to conduct its investigation in private, on the Congressional model, or in public with full rights of representation by counsel. On May 3, 1962, the Commission denied the motion, Commissioner Elman again dissenting.

In that focus we decided to try a novel strategy. At the time suit could be brought against the Commission -- or any or all of its members for official acts -- only in the United States District Court for the District of Columbia. Most of the judges of that court were notoriously pro-government.

Accordingly, rather than sue in the District of Columbia, we decided to proceed instead against William Lemke, the FTC official presiding at the public investigation. He resided in Illinois. We filed suit against him in the United States District Court for the Northern District of Illinois, sitting in Chicago, the jurisdiction of his residence.

Our complaint asked a judicial declaration that the conduct of "the proposed public hearing" violated the constitutional mandate that legal proceedings be conducted solely by "due process of law" (Fifth Amendment) -- specifically full right to counsel -- and that the extraordinary breadth of the investigation, as defined by the subpoenas, was in breach of the constitutional prohibition against "unreasonable searches and seizures (Fourth Amendment). In addition, we asked that the defendant be enjoined from proceeding with the hearing under the conditions prescribed by the Commission.[8]

So far as I knew then, and know now, such a complaint, directed against an FTC hearing officer, rather than the administrative agency involved, or its members, was the first of its kind. We grounded the suit on precedents holding that the superior body or officer responsible for a challenged order need not be joined as a defendant "where the decree which is to be entered will effectively grant the relief desired by expending itself upon the subordinate official who is before the court."[9] In other words, when negative relief is the object and can be effected by inhibiting a subordinate's action, the remedy is available. That is not the case when a party seeks affirmative relief. By way of example, Lemke, the Hearing Officer, could not have been sued to compel him to grant Kroger witnesses affirmative relief, such as the provision of full rights of representation by counsel.

In the course of further research, we uncovered a real gem. This was a precedent from the highest English judicial authority -- the House of Lords. The case was squarely in point with regard to our claim that a public investigation into a corporation's compliance with law would entail injurious practical consequences.[10]

The case involved a successful challenge to that process by an insurance company suspected of illegal activities. Two of the opinions are particularly apropos. Lord Thankerton stated:

> . . . If the examination were to be held in public, it might well be that unfavorable opinions as to the financial position of the society or company might be prematurely and wrongly formed in the minds of the public or the policy-holders either through reports in the press or as the results of attendance at the examination of some of the persons to be examined on oath.[11]

Lord MacMillan emphasized the Commission's long-term practice of conducting pre-complaint investigations in private:

If Parliament had intended that inspection should or might be conducted as a public inquiry, one would have expected to find in the Act the familiar provisions which are inserted when a public inquiry is contemplated....This system of inspection has thus been in existence for some seventy years. *Your Lordships have been informed that such inspections under the Companies Acts have from the inception of this legislation been invariably in practice conducted in private.*

The Attorney-General urged that it was desirable that abuses where they existed should be made known at the earliest moment, and that publicity might have the advantage of bringing forward witnesses who could give useful evidence. I can see every reason for speedy action in the interests of the numerous policy-holders of such companies whenever abuses have been ascertained to exist, *but it is quite a different matter to give publicity to the process of obtaining the information on which the Commissioner has to decide whether or not an offense has been proved to exist and on which action may or not follow.*[12]

The case against Lemke was assigned to Judge Hubert Will, a native of Illinois and an able man. He was newly appointed, after service at the Securities and Exchange Commission and the United States Treasury Department in Washington, D.C. Our local counsel, Stuart Ball, a senior partner of the preeminent Chicago firm of Sidley, Austin, Burgess & Smith, considered the assignment unfortunate, fearing that Will would lean in favor of the government.

Ball's fears proved groundless. On May 7, we filed motions for a temporary restraining order suspending the public hearing for a period of 10 days; for a preliminary injunction preventing conduct of that hearing until final judgment; and for summary judgment, granting final relief without trial. (The restraining order could be granted for a period of ten days without notice to the other side).

Judge Will granted the restraining order.[13] He further ordered the defendant -- represented by the United States Attorney for the Northern District of Illinois -- to file responsive documents by May 13, 1962. Meantime, the Judge suggested that the parties meet in an effort to achieve a mutually satisfactory resolution of the matter.

On May 10, 1962, I met for that purpose with J.B. Truly, the FTC's Assistant General Counsel. We reached a stalemate when he said he was not authorized to depart from the Commission's position on the prescribed public procedure. The court was so notified.[14]

On that same date, I also received a telephone call from Lawrence Speiser, Washington Representative of the American Civil Liberties Union (ACLU). After inquiring about the status of the case in Chicago, he advised me that the ACLU had written to Chairman Dixon protesting the public procedure adopted by the Commission for the Indianapolis investigation. This was astonishing. It was unsolicited, inspired by a news report in the *Washington Evening Star*, then a leading D.C. newspaper. It was a true rarity -- the ACLU going to bat for a commercial corporation.

At my request, Speiser provided a copy of a three page letter from the ACLU to Chairman Dixon. It was dated April 20, 1962 and signed by John J. de Pemberton, Jr., Executive Director. I filed it with the court, as an attachment to my own affidavit. It stated in part:

> There are two civil liberties aspects of this controversy which gravely disturb the Union and which we urge the Commission seriously to consider. One is the holding of an investigatory hearing, analogous to a grand jury investigation, in public. The second concerns the failure to allow counsel for companies under investigation adequate participation in the hearing in behalf of their clients. Both combine to create a breach of the safeguards embodied in the idea of due process of law, the touchstone of our democratic system which should be especially respected in the relationship between the government and the citizen.

> The analogy between an administrative investigatory proceeding and a grand jury investigation has been often made. One of the more emphatic statements on the subject was made by the late Justice Jackson of the United States Supreme Court in *United States v. Morton Salt Company, 338 U.S. 632 (1950)*:

> . . . It [the administrative agency] has a power of inquisition, if one chooses to call it that, which is not derived from the judicial function. It is more analogous to the Grand Jury, which does not depend on a case or controversy for power to get evidence but can investigate merely on suspicion that the law is being violated, or even just because it wants assurance that it is not. When investigative and accusatory duties are delegated by statute to an administrative body, it, too, may take steps to inform itself as to whether there is probably violation of the law.

*   *   *

. . . Unlike the congressional committee whose authority rests on obtaining information on which the Congress can act to write new laws, the FTC itself can use the information it gathers in investigatory hearings in a later adjudicatory hearing which can result in an order or the imposing of sanctions where a violation is found to exist. *As the Commission serves as investigator, grand jury, and judge, it should take special pains to afford all the due process protections of a judicial proceeding.*[15]

We then argued the motions for preliminary injunction and for the entry of final summary judgment in Kroger's favor -- the latter remedy being available without trial when the facts are undisputed and the law favors the moving party. During the argument, Judge Will seemed favorably inclined to our view. But before he could issue his decision, the Commission withdrew the contested subpoenas. On that basis, the United States attorney, on June 21, 1962, moved to dismiss the case as "moot" -- meaning that there was no legal issue on which the court could act. We disputed that contention, emphasizing that the investigation had not been terminated and that the Commission could reissue the same subpoenas at any later time.[16]

At that point Judge Will again directed the parties to consult with an eye toward settling the matter. The consultation resulted in a total and final victory for Kroger. This is shown by the following record of the proceedings before Judge Will on July 24, 1962, in which Stuart Ball appeared for the Kroger plaintiffs:

THE CLERK: 62 C 942, Hall v. Lemke, further hearing re supplement to motion to dismiss.

MR. BALL: We have a statement to make that I think will please the Court. The Court gave injunctions to the Commission and ourselves some time ago to see if we could reach an amicable disposition.

THE COURT: I begged you to. I didn't order you to.

MR. BALL: Well, I am happy to report that we have received this assurance from the Commission: That if subpoenas are issued to Kroger or its officials in lieu of subpoenas previously issued, they will be made returnable at a non-public hearing.

Now, I think that counsel can confirm that. It seems to me that an order of dismissal based upon that representation is in order.

THE COURT: Is that accurate, Mr. James?

MR. JAMES: Yes, sir.

THE COURT: I am delighted because, apart from the disposition of this case, I subscribe to the philosophy indicated in that position.

So you are now moving -- Well, you have a motion on file?

MR. JAMES: Yes, it is pending.

THE COURT: The motion will be granted with the understanding as stated in the record that that is to be the procedure in the case.

Thank you, gentlemen.

So ended Chairman Rand Dixon's attempt to revolutionize the investigative procedure to be followed by the Federal Trade Commission. *Sic transit gloria mundi.* Dixon should have yielded to the superior wisdom of Commissioner Elman, instead of undertaking an arrogant abuse of government power.

James P. Herring, SuperX CEO, when it was
acquired by Kroger, and later Kroger CEO

CHAPTER NINETEEN

FOX HUNTING

Whenever a case looks like a sure thing, watch out for Murphy's law -- which admonishes that "whatever can go wrong will go wrong." I learned its validity from litigation triggered by a routine application, in 1962, for a renewal of a pharmacy license from the Michigan Board of Pharmacy. It was needed by a Kroger subsidiary -- SuperX Drug Corporation -- to enable it to enter the Michigan market. For that purpose, Kroger had purchased a local pharmacy, operated in Battle Creek, by a corporation named Owl Drug Company, whose name was then changed to SuperX. That purchase provided exemption from a 1948 Michigan statute requiring that, except for preexisting businesses, registered pharmacists had to own 25% of a corporate drug store. Kroger also prepared three other SuperX pharmacies for business. However, renewal of the license was denied after "a hearing held before some 900 pharmacists presumably opposed to the application."[1]

SuperX immediately applied to the Michigan Supreme Court, for a writ of mandamus, by which the Board would be directed to grant a license. The composition of that Court proved to be the first step in the Murphy's Law saga which continuously bedeviled the matter. It was an even-numbered eight man body, almost unheard of for a multi-membered court. (Parenthetically, the court was later increased to nine members).

At the outset, that seemed inconsequential. After enjoining interference with the store's operations, the Court granted the writ by a 5-3 vote. The majority opinion rejected the Board's finding that SuperX had illegally dispensed barbiturates and amphetamines on oral prescription.[2] SuperX then suffered its first misery under Murphy's law. Before a mandate could issue to the Board, there was a change in the Court's membership, when the term of the Chief Justice expired. Meanwhile, the Board had moved for rehearing of the original decision. The new justice sided with the original minority on that motion, creating a 4-4 tie. The two factions then issued contradictory instructions to the Clerk of the Court. One instructed him to issue the mandate and the other ordered him not to do so. In the circumstances, the Clerk merely entered a note on the docket that the motion for rehearing had been denied.[3] That left the SuperX application in a state of suspense.

We were then called into the case. After high-pressure research, we filed the federal case -- cited in note 1 -- in the United States District Court for the Western District of Michigan. The complaint alleged that refusal of the license violated SuperX's rights to equal protection and due process of law under the 14th Amendment to the Constitution. Along with it, we filed motions for a preliminary injunction to prevent interruption of the pharmacy's business and for summary judgment resolving the case for SuperX. A motion for a preliminary injunction -- which is operational until the case is finally decided -- commands expedited consideration by the Court under the provisions of the United States Code governing Civil Judicial Procedure.[4] Summary judgment is available without a trial when the facts are undisputed and dictate the legal result.

The case had originally been assigned to Judge Kent, the Chief Judge of the Western District sitting in its Kalamazoo Division. It had then been reassigned to Judge Noel Fox, sitting in the Grand Rapids Division of the same Court.

Our research pointed to a quick victory before Judge Fox. Less than a year earlier, he had issued a ringing erudite decision -- in the *Lewis* case[5] -- which seemed to guarantee a ruling in our favor. In it he had reversed on the very same constitutional grounds we had raised, a decision of the local authorities denying the transfer of a liquor license to an African-American. In the process, he had overruled the holdings of a number of state courts, including Michigan's, that constitutional protections did not extend to liquor licenses because their enjoyment is a privilege not a right.

Since pharmacy licenses were immune to any such claim of "privilege," our case looked like a cakewalk in Judge Fox's court. At that point, I should have thought of the truism that if something sounds too good to be true, it probably is. In terms of the law, the SuperX case taught me that if winning a case seems like a "no brainer," it's time to flash a yellow light in your mind.

Instead of granting SuperX prompt relief, Judge Fox confronted us with a two-part roadblock. First, he improperly held the SuperX case for six months before taking any action, in contravention of the statute dictating expeditious resolution of preliminary injunction issues.

Next, when he finally acted, he threw us a real curve ball. This was an extensive, convoluted opinion, saturated with arcane legal verbiage, by which the judge declined to decide the matter for or against SuperX. Rather, after taking pains to note that Kroger owned SuperX,[6] he immobilized us by a "no decision" opinion which foreclosed opportunity to seek appellate reversal of a negative ruling. This was accomplished by a determination that the parties should return to the Michigan Supreme Court to institute proceedings for a declaration whether its original 5-3 decision for mandamus was final and determinative (in legal jargon whether it was "*res judicata.*)[7]

At that juncture, Judge Fox, of course, was aware of that Court's 4-4 split on that very issue. As I belatedly learned -- for a reason outlined below -- his object was to settle a score with Kroger by undermining the original 5-3 ruling for SuperX.

For that purpose, his opinion undertook to spell out in great detail how that could be accomplished. In that ploy he failed. In the end, the Michigan Supreme Court resumed jurisdiction and again directed the Board to issue the license.[8]. This time, the Board finally complied -- four years after SuperX had filed an application, which should have been affirmed in a day or two. In the process, the Michigan Supreme Court treated Judge Fox as a non-person, despite his obsequious deference to the priority of its jurisdiction on constitutional issues involving state law -- in contrast to his defiance of its precedents in *Lewis v. Grand Rapids.*

Because the uncertainties of the law are so graphically illustrated by the shocking turn of events in *SuperX v. Board*, the details deserve full recital. To begin with, the force of the *Lewis* opinion as a source of our unlimited optimism is impossible to exaggerate. Next, the "Murphy's Law" incident which impelled Judge Fox to ignore *Lewis* in composing his "no decision" result in the *SuperX* case still seems beyond the pale of any remotely imaginable contingency. Third, the vindictiveness betrayed by Judge Fox in reaching that result not only demeans him, but reflects adversely on the federal bench.

The opinion by Judge Fox in *Lewis v. Grand Rapids* began by emphasizing that the case involved "the only negro-owned-operated, Class C liquor license -- [*i.e.*, authorizing operation of a bar] -- in a city of over 200,000 population."[9] Judge Fox then embarked on a 47-page opinion excoriating the local officials on a variety of constitutional grounds. In essence they were condemned for "conspir[ing] together under the 'color of law' to deny the [plaintiff] due process and equal protection of the law [by] invidious discrimination."[10]

The intervening analysis began by rejecting the admitted holdings of the Supreme Court of Michigan, along with other jurisdictions, that liquor licenses are privileges, not property, and hence are not protected by the Fourteenth Amendment. As Judge Fox put it:

> We recognize that the Michigan Supreme Court and the courts of the other states have held consistently that the due process clause of the United States Constitution does not apply to matters concerning liquor licenses.
>
> Various reasons for this position have been given. Licensees are said to have no vested interest in their license. *People v. Schafran*, 168 Mich. 324, 134 N.W.29 (1912); *Case v. Michigan Liquor Control Commission*, 314 Mich. 632,23 N.W.2d 109; *Fitzpatrick v. Liquor Control Commission*, 316 Mich. 83, 25 N.W.2d 118, 172 A.L.R. 608; or the court holds that a license is merely a "privilege" and not property. *Johnson v. Liquor Control Commission*, 266 Mich. 682, 254 N.W. 557. And the Michigan courts have flatly stated that the exercise of the state's power in regard to liquor license is not affected by the Fourteenth Amendment. *People v. Wheeler*, 185 Mich. 164, 151 N.W. 710; *Gamble v. Liquor Control Commission*, 323 Mich. 576, 36 N.W.2d 297.[11]

*   *   *

Judge Fox rejected that doctrine, concluding:

> The Federal Constitution, as interpreted by the United States Supreme Court, designates the rights which shall be protected. It is the duty of this court to determine whether the right here involved was intended to be protected.[12]

*   *   *

So long as it is legal to engage in licensed liquor traffic, and, so long as such licenses have a substantial monetary value, their transfer cannot be denied without due process of law.[13]

*   *   *

For the reasons stated in this opinion, the revocation of the license denied . . , Mr. Lewis equal protection of the law.[14]

*   *   *

In this court's opinion, plaintiff has no adequate administrative remedy; and if so the court would not require its exhaustion. *McNeese v. Board of Education*, 373 U.S. 668, 83 S. Ct. 1433, 10 L. Ed. 2d 622.[15]

*   *   *

These ultimate conclusions were buttressed by a plethora of pronouncements derogating the municipality's authority to regulate liquor licenses free of constitutional restraints. These were the rulings of Judge Fox on that issue:

The City Commission claims that its action on the applications for transfer of the liquor license is a privileged exercise of police power. It is their contention that they may deny such applications without stating reasons for such denial.

The police power of the state or any of its agencies is not a sanctuary from which constitutionally protected rights of citizens may be violated with impunity.

The police power of the state is not a license to ignore the constitutionally protected rights of equal protection of the law, of equal enforcement of the law, and of due process of law.

What Judge Miller said (160 F.2d at page 100) in the Glicker case may be paraphrased: It is well settled that under the decisions of the United States Supreme Court a state police regulation is, like any other law, subject to the equal protection clause of the Fourteenth Amendment.

The City may not under the guise of protection of the health and welfare of the city, ignore these fundamental, constitutionally protected rights.

While it would be sufficient for this court to rest its opinion on the finding of denial of equal protection of the laws and thus a violation of a constitutionally protected right of the Fourteenth Amendment, the court is compelled to further hold that the method of disapproval was a denial of the process.

*   *   *

To deny the transfer without due process, on the ground that a privilege only and not property is in issue, is to close the eyes of justice to realities. Other courts have overcome this judge-made hurdle.

*   *   *

Liberty includes the right to pursue a lawful occupation. To prevent this without due process is to violate the Fourteenth Amendment to the United States Constitution.

*   *   *

Although Mr. Lewis insisted upon due process, confrontation and a declaration of reasons, Mr. Lewis was never informed of the specific reasons for the disapproval and denial of the transfer of the liquor license to himself and Dr. English.   They were never given an opportunity to formally challenge the ex post factum purported reasons. For these reasons alone, Mr. Lewis was denied procedural due process.

*   *   *

It is ordered that the City of Grand Rapids, through its Constitutional officials, approve the transfer of the license   at Barnett's Bar to Mr. Lewis and Dr. English.[16]

With this cornucopia of supporting doctrine, I should have recalled an incident involving Judge Arnold which occurred many years earlier. One morning, abut 8:30, as I entered the office, I saw him and an associate on their way out, with bulging briefcases under their arms. The following dialogue ensued when I asked where they were headed:

Judge Arnold: To the District Court to try the [XYZ] case.

Diamond: How do you think you'll make out?

Judge Arnold: We're sure to lose.

Diamond: What makes you say that? I thought we had a pretty strong case. [In those early days, everyone in our small office knew just about everything that was going on.]

Judge Arnold: Because I'm so sure we'll win.

But my confidence in the controlling force of the *Lewis* opinion precluded the possibility of any cautionary thoughts.

Shortly after the Pharmacy Board moved to dismiss the SuperX complaint in the district court, oral argument on that motion and our pending motions was held before Judge Fox. I appeared for SuperX in the company of one of Kroger's in-house attorneys -- Arthur Ferguson. He had informed me in careful detail of the preceding events before the Board and the Michigan Supreme Court. Following opposing counsel's argument in support of the Board's motion to dismiss, it was my turn. My presentation began with a careful review of the circumstances which led us to the federal court.

Then it was time to refer to Judge Fox's opinion in the *Lewis* case. Scarcely able to control my satisfaction, I recited the principles he had enunciated, emphasizing his recognition that the guarantees of the Fourteenth Amendment comprehend "the right to pursue a lawful occupation." However, I keenly sensed, to my surprise, that he seemed totally unreceptive to anything I had said, although he never asked a question or uttered a word during my argument.

As we left the courtroom, I turned to Ferguson and expressed mystification at the court's chilly reaction. Ferguson, a slow speaking mid-westerner, then solved the mystery. I'll never forget his answer. This is close to a verbatim recitation of what he said:

Well, I guess I should have told you this before. A while back Kroger had a case in Judge Fox's court. We were suing one of our supermarket landlords for breach of his lease commitments. A few thousand dollars were involved. It turned out that the landlord's lawyer was a close friend of Judge Fox. So as soon as the answer was filed, the Judge called a conference and urged the lawyers to settle the case.

Kroger's counsel said he had been instructed not to settle under any circumstances. When the Judge asked who gave the instructions, he was told it was a Kroger lawyer at its Cincinnati headquarters, named Mitchell [to my knowledge, very young and very feisty]. The Judge immediately got Mitchell on the phone and asked him to come to Grand Rapids for a settlement conference. Mitchell answered that he wouldn't come: "It would just waste my time and my employer's funds, because there is no chance Kroger will settle the case."

This was Murphy's *coup de grace.* To paraphrase an American classic, written by Ernest Laurence Thayer and popularized by DeWolf Hopper: "The outlook wasn't brilliant for the SuperX team that day."

More prosaically, Ferguson's belated eye-opener brought to mind Judge Arnold's maxim about sure winners. The Mitchell incident, of course, explained the entire pattern of events following our recourse to the federal court.

I knew Bob Mitchell. He was impulsive and immature. He didn't last long at Kroger. In effect, he had told Judge Fox to go fly a kite. That was a genesis one "no no." A federal judge is an icon, almost a deity in a small town. In my book it's a 100 to 1 shot that as soon as he noticed the SuperX case on the Kalamazoo docket, Judge Fox had grasped the chance to get even with Kroger by arranging for transfer of the case to his court.

Although the milk had been spilled, I couldn't help wondering what could have been done with advance information of the potential problem posed by Judge Fox in the Western District. There were alternatives: we could have sued in the Eastern District of the Michigan federal court or possibly in a Michigan State court. But it did no good to look back.

For better or worse, we were in the Fox's den, my expectation of a cakewalk win for SuperX gone with the wind. We now faced the reality that he would somehow find a way to avoid a decision for SuperX. We desperately contemplated the possibility of a way out. I sensed a chance to do so when a month of silence went by, for, as already noted, an expedited disposition is the norm when a motion for preliminary injunction is in issue.

This led me to suggest that we appeal to the United States Court of Appeals for the Sixth Circuit for reversal, on the theory that Judge Fox's weeks of inaction was a "*de facto*" [an actual] denial of our motion for such relief. Alternatively, we would seek an order requiring him to rule on our motion for by a specified date. If he then denied it, we could promptly appeal. But my proposal didn't sell. At that point, the head of Kroger's public relations unit intervened, stating that he was well-connected with the reigning Michigan politicians and would quickly take care of the pharmacy license problem. Unfortunately, he didn't live up to his billing.

On the other hand, Judge Fox more than fulfilled my worst fears. To paraphrase the great 18th Century dramatist, William Congreve, he proved that like a woman, "Hell has no fury like a Federal Judge scorned." (Mourning II).

Judge Fox was, of course, aware that denial of a motion for a preliminary injunction is immediately appealable by the losing party. He was also doubtless concerned, for good reason, that a ruling by him denying the SuperX Motion would invite reversal by the Court of Appeals. So he contrived a no-decision strategy.

This is what he did: About six months after SuperX complaint filed its complaint in his Court, he promulgated a convoluted, esoteric opinion which neither granted nor denied the SuperX motions, nor the Board's motion to dismiss.[17] Instead, it remitted SuperX to the pursuit of further proceedings before the Michigan Supreme Court. The one and only mention of the *Lewis* case was this peremptory comment:

> At this point, I wish to remark that the case of *Lewis v. City of Grand Rapids, et al.*, 222 F. Supp. 349, cited extensively in plaintiff's brief, contains many important factual distinctions.[18]

Judge Fox did not specify a single one of those alleged "important factual distinctions." Indeed, the only one of significance favored SuperX -- the fact that a pharmacy license, unlike a liquor license, could not be deemed an unprotected "privilege" for purposes of constitutional law. Rather, on the contrived hypothesis of such ostensible "distinctions," Judge Fox returned the case to the Supreme Court of Michigan to seek its guidance on the status of its 5-3 decision on the mandamus issue, in light of its 4-4 division on the Board's motion for rehearing.

That aspect of the opinion began with a declaration that "no formal writ has ever issued" from the Supreme Court of Michigan. He followed with a reminder of the various motions pending before him in the *SuperX* case. At that point he fashioned a variety of pretexts, purportedly requiring additional advice from the Michigan Supreme Court.[19]

He next created the fantasy of "a vortex of uncertainty," based upon the three routine motions pending before him. In that process, he simultaneously acknowledged, but ignored, the self-enforcing quality of a judgment of mandamus, stating that a "timely motion for rehearing . . . stayed the operation of the writ." From those premises, he concluded that the consequences of the equal division on the motion for rehearing "are unsettled." Because this rationale seems so fanciful, it deserves to be read in the original text:

> Plaintiff now seeks a preliminary injunction and summary judgment from this Court, while defendants move to dismiss.
>
> The beacon to which the court is drawn by this vortex of uncertainty is the 4 - 4 tie on the motion for rehearing and the effect which this has on the 5 - 3 decision granting the writ in December of 1963.
>
> While it is true that under General Court Rules of 1963 (M.S.A. § 714.5) *a writ of mandamus is contained in the order of judgment*, a timely motion for rehearing was filed, which stayed the operation of the writ. The hearing on that motion resulted in a 4 - 4 vote and the consequences of that vote are unsettled.[20]

The fallacies of the quoted rationale are easily discerned. The fact that no "writ" ever issued should have been meaningless in light of his quotation of the rule that "a writ of mandamus is contained in the order of judgment." No one ever questioned the fact that judgment for SuperX had been entered on its mandamus case. Otherwise, there would have been nothing to rehear. Consequently, it was fatuous to assert that the motion for rehearing "stayed the operation of the writ." Properly construed, the Board's motion sought a stay of the operation of the writ already in force by reason of the judgment. In that context the 4-4 split could not have suspended the writ.

A truly innovative notion marked the next move in the Judge's ploy to steer the case back to the state court. Here he cited the conventional Michigan statute stating that in the event of a tie vote in the Supreme Court, the decision below "shall be affirmed." To that elementary legislation, Judge Fox attached this truly novel proposition: that in such a case, the "tie-breaking vote is that of the trial judge in the court below." By this original technique of putting the Supreme Court cart before the lower court horse, Judge Fox arrived at the following judicial destination:

> The question, therefore, is whether or not an equally divided Supreme Court affirms its own judgment, rendered in an exercise of its original jurisdiction, when there is no Circuit Judge to break the tie.[21]

Judge Fox now jumped to extraneous events. These were the change in the composition of the court by the substitution of a new Justice for the one whose term had expired, coupled with the adoption of a new State Constitution "in the hiatus between the December decision and the February vote." Concerning those changes, he emphasized two points: First, that the new Constitution had revised older language "designating individual writs to language which provided simply for prerogative and remedial writs".[22]

Second, referring to the tie on the motion for a rehearing, he described the resultant situation and what he deemed the resultant puzzle:

> Under these circumstances, four Justices of the Supreme Court indicated that the original judgment should not stand, four held that it did. From an examination of the record, therefore, it is apparent that at least four Justices of the Michigan Supreme Court are convinced that the first decision is not res judicata.
>
> *In this unique situation, can it be definitely said that the December 1963 decision is res judicata? . . .*[23]

In other words, Judge Fox treated a vote on a procedural issue -- *i.e.*, on the motion for rehearing -- as the equivalent of the previous substantive vote on the mandamus issue. He cited no precedent for that view. To my knowledge, there is none.

From his above underscored query -- whether the December 1963 decision was *res judicata* -- the Judge proceeded to demonstrate the power of a court to convert a simple legal issue into an arcane dissertation of intricate judicial principles. Whether or not Judge Fox was so motivated, the result was to frustrate SuperX's opportunity for a timely determination of the merits of its claims.

In contrast to his emphatic affirmation of the supremacy of the federal constitution over state adjudications in the *Lewis* case, Judge Fox now declared the prudence of awaiting a ruling by the Michigan Supreme Court on the status of its mandamus decision:

> Under these circumstances, it is prudential jurisprudence to have the Supreme Court of the forum state clarify the relevant issues. When a Federal District Court is presented with a claimed breach of a constitutionally protected right, which may spring from the action or inaction of a State Supreme Court in a given case, it is sound jurisprudence for the Federal Court to forebear so as to give the highest Court of the forum state a reasonable opportunity to write the law of the State which is to be applicable if controlling on the issue before the Federal Court.[24]

From this expression of deference to the state courts, he moved to a complex discussion of the types of writs authorized by various Michigan rules of procedure. If what follows is confusing to the reader, it is no less so to the author.

Upon delving into Michigan law, he found an "apparent conflict between the Michigan General Court Rules and the decision of December 1963." (*i.e.*, the 5-3 decision granting mandamus). He based this discovery on the premise that "[w]hile their scope has not been expanded, the prerogative writs have been absorbed into the new order of superintending control, which permits a broader exercise of powers."[25] His resultant perception of conflict arose from "the [Preliminary] Committee Comment to Rule 711.1, the General Court Rules."

He cited these declarations from the Comment's text:

> The power of superintending control is an extraordinary power. . . . It is unlimited, being bounded only by the exigencies which call for its exercise. Moreover, if required, the tribunals having authority to exercise it, will by virtue of it, possess the power to invent, frame and formulate new and additional means, writs and processes whereby it may be exercised . . . Furthermore, it is directed primarily to inferior *tribunals* and its relation to litigants is only incidental.[26]

Judge Fox now invoked a quotation from the new Constitution providing for judicial review of "all rulings and orders of any administrative official or agency . . . . which are judicial or quasi-judicial." This led him to cite the State Administrative Code, defining an "agency" as any state body "authorized to adjudicate contested cases" (with exceptions immaterial in this case).[27] He next derived from the Supreme Court's General Rules 711.1 and 711.3 the following rationale:

> Thus, we see Rule 711.1 calls for the writ of superintending control to be used in exercising power over *inferior tribunals*. It appears that the writ of December 1963 should have been one of superintending control, and not of mandamus, in view of the fact that mandamus when directed to an inferior tribunal or officer thereof, is *superseded by the order of superintending control*. General Court Rule 711.3. It appears reasonably certain that the Michigan Supreme Court would have the authority to exercise superintending control over an agency when its action may involve questions of Fourteenth Amendment constitutionally protected rights of due process, confrontation of witnesses, hearings, and equal protection of the law.[28]

In my view, this analysis smacks of an effort by Judge Fox to escape any responsibility for the SuperX case, since no "writ of superintending controls" had been issued to the Pharmacy Board. His opinion at least implies a purpose to shift authority to decide the Fourteenth Amendment issues to the Michigan Supreme Court, then deadlocked 4 to 4 on the license issue.

For this purpose, Judge Fox next continued his review of Michigan writs to buttress his point that the Michigan Court had erroneously approved issuance of a writ of mandamus in its original 5-3 decision. To that end he injected a reference to Michigan Court Rule 714.1. That Rule, he said, supported his view -- presumably that the "writ of superintending control," instead of mandamus, should have been utilized by the Michigan Supreme Court in its 1963 decision. In his words:

> This conclusion is further enforced by Michigan Court Rule 714.1, which appears to call for use of the writ of mandamus against state officers. *State officers in the context of Rule 714.1 must be distinguished from those who constitute inferior courts or tribunals --* agency tribunals acting in a judicial or quasi-judicial capacity.[29]

He next addressed "Rule 714, section 5," describing it as the only one which mentioned a judgment free from the need of an enforcing writ.[30] He thereby came to these interpretations of the two different writs:

> In view of this dichotomy drawn between the objects of the writs of mandamus and superintending control, the two appear to be mutually exclusive when considered in light of this distinction between state officers and "tribunals."

> The proviso that the writ shall be contained in the judgment, in the form of an order, and a separate writ need not be issued or served is found only in Rule 14, Section 5. [*i.e.*, applicable only to mandamus judgments against individual state officers.][31]

Here Judge Fox reiterated his newly adopted respect for state court prerogatives:

> From any standpoint, this is a highly unusual case, and were a one-man Federal Court to render a decision in such a case, involving, as it apparently does, the nascent writ of superintending control, it could conceivably have a heavy bearing on future interpretations of that writ, and thus in some measure determine the course of future state law. The undesirability of this result is too obvious for further comment, and provides an added reason for deferring, for the time being, to the Michigan Supreme Court.[32]

The foregoing quotation served as a launching pad for another lengthy dissertation on the virtues of the "abstention" doctrine. To emphasize it he cited various precedents of the Supreme Court of the United States for the "principle . . . that the federal courts should not adjudicate the constitutionality of state enactments fairly open to interpretation until the state courts have been afforded a reasonable opportunity to pass upon them."[33]

Judge Fox next described the rudimentary principles governing the availability of summary judgment under Rule 56 of the Federal Rules of Civil Procedures. These are the simple rules that undisputed facts must dictate a particular legal result. He then concluded that the facts before him were uncertain and required clarification:

> Thus, if as a matter of law the facts are not resolved by SuperX v. Pharmacy Board, supra, then summary judgment, as urged by plaintiff, cannot be granted by this Court. There is substantial question and doubt on the present record.

The decision on the motion for summary judgment will be held in abeyance until some final or further disposition by the Michigan Supreme Court.[34]

The hostility of Judge Fox towards Kroger/SuperX was overtly manifested in several passages of his opinion. Among other things he stated that SuperX had invoked "the original jurisdiction . . . of the Michigan Supreme Court with full knowledge of [its] eight man composition . . . and the possibility that it might divide equally over a proposition . . . ."[35]

The inference of that proposition is that a litigant ought never resort to the court's original jurisdiction for fear of a split decision. If anything, faced with a threat of litigation to close the Battle Creek pharmacy, and its idle investment in three other pharmacies, prudence dictated recourse by SuperX to the quickest possible means of judicial decision. Delay was inherent in the slower method of resorting first to an intermediate appeal and then to the Michigan Supreme Court. Moreover, Judge Fox failed to consider the possibility that a loss before an intermediate tribunal might likewise be affirmed by an equal division of the Michigan Supreme Court, which would mean denial of the license.

Besides criticizing SuperX's procedural choice, Judge Fox also asserted that it had created its own problem by establishing the three additional pharmacies before it received the Battle Creek license.[36] This was hardly imprudent since that pharmacy had been routinely licensed for some 50 years.

Stymied by Judge Fox, SuperX returned to the Supreme Court of Michigan by way of a pleading entitled "Petition for Affirmation that Decision of December 5, 1963 is Res Judicata."[37] All pertinent documents were attached to it, including the Court's original decision ordering issuance of the license, our complaint against the Board and Judge Fox's opinion. Here the case took a turn which I suspect surprised Judge Fox.

As I read his opinion, he had a threefold purpose in ordering the case returned to the Michigan Supreme Court. Overall, with the Supreme Court divided, he searched for a method of denying the license permanently, in order to get even with Kroger. This generated his perceived "dichotomy" between Michigan writs in order to establish that the original writ of mandamus to the Pharmacy Board was ineffective, because it was susceptible only to a "writ of superintending control." Third, he tried to cajole the Supreme Court of Michigan by softening his arrogant defiance in the *Lewis* case of its view that liquor licenses did not enjoy constitutional protection.

But instead he hit into a triple play. The Michigan Supreme Court decided that the case should be reheard, but went out of its way to state that in so deciding it acted "on its own motion . . . without further argument or briefs."[38]

After remanding the matter to the Board for reconsideration,[39] it overruled a second attempt to deny the license, again by 5 - 3 vote. This time it rejected the Board's ruling that SuperX's predecessor had forfeited its "grandfather" status by discontinuing operations for remodeling during the period August 30 to November 24, 1958.[40] Ignoring Judge Fox's disquisition on the nuances of Michigan writs, the 5 - 3 majority decided: "Let the writ of mandamus issue."[41]

In the end, the Michigan Supreme Court treated Judge Fox as a nonperson and his supposedly learned opinion as a nonentity. Both were ignored by all four separate opinions written by members of the Michigan Court in connection with its ultimate decision to grant the license.

Judge Fox's intricate maneuvers to avoid deciding the simple issue in SuperX reminded me of a classic response by Governor Ellis Arnall of Georgia to Chief Justice Stone during the argument in *Georgia v. Pennsylvania Railroad*.[42] That was an antitrust case in which the State of Georgia sought an injunction against an alleged ratemaking conspiracy among the defendant railroads.

Specifically, the complaint charged that the defendants and their affiliated rate-fixing agencies, conspired to discriminate against Georgia ports and its industries by fixing joint-through rates at levels 39% higher than comparable rates in the north. The State sued both as "*parens patriae*", that is as the sovereign on behalf of its citizens, and in its "proprietary capacity," as the owner of a railroad and other entities. A major issue was the standing of a state to sue for antitrust relief by way of the Court's original jurisdiction -- on which the Court divided 5 to 4 in Georgia's favor.[43]

The argument for Georgia was personally made by its Governor Ellis Arnall, a former Attorney General of the State. He urged that since the State was a party, the Court had original jurisdiction under Article III, Section 2 of the Constitution which provides; "in all cases. . . in which a State shall be a party the Supreme Court shall have original jurisdiction." This means that it had to act as a trial court to hear the matter. As Arnall made that point, Chief Justice Stone asked: "Governor, are you telling us we have to take this case?" "Why no your Honor", the Governor replied, "I'm merely stating that the Constitution says you have to take it. However, not for a moment do I underestimate the power of this court."

Timewise, Georgia was more fortunate than SuperX, although its case involved complex legal issues. After argument on January 2, 1945, the Court resolved the original jurisdiction issue in favor of Georgia on March 26, 1945.[44] On December 17, 1945, the Court appointed Lloyd K. Garrison, a prominent New York attorney, as "Special Master" to hear the evidence.[45]

SuperX taught us not to underestimate the effect of a federal judge's vanity upon the discharge of his adjudicative function. His maneuvers delayed the development of SuperX's Michigan business by four years, during which it suffered a substantial monetary loss. But perhaps the Judge also learned that a wily Fox could lead the litigation hounds on an extended chase for just so long. In the end, they would bring him to bay.

CHAPTER TWENTY

UNINTENDED CONSEQUENCES

This is the story of how a seemingly impossible litigation dream turned into an unexpected judicial reality. Beginning in 1948, I started doing the labor law work for the now defunct *Washington Evening Star*. At one time, it was by far the leading Washington newspaper. A family enterprise owned by the Kauffmann and Noyes families, it may have been the most prosperous newspaper in the country, before television killed the evening versions of the print media. I remember hearing that *The Star* carried more advertising lineage than *The New York Times*.

The representation came to me from Jack Kauffmann, son of the publisher, Sam Kauffmann. Jack and I had become close personal friends. Good-natured banter was Jack's typical speaking style. He was every woman's dreamboat: young, blond, extremely handsome, a free spirit, a bright Princeton graduate with a smiling carefree manner and a keen sense of humor. The social status of his family never influenced his associations or his activities.

The morning of May 5, 1958, I received a call from him that was out of character. At the time, Jack was *The Star's* Business Manager. He was obviously troubled. He explained that due to a wage dispute, *The Star* had been struck by its reporters' union, the Washington Newspaper Guild. He feared that the strike would force the paper to shut down because the Guild's pickets were blocking the entrances to its building. He wanted us to get a court order to stop the picketing.

Jack's request seemed to call for an exercise in futility because of the Norris-LaGuardia Act.[1] To quote the outstanding judge who eventually heard the case -- the Honorable David Pine -- about the effect of that statute when labor unions went on strike: "It has taken almost complete jurisdiction away from the courts." He did not exaggerate. As intended by Congress, the statute virtually eliminated the injunction as an instrument for an employer's legal counter-measures against striking employees.

The Act validated any and all collective or individual activities by employees engaged in a labor dispute, absent proof of "fraud or violence."[2] A temporary restraining order could be issued against striking employees or their unions only in extremely limited circumstances. Very specific "findings of fact," based only on live testimony -- affidavits wouldn't do -- were made prerequisite to the issuance of a temporary restraining order -- good for only five days -- against a strike. Among the findings prerequisite to the entry of such an order were the following:

> That unlawful acts have been threatened and will be committed unless restrained or have been committed and will be continued unless restrained . . . .;

> That substantial and irreparable injury to complainant's property will follow;

> *   *   *

> That the *public officers* charged with the duty to protect complainant's property *are unable or unwilling to furnish adequate protection.*[3]

The Act further declared that any injunction issued within its constraints should be limited to organizations or individuals "committing or actually authorizing or ratifying" the illegal acts.[4] By judicial precedent, a going business constitutes "property" for purposes of the statute.[5]

In brief -- as Jack explained the facts to me -- this was the situation confronting the Star: Ordinarily a reporters' strike wouldn't close down a newspaper. The management staff could substitute at least in part for the reporters. Syndicated material plus A.P. and U.P. news wires could fill the balance of the columns. But the strikers were using unusual tactics. There were two picket lines, with strikers stationed about one foot apart. The lines moved continuously in elongated ellipses at the two entrances to the Star's Building, in a manner which maintained an almost solid human wall in front of them.

At least in those days, a newspaper couldn't publish without the services of its craftsmen who performed the mechanics of preparing the paper -- *i.e.*, printers, pressmen, photoengravers, stereotypers and mailers. Each of their local unions had signed labor contracts with *The Star* containing no-strike clauses. These required them to cross the Guild picket lines. But they were not doing so. Doubtless in cahoots with the Guild, the presidents of the craft unions all asserted that they had ordered their members to honor their contracts by crossing the Guild picket lines. However, each claimed that his members had declined to do so, as individuals, for fear of physical harm. This avoided the obligation imposed on a union by a no-strike clause. Only a group refusal was prohibited.

After describing the situation, Jack requested that I come to his office as quickly as possible. Judge Arnold agreed to join me. We went right over, wedging our way through the picket lines. To put it mildly, the situation was difficult. Injunctive relief was the only solution, but Norris-LaGuardia stood in the way.

As a first step, we carefully explained the restrictions imposed by the Act. To our surprise, Kauffmann and Harold Boyd, *The Star's* Director of Labor Relations, then informed us that there had been some violent incidents on the picket line. Although we suspected that the Guild had staged them as pretexts to justify the refusal of the craftsmen to cross the lines, they opened an inviting line of inquiry. We quickly ascertained the names of the actors and victims plus -- to our absolute astonishment -- the identities of two police officers who had witnessed the incidents.

After verifying the facts, we immediately drafted and filed a complaint, together with a motion for a temporary restraining order without notice (limited to five days under the statute); subpoenaed the two designated police officers; brought the matter to hearing in the federal district court and obtained a restraining order. All this was done on the same day -- May 5, 1958.[6]

The principal content of the hearing was the testimony of the two police officers. The first was Lieutenant James E. Stargel. After describing the congested picket line, he testified, as follows, under my examination:

Q Did you observe any acts of violence while you were stationed at that point?

A Yes, sir.

Q Will you describe it, please?

A At 8:45 a.m., while standing adjacent to the entrance to The Star Building, I had occasion to arrest, place under arrest a Mr. Harris Monroe for assaulting a Mr. Eugene C. Tanner.

Q Was Mr. Tanner injured?

A I beg your pardon?

Q Was Mr. Tanner injured?

A No, sir.

Q Was he thrown to the ground?

A Yes, sir.

Q By Mr. Monroe?

A Yes, sir.

Q Were there any charges preferred against Mr. Monroe?

A Yes, sir.

Q Was Mr. Tanner as far as you know attempting to cross the picket line at that time?

A He appeared to me to be, sir. He approached from the direction of Eleventh Street and was entering or attempting to enter the door at the time it happened.

Q And Mr. Monroe, shall we say, impeded his progress?

A Yes, sir.

MR. DIAMOND: That is all, Lieutenant. Thank you very much.

BY THE COURT:

Q What sort of an assault was it, Lieutenant?

A Your Honor, I was immediately adjacent to Mr. Monroe, he being on my right, and the door slightly on my right.

I observed Mr. Tanner approaching. They apparently looked, at least Mr. Tanner looked toward me and toward Mr. Monroe, and at that time Mr. Monroe made an assault with his left shoulder and his right fist substantially blocking Mr. Tanner's entrance; and Mr. Tanner moved back rather rapidly, and Mr. Monroe following him, and they ended up on the sidewalk, approximately thirty feet from the original point of contact.

Q Was a blow struck?

A Yes, sir.

Q Where?

A It appeared to me to strike Mr. Tanner on the face or very close. The impact was with Mr. Monroe's left shoulder, and at the same time he crossed with his right fist or right hand, which went in the direction of Mr. Tanner's face.

Mr. Tanner said that he was not injured, so apparently the blow did not strike to any great extent. However, they both ended up back some distance and on the sidewalk.

Q He was not knocked down?

A Yes, sir, he was knocked down, with Mr. Monroe on top of him.

THE COURT: I see.[7]

The second police officer was Corporal Patrick Sochocky. Under my questioning, he similarly described the picket line and then testified:

Q Did that picket line interfere with access to the entrances to the Star Building?

A Some of the people going in had to, well, were brushed against by the pickets, moving across, down the street; yes, sir.

Q During your observation of that picket line, did you observe any act of violence, Corporal?

A Yes, sir, I did.

Q Will you describe it, please.

A About 12:45 p.m., I was standing along the curb, facing the doorway of The Star Building, on the Eleventh Street side, and I observed a body of men coming from across the street, across Eleventh Street, going to enter the doorway, and in so doing that they had to pass between the pickets.

Some of these men went through the first line, the line that was going northward or the line that was toward the curb, and then I observed a man rushing towards another man, bumping him and striking him in the face with his fist.

I immediately rushed to the scene, which was only a couple of feet from me, and I grabbed the man's arm again as it was coming down to strike the other man.

I wrenched him free and pulled him out into the street.

Q Do you know who the assailant was in that instance?

A Albert Wesley Barthelmes, something like that.

Q Do you know who the man was that was struck?

A Mr. Boswell, David S. Boswell, I believe.

Q Was he an employee of *The Star*?

A He stated to me afterwards he was a pressman employed at *The Star*.

Q Was Mr. Boswell injured by this assault?

A He stated that the blow struck him on the side of the fact [sic] and neck, temporarily knocking the wind out of him, but I asked him if he required any hospital treatment, and he said, No, that he was just, the wind knocked out of him and startled and shocked.[8]

Another witness was James J. Rose, *The Star's* Assistant Production Manager. He testified to the following events when he attempted to get into The Star Building:

> The pickets were so close together, and they were moving, that I had to stop and pick a place to cross the line.
>
> Well, I waited for a particularly large opening, which did occur occasionally, and I gave a little skip across the line; but just as I had crossed the line an umbrella, which was carried by a woman, struck me, or the crown of the umbrella struck me in my right temple.
>
> Q Had she quickened her pace to accomplish that?
>
> A Yes, sir.
>
> MR. DIAMOND: I have no further questions. Thank you, Mr. Rose.
>
> BY THE COURT:
>
> Q Was she part of the picket line?
>
> A Yes.
>
> Q Are you sure of that?
>
> A Yes.[9]

Whether contrived or not, the described "violence" got the job done. On that basis, plus testimony from *Star* officials that a shutdown would cause a severe loss of revenue, United States District Judge Pine issued a restraining order. In drafting it, he lived up to his reputation as an outstanding jurist. He meticulously followed the precise text of the statute in composing the required findings, resisting our efforts to expand them as unauthorized. But he did add one important exception, after prolonged argument, by including the succeeding italicized reference in his order enjoining the Union not to "prevent by physical violence or *physical hindrance* access to the plaintiff's premises by plaintiff's employees.[10]

That addition -- unmentioned in the text of Norris-LaGuardia -- not only brought *The Star's* mechanical staff back to work, but became a lasting restraint on permissible picketing in the District of Columbia. As I recall it, sometime afterward the U.S. Attorney, Oliver Gasch -- (later himself a United States District Judge) -- told me that the "physical hindrance" prohibition -- which became known as "The Star rule" -- was interpreted to mean that pickets had to be separated by at least six feet. When last I heard, it was still in force.

I subsequently represented *The Star* in several other labor matters before the National Labor Relations Board. These involved both unfair labor practices and jurisdictional disputes -- the latter involving claims by one union that the paper was illegally assigning its work to another labor organization. Our position was sustained in every one of them. Looking back, that was pretty amazing, since the Board in those days was so pro-labor it almost automatically ruled against employers. In representing *The Star*, I was assisted on occasion by Mel Spaeth, then one of our young associates. Later a highly valued partner, his gift for profound analysis of legal problems has always been and still is, an enormous asset to the firm's capacity to handle "oxygen tent cases."

I can't help adding one other facet of my friendship with Jack Kauffmann. He was my client in the only divorce case of my entire career. He had to file in Maryland, where he and his wife were domiciled. That made it a hard sell. At the time in Maryland, the grounds were not only very limited -- adultery, failure to consummate and mental illness -- but a decree could not be obtained on the testimony of the parties. The corroboration of an independent witness was required. I managed to obtain it. Divorce cases are not pleasant under any circumstances. They are miserable when contested. Jack's wife never dreamed he would take the step. Since I knew her, the process was particularly unpleasant. Domestic relations cases are too painful for my taste. Thankfully, the office is rarely involved in that branch of the law.

**Nelson Poynter, Editor and Publisher
of the *St. Petersburg Times*; founder of the
Poynter Institute for Media Studies**

CHAPTER TWENTY-ONE

CITIZEN POYNTER

When I met Nelson Poynter in 1946, he was the editor of the *St. Petersburg Times*. Although it served a small southern community -- a village by modern standards -- the *Times* was a liberal newspaper with a national reputation for integrity and excellence.

Nelson Poynter was a truly remarkable person. He was a small, affable soft-spoken man, whose quiet manner belied his fierce independence and his truly passionate convictions. He was an old-fashioned liberal -- a true "New Dealer" -- as attested by the editorial page of the *Times*.

He lived his business life in accordance with his belief that integrity and independence constituted a newspaper's obligation to its readers. For fear of compromising the integrity of his newspaper, he had no business interests except for his ownership shares in the Times Publishing Company, the corporation that owned *The Times*. As I later learned, among the opportunities he rejected was an invitation to participate as an investor in the original commercial venture to develop orange juice concentrate. He was well aware at the time that the product would be a proverbial gold mine.

As a result of Poynter's foresight, *The Times* survives today as one of the nation's few remaining independent publication. It still enjoys its national reputation as an exemplary newspaper.[1] In order to "keep control of the newspaper in local hands and protect it against chain ownership," Poynter established a tax exempt organization -- "The Poynter Institute for Media Studies." He gave the Institute -- a non-profit educational organization -- his majority ownership of the stock in Times Publishing Company.[2]

Under that control the paper flourished. It prospered to the point that Robert Bass -- the Texas billionaire -- bought the minority interest of 40 percent of the Publishing Company's stock from Poynter's nieces for almost $28 million and offered $270 million for the majority interest. The trustees of the Institute declined, notwithstanding a suit alleging breach of trust among other things. When this ploy failed, the minority interest was sold to the Institute for upwards of $50 million.[3]

What brought Poynter to our office was a truly quixotic legal proceeding against the *St. Petersburg Times.* To defend it he retained Judge Arnold, who enlisted my assistance. Specifically, *The Times,* along with the *Evening Independent,* the other local St. Petersburg daily, was charged with violating the National Labor Relations Act (the "Act"), by the National Labor Relations Board (the "NLRB"), the agency established to enforce the Act.[4]

The Act was the New Deal's "Emancipation Proclamation" for labor unions. In brief, it required employers to bargain collectively with unions which represented a majority of their employees working in a particular labor "unit" or craft. It also prohibited discrimination or threats against union members or pro-union employees.[5] (At the time, the statute imposed no reciprocal obligations on labor unions.)

The complaint against *The Times* and the *Independent* alleged that the newspapers had unlawfully refused to bargain with the local branch of the International Typographical Union. That union represented the newspapers' printers -- or "typographers" -- who set the type for reproduction on the newspapers' presses. The paradoxical quality of the complaint is evident from the following excerpt of the "Intermediate Report" of The Trial Examiner -- *i.e.,* the hearing officer. In it he lauded the pro-labor attitudes of the editors of the respondent newspapers, but nevertheless sustained the charge of violation:

> From their past record as employers it appears that both Poynter and Brown preferred to have their employees unionized and to deal with the Union as the representative of such employees. Far from being anti-union, they are pro-organized labor. Poynter, especially, enjoys among newspaper editors and publishers a reputation for being very progressive and liberal because of his numerous editorials in support of the Wagner Act and against anti-labor legislation. While Brown has not been as vocal on the subject, his actions have always shown him to be equally as friendly towards unions as Poynter.[6]

What precipitated the case was a collective bargaining impasse resulting from a series of the Union's demands: a wage increase; the discontinuation of the arbitration procedures historically followed by the union and the St. Petersburg newspapers to resolve stalemated issues; and insistence that the "laws" of the international union would govern "working conditions of its members, without negotiation."[7] The "laws" were all-inclusive. They were contained in a 164 page booklet entitled, *"Book of Laws of the International Typographical Union."* Among other things, they required the employment of five journeymen for each apprentice and six years for progression to journeyman; detailed the manning of overtime work; outlawed arbitration of the union's laws; and dictated certain "featherbedding," requirements referred to in the laws as "make-work."

On November 20, 1945, the union went on strike to enforce its demands.[8] The strike was admittedly "economic" in nature, as distinguished from a protest against unfair labor practices.[9] As a matter of law, this entitled the employers to hire permanent replacements for the strikers.[10] However, such a strike does not relieve the employer of a continuing duty to bargain with the union. The Union retains the right to negotiate for reinstatement of its members regarding subsequently available positions. Unfamiliarity with that odd feature of the governing labor law trapped Poynter into an ostensible refusal to bargain.[11]

This is how it happened: *The Times* and the *Independent* responded to the strike by organizing a jointly owned third corporation -- News Printing, Inc. (*"The News"*) -- to do the mechanical work, including printing, for both newspapers. The News then informed the union that it would soon start hiring printers under posted conditions of employment.[12] The entire membership of the union was simultaneously invited to a meeting at which the "conditions" would be presented "and all questions pertaining to them" would be answered.[13] The meeting was held on January 12, 1946.[14] In the course of that meeting, Poynter made the misguided statement which resulted in the refusal to bargain complaint. It consisted of this response, when he was asked whether "the new company would negotiate with the union":

> "The new company is not willing to negotiate with strikers. We are not willing to negotiate with strikers but we are willing, I repeat, to negotiate with the employees about anything. We will not negotiate with

strikers because we have demonstrated that we do not depend on your union to get along -- we can publish a paper without it . . . Remember we have no printers . . . we are posting conditions whereby they can become our employees.[15]

According to the Intermediate Report of the Trial Examiner, these events occurred at the conclusion of and after the meeting:

> Poynter ended the meeting with the assurance that the Respondent News would not make any long term employment contracts before January 21, urged the membership to study carefully the January Conditions so that the Union would vote to liquidate the strike and accept the positions under the January Conditions to which they were being given first chance.
>
> That afternoon at 3 p.m. following a talk by Carter [a representative of the International Union] against the January conditions, the membership of the Union voted to reject them. The Respondents were so informed by the following letter dated that day:
>
> This is to inform you that St. Petersburg Typographical Union, Local 860 voted this afternoon to reject your ultimatum.
>
> The vote was 54 to 1.[16]

Subsequently, *The News* hired other personnel in place of the strikers. However, it advised a representative of the International Union that it would hire members of the union as vacancies occurred, if "the union would remove [the newspapers] from its unfair list."[17]

Upon an initial analysis of the facts -- knowing of the board's pro-union bias -- we were seemingly faced with the proverbial smoking gun by Poynter's misguided statement that the News "is not willing to bargain with strikers." Nevertheless, we searched for a viable defense rationale, encouraged by Poynter's established reputation as a pro-union employee. We defended the complaint on two grounds: first, that viewed in full context, the facts of the dispute -- including the background of the employers -- rebutted the reality of an actual refusal to bargain. Secondly, we argued that by unilaterally imposing the union laws as working conditions and refusing to arbitrate them, the union itself had refused to bargain, thereby absolving the employer of any liability for refusing to negotiate with it.[18]

Both defenses were rejected by the Trial Examiner in his Intermediate Report. He first ruled that wages and hours were the only matters at issue between the parties at the time of the strike. He further held that the unilateral proffer of terms of employment by *The News,* coupled with Poynter's verbal refusal to negotiate with strikers, violated the employer's duty to bargain collectively.[19]

Regarding the laws of the international union, the Intermediate Report found as follows:

> "Respondents then point out, as the evidence at the hearing showed, that the general laws of I.T.U. cover numerous working conditions in the composing room and provide, in some instances, for what may be called "make-work" conditions. They also show that the I.T.U. laws further prohibit interpretation of any of those laws by arbitration. It can further be assumed that arbitration is a matter of great concern to the Respondents and a proper subject for negotiation."[20]

However, the Examiner held that because the newspapers allowed the laws to be posted in the composing room, an agreement had been reached, although the union's president had declared "that it was not a contract."[21] Further, when asked whether the newspapers had agreed to the laws, L. Chauncey Brown, the editor of the *Evening Independent*, testified: "We did not and we could not have."[22] The Intermediate Report characterized him as an "absolutely trustworthy witness."[23]

On review, the NLRB reversed the Trial Examiner. In the process, it recognized that despite the absence of a statutory duty to bargain on the part of a union, its failure to negotiate "in good faith may . . . preclude the existence of a situation in which the employer's own good faith can be tested. If it cannot be tested, its absence hardly can be found."[24] [Oddly enough, within four months of the decision in *The Times* case, on February 17, 1947, the National Labor Relations Act was amended by the Taft-Hartley Act. Among other things it provided that a union's refusal to bargain collectively with an employer was an unfair labor practice.][25]

Although it had recognized the problem, the Board nevertheless refused to decide the significance of the Union's refusal to bargain, prior to Taft-Hartley's enactment. It reasoned:

. . . Even assuming, arguendo, a "refusal to bargain" by the union about an arbitration clause and I.T.U. laws on August 1, 1945, such fact alone could not eliminate the duty of the employer to bargain on January 12, 1946.[26]

However, the Board dismissed the complaint. It ruled that the newspapers "were clearly entitled to replace the economic strikers," had no "duty to inform the union of their intention to hire replacements," and had offered to rehire them "should the union elect to terminate the strike before the replacements were hired."[27] On those premises, it rationalized the propriety of the Respondent's conduct in organizing *The News* to run a joint printing shop and advising the union membership of its intended program:

. . . To penalize this employer [*The News*] for proffering the jobs once again to economic strikers on the same terms to be offered replacements, would penalize open dealing and invite silent displacement of striking employees, a result which seems to us more likely to be productive rather than preventive of industrial strife and thus not to effectuate the purposes of the Act.[28]

The Board then went on to excuse Poynter's statement that the meeting of January 12, 1946, that "[t]he new company is not willing to negotiate with strikers," on which the Trial Examiner had based his adverse ruling. In this connection, it reasoned:

. . . We agree with the Trial Examiner's findings that "When Poynter made his statements . . . he in good faith believed this to be the law." Such statements standing alone would normally provide the basis for a finding of refusal to bargain with the Union as the representative of the striking employees. Yet as we have previously noted, we believe these statements must be appraised in the total context of the case and not in isolation. In the light of the background of relations between the parties, we do not believe that the statements were reasonably calculated to block or deny collective bargaining. The Union did not actually ask, nor did the respondents actually refuse, to bargain on January 12, 1946. As we have already observed, we believe that on that date Poynter would have been not only willing as usual to bargain, but would have welcomed bargaining with the Union to settle the dispute, and that the Union did not understand differently, but preferred instead to continue its strike to force acceptance of its original demands.[29]

As a result, following a lengthy proceeding, *The Times* and *Independent* were freed from the presence of the union printers and from the burdensome I.T.U. laws. What bothered Poynter was not merely the content of those "laws" in eliminating working conditions and arbitration from the collective bargaining process. He was more deeply troubled by their uniform application to all newspapers -- large and small alike -- regardless of circulation and advertising revenues. Consequently, the impact on smaller newspapers was much more severe.

The requirements of those "laws" were totally glossed over in the Board's opinion. They had been barely mentioned by the Trial Examiner in his brief reference to their "make-work" feature, obligating the employer to pay for useless production.[30]

In Poynter's opinion the "laws" were so onerous and expensive as to threaten the survival of all but the richest and most widely circulated newspapers such as the *Chicago Tribune* and the *New York Times*. He objected in particular to the mandatory specification of the ratio of apprentices to journeyman printers -- 5 to 1 -- and to the dictation of six years of service as an apprentice as a precondition to qualification as a journeyman. The "make work" law was a total waste. For example, it applied to mats received from some advertisers -- notably department stores -- which were ready for the newspapers' presses. The union's law required that union printers reproduce them, at full pay, after which the reproductions were broken up and discarded.

Poynter proved prophetic. Not too many years later, the I.T.U.'s enforcement of its exorbitant demands concerning wages and its "laws" killed off five New York newspapers when it insisted that they accept the same terms as the highly prosperous *Times* and *Daily News* (then a big time moneymaker). The victims were *The Herald-Tribune*, *The World Telegram* and the three Hearst newspapers -- *The New York American*, *The Daily Mirror* and *The New York Evening Journal*. They lacked the advertising and circulation to make ends meet under the terms accepted by *The Times* and *The News*. By demanding such equivalence, the ITU seemed determined to shoot itself in the foot.

More recently, in the *"Week in Review"* section of the *Sunday Times* of July 30, 1995, the lead article on the first page was entitled *"The Press: Bought and Sold and Gray All Over."* It spoke of the Gannett Company's purchase of "another eleven daily newspapers last week" and stated:

With chain-owned newspapers in most cities looking more and more alike, as though stamped from some giant corporate cookie cutter, many no longer play the vibrant role they played when there were more of them and they answered to more different kinds of owners.

In the case of his own newspaper, Poynter soon proved the validity of his observation to me that he could train ex-GIs to qualify as journeymen printers within a period of six months. Freed from the excesses of the I.T.U. laws, *The Times* and the *Independent* soon had a composing room working at an improved level of efficiency and at much lower expense.

This was only the beginning of the *St. Petersburg Times'* liberation from the extravagant wage and working conditions demanded by the craft unions. Within about six years, *The Times'* pressmen went the way of its printers, likewise in the context of an NLRB complaint. This one was based on a charge filed by the International Printing Pressmen and Assistants Union. It alleged that several named members of the union had been discharged and denied reinstatement because of "concerted activities with other employees for the purposes of collective bargaining" -- *i.e.*, a strike. There was an express allegation that Poynter -- then publisher, as well as editor, of *The Times* -- had "threatened its employees that it would close the plant before it would recognize the union."[31]

The scenario on this occasion was altogether different. There had been advance consultation with us concerning Poynter's every move before and during the strike. As events soon proved, there was not the semblance of a smoking gun. In fact, it was soon evident that the Board had abused its process in issuing the complaint.

The history of that proceeding was a defense lawyer's delight. In accordance with routine practice, the complaint was accompanied by a *"Notice of Hearing,"* which scheduled a hearing to begin sixty days later, on June 29, 1953. It was equally routine for all employer-respondents to move for a substantial adjournment of the hearing date. But not Nelson Poynter. Much to the amazement of the agency's trial attorney, there was no such motion. We filed Poynter's answer to the complaint and were prepared to go forward at the originally designated time. The hearing was nevertheless adjourned until October 19, 1953, by order of the Board's Regional Director in Atlanta.[32]

The succeeding events were a bureaucratic travesty. But for us it was fun and games. Soon after the adjournment an NLRB attorney called. He proposed a consent order so innocuous that it was laughable. No reinstatement, no back pay, not even a "cease and desist" order. The Board would settle for a notice to be posted on the pressroom bulletin board of *The Times* stating something to the effect that "The Times Publishing Company recognizes its obligations under the National Labor Relations Act." I could hardly believe my ears and immediately called Poynter to tell him the good news. He wouldn't accept the Board's terms. His instructions were to state his position to the Board in these words. "Either I'm right or I'm wrong. I'll meet them on the courthouse steps." When I relayed Poynter's response, it was the Board attorney's turn for disbelief, which he voiced with utter astonishment.

But the Board's incredulity was yet to peak. Soon after, while Poynter was in my office preparing for his testimony, the Board's attorney called again. This time he offered to settle for an order which required *The Times* to post an even more innocuous statement on the bulletin board. My recollection is that it read something like this: "that the Times Publishing Company supports the Constitution and laws of the United States." I gleefully asked the caller to hold a minute. I then turned to Poynter saying the Board had thrown in the sponge and recited its newest proposal. "It's no go," said Poynter. When I communicated the rejection to the caller, he asked, "How can he turn it down?" I replied: "He's here in my office, I'll put him on. You can ask him yourself." Poynter got on, listened a moment, and said: "I won't put anything on a *Times* bulletin board that I wouldn't put on its editorial page."

Soon afterward, we received the following order from the Board's Regional Director in Atlanta:

Order Withdrawing Complaint
And Closing Case

A Complaint in the above-styled case having been issued on April 29, 1953, by the undersigned Regional Director, and

The charging party, International Printing Pressmen & Assistants' Union of North America, having requested withdrawal of its charges in the matter, without prejudice, which request has been approved by the undersigned,

IT IS HEREBY ORDERED that the said complaint be, and it is hereby, withdrawn, and the case be, and it hereby is, closed.

DATED, Atlanta, Georgia this 31st day of July, 1953[33]

Such a disposition -- from complaint to final order in three months -- may have set an all-time NLRB speed record.

I question whether anybody but Nelson Poynter would have stuck so unflinchingly to his sense of right and wrong, no matter what the expense. As I mentioned earlier, he was a truly remarkable man.

There's another significant achievement to his credit. One evening as we walked to dinner, following a preparatory session for the anticipated hearing, he told me of an idea for a new publication. It would report exclusively on the nuts and bolts operations of Congress. He felt that media coverage of events on Capitol Hill was largely confined to sensational investigations -- *e.g.*, the McCarthy hearings -- and blockbuster legislation, such as the revolutionary pay-as-you-go income tax law. In his view, broader public awareness would improve legislative performance and responsiveness to the nation's needs. He had no expectation of profit. He thought the subscription list would consist mainly of libraries. How nice to know that Poynter's *pro bono* project bore profitable fruit. The idea became reality as the *Congressional Quarterly,* now the bible of every lobbyist in the country and a real moneymaker.

The esteem in which Nelson Poynter and the *St. Petersburg Times* were held by the journalism community was eloquently recited in a column by Mary McGrory, my all-time favorite newspaper columnist. It appeared in the *Outlook* section of the *Washington Post* for Sunday, March 11, 1990. It was entitled *"Raiders Versus Readers"* and addressed the attempted takeover of *The Times* by Robert Bass. After describing the reportorial responsibilities of the press, Ms. McGrory stated:

In other words, a newspaper, particularly one like the *St. Petersburg Times,* is not just a 7-Eleven to be knocked over by any wandering gunman. Its newsroom is an unlicensed journalism school, where beginning reporters learn their trade and what they need to know about journalistic ethics. Alumni of *The Times* have carried its high standards to larger newspapers all over the country.

Its previous owner, Nelson Poynter, a statesman of the newspaper trade, also founded an official school of journalism, the Poynter Institute, where good reporters are taught how to be better ones. Poynter also founded *Congressional Quarterly,* an indispensable, meticulous journal of fact. He believed passionately in local and independent ownership of newspapers. His nieces believed that they should be paid more than Barnes' predecessor [as head of the Institute] offered them for the 40 percent of the stock they inherited. They peddled their holdings on the open market. Enter Bass, who snapped them up.

I hope the people of St. Petersburg are following these events and have doped out what it is all about. I hope they value their newspaper. I remember the day *The Washington Star,* after more than 100 years of publication, breathed its last. As we left the last time, we went through the lobby, which was jammed with would-be buyers of the final edition. With me was Phil Gailey, who is now the *St. Petersburg Times* Washington bureau chief. He turned to the crowd and said, "Where were you when we needed you?"

I hope no one has to ask St. Petersburg that question any time soon.

The Poynter representation exemplified the uninhibited ease of working with Judge Arnold. It's impossible to overstate his inherent sense of equality with all people. No junior had to defer to his eminent stature in the profession. Working with him was just a lawyer-to-lawyer process -- as if he were a junior's contemporary. He vigorously debated legal issues on a man-to-man basis. I often responded in kind. During our preparation for the Poynter matter this was routine. One day we went at it especially hard until the Judge bellowed: "If you say that once more, I'll throw you right out of the window." As I left his office, I noticed that Marguerite O'Brien was pale and shaking. I asked, "What's the matter, Marguerite?" She answered: "I wasn't sure you would come out of there alive."

Of course, the way we worked together was no secret around the office. It was not only familiar, but a source of amusement. One of our partners, Reed Miller -- also gifted in verse -- along with a sly sense of humor -- was moved to memorialize the Arnold/Diamond

Debating Society by a poem. It seems worthy of quotation, so here
goes:

The Nite Before Brief Day
Or Norman's Revenge

Twas the night before brief day
When all thru the shop
Our Norman was spinning
Around like a top.

The galleys we proofed with great
    care and some dread
To split an infinitive might cost you
    your head.
All faces were grim -- no sign of
    a laugh
As we all settled down for the last
    paragraph.
When down in the round room there
    arose such a clatter
I sprang from my desk to see what was
    the matter.

Away to the stairwell I flew like a
    flash
Bent over the railing and batted
    a lash
For what to my sleepless eyes should
    appear
But Norman and Thurman -- the battle
    was near!

Twixt Norman the younger, so nimble
    and quick
And Thurman, the sage -- a hard man
    to lick
The Judge opened fire with a most
    awesome shout
But Norman, undaunted, cried "Wait,
    hear me out!"

Louder and louder their shouting became
As they screamed and berated each other
    in vain.
Ask Rogers! Call Charley! He's busy!
    Try another'n!
Get Freeman! Where's Fortas? Let's
    try it on McGovern!

Away to the top floor, dash down the
    hall
Let's hurry, yes hurry, we might catch
    them all.
As dry leaves that before the wild
    hurricane fly
When they meet with an obstacle, mount
    to the sky,
So thru the offices Norman he flew
Collecting his partners and associates,
        too.

And then in a twinkling, I heard on the
    stair
A chorus of voices that made blue the
    air.
As I pulled in my neck and was turning
    around
Down the stairs they came with a bound.

Our Norman, so natty, from head to his
    foot
Had Thurman's cigar ashes all over his
    suit.
The weight of the world was now on his
    back
A harried look -- his countenance black
His eyes . . . oh how bloodshot, his
    manner now nervous
But this is our Norman -- he really
    gives service.

His droll little mouth was drawn up
    like a bow

His five o'clock shadow beginning
  to show.
The stump of a pipe he held tight in
  his teeth
He looked so forlorn that it even moved
  Vieth.

Then Thurman, the elder, gave forth a
  stout howl
Let's change the last paragraph -- I'll
  do it right now.
He spoke not a word but went straight
  to his work
Revised Norman's language, then turned
  with a jerk
And laying his pencil down with a boom
Clipped his cigar and strode from the
  room.

Norman sprang in a cab, to the driver
  did shriek,
And off to the printers they went like
  a streak.
But I heard him exclaim, e'er he drove
  out of sight,
I'll change it on page proof if it
  takes me all night!

One day the Judge told me, "I like to work with you, Norman. When I holler at you, you holler right back. When I holler at "Hammy", tears come to his eyes." (Walton Hamilton was a gentle former law professor at Yale who had joined us on his retirement). Arnold was truly a one-of-a-kind human being. He had no predecessor and will never have a successor.

James J. Ling, the conglomerate king, who built a small electrical contracting business from scratch in 1947, into the giant LTV Corporation, listed 14th in the Fortune 500 list in 1969

CHAPTER TWENTY-TWO

THE SWING AT LING

James J. Ling was a legendary figure in the business and financial worlds, long before 1969, when the government challenged the acquisition of Jones & Laughlin Steel Corporation ("J&L") by his company -- Ling-Temco-Vaught ("LTV") -- in which we defended the transaction.[1] He was the leading proponent of the joinder of corporations engaged in wholly unrelated businesses, known as "conglomerate mergers". Such consolidations were as common in the business community during the 1960s as were leveraged buyouts -- LBOs -- in the 1980s. The theory was that the resulting diversification would insure sustained profitability. If the welfare of one component weakened, the strength of the others would offset the losses. Additionally, common top management supposedly promised a profitable synergy.

Jim Ling won the gold medal for conglomerate mergers in the 60s, much as Henry Kravis earned it for LBOs in the 80s. Through a series of eight conglomerate acquisitions, during the 1950s and 1960s, Ling had built a small, personally-owned electrical contracting business into the giant LTV corporation. In 1969 it did more than $3,750 billion in sales and ranked #14 on the Fortune 500 list. Ling accomplished all this before he was forty-seven years old.[2]

The authorized biography by Stanley H. Brown, sets out in great detail Ling's history up to 1972. It covers many surrounding facets of the LTV-J&L litigation which were previously unknown to me, although I led LTV's defense. First person quotations by Ling are of particular interest.

247

In June 1968, LTV had acquired 63% of the stock of J&L for $85 a share or $425 million, all in cash.[3] The funds for the tender offer were assembled by a group of Wall Street investment bankers headed by Goldman Sachs, and in particular its legendary Chairman, Gustave Levy, an LTV director and one time Chairman of the Board of Governors of the New York Stock Exchange.[4]

The merger precipitated a suit by the Antitrust Division of the Department of Justice to undo the transaction as a violation of the antimerger statute -- § 7 of the Clayton Act. In terms, that section prohibits one corporation from acquiring the stock or assets of another

> "where in any line of commerce . . . in any section of the country the effect . . . may be substantially to lessen competition, or to tend to create a monopoly."[5]

My involvement with the J&L case began on Saturday evening, March 22, 1969 at about 6:00 p.m., while I was watching the telecast of one of the semifinals of the NCAA basketball tournament (now known as the "Final Four"). My focus on the game was then interrupted by a call from Jack Landau, the Press Relations chief of the office of Attorney General Mitchell. He told me that the Antitrust Division would sue LTV to compel it to divest J&L. After passing the bad news to LTV's General Counsel, Dan Burney, I was instructed to set up the earliest possible meeting with Richard McLaren. He was the Nixon Administration's newly appointed Assistant Attorney General in charge of the Antitrust Division. The meeting was set for the afternoon of March 24.[6]

My first view of Ling occurred on the morning of that day when we met at my office to prepare for the session with McLaren. I took an instant liking to him. He seemed smaller than the "compact man standing six-foot-two and weighing between 190 and 200," described by Brown.[7] Friendly and unassuming, he radiated energy and a quiet dynamism, yet seemed wholly relaxed. I later learned that he was a qualified jet pilot who had flown LTV's falcon jets all over the United States and across the Atlantic.

I was pleased to learn from Brown's book that my liking for Ling was apparently reciprocated. As Brown quoted him:

> "Norm made quite an impression on me. He's a tough fighter, a real professional. I have no idea what a trial lawyer ought to be or what his

capabilities are, but I could see that he would acquit himself well in a courtroom."[8] (Exaggerated, but welcome).

It did not take me long to realize the full extent of Ling's celebrity. During our meeting on the morning of March 24, my secretary slipped me a note. It stated that my wife was parked outside and wondered whether she could come in and meet Mr. Ling. I haven't the faintest idea how she knew of him or how she learned that he was in my office. It was the only time she initiated a meeting with any of my clients. Anyway, when I mentioned her interest to Ling, he immediately said: "I'll go out and meet her." At that point I escorted him to my wife, Luna. He couldn't have been more gracious.

On March 24, 1969, the scheduled meeting with McLaren and his staff was held. Ling and Burney were present, along with three of us from Arnold & Porter. Ling had two objectives: first, to get the case tried as quickly as possible, without delaying tactics of any sort; second, to have McLaren acquiesce in LTV's pursuit of the outstanding tender offer for additional J&L stock until it acquired 81%. Under IRS rules that would permit LTV to file a consolidated tax return incorporating some $16 million of J&L's earnings.[9] Such a consolidation also permits the offset of gains and losses of the consolidated entities and avoids taxation of transactions among them.

Later that week -- on March 26 and 27 -- a written agreement was reached which allowed LTV to acquire up to 81% of J&L's stock and specified that the antitrust action would be filed no later than April 15, 1969.[10] As Brown emphasized, McLaren imposed harsh terms for his consent to the acquisition of the additional stock:

> ". . . As part of the agreement, LTV had to withdraw its representatives from the steel company's board of directors and from the stock-voting trust and not participate in the company's management. That meant that LTV had nothing to say about the operation of its largest single investment and its biggest management problem. . . ."[11]

This proved to be a real body blow. Its impact is evident from *Business Week*'s report of the effect of the antitrust action on J&L's operation and the state of the management of the company under its prior CEO -- Charles M. Beeghly -- who resigned when LTV acquired its controlling interest:

"Everyone is acting in good faith," says a former director sadly, "but J&L has been run like a company that isn't owned by anyone."

*   *   *

J&L has been a laggard in the steel industry's recent push for diversification into more profitable fields. Says a former employee sarcastically: "We could make acquisitions. Beeghly was not opposed. The only conditions were that the company we acquired had to have a lower price/earnings ratio than J&L, had to be in a commodity with a high capital investment, had to have a proprietary position in its industry, and had to be low in labor content because J&L was bad with labor. The only thing left after those conditions was the cement industry."[12]

If ever there was an unprecedented and meaningless antitrust case -- with destructive consequences -- it was *U.S. v. LTV*. Conventionally its purpose was to force LTV to divest J&L. But its ulterior objective was unprecedented: to reverse preexisting antitrust policy by extending the compass of Section 7 to reach purely "conglomerate" mergers. That provision had not previously been deemed applicable to such mergers. In financial parlance "Conglomerates" refers to corporations which are not actual or potential competitors or existing or prospective participants in a customer-supplier relationship. Reduced to it's essence, the theory of the case reflected the pure and simple hypothesis that big business is bad business -- the acrimonious charge often made by the major industrialists against Democratic antitrust administrations. But incredibly the attack was brought by a Republican administration.

As the case developed, neither the routine divestiture nor the innovative conglomerate objective was achieved. The case was pursued at huge cost to both LTV and the government without entry of an order divesting J&L or a decision sustaining McLaren's radical goal of extending Section 7 to comprehend conglomerate mergers.

Instead, *U.S. v. LTV* was settled on terms allowing LTV to divest two earlier acquired subsidiaries. One was a floor covering and cable manufacturer named Okonite and the other Braniff, an airline carrier which ultimately became bankrupt. According to his authorized biographer, Ling had been trying to sell those companies anyway, so the settlement terms represented a "neat coup" for him.[13] But in the process the case drove LTV into bankruptcy and ruined Ling's career.

In sum, the case proved a doctrinal zero. It devastated LTV; frustrated any hope of reviving J&L as a vigorous competitor in the steel industry; and prematurely derailed the Horatio Alger career of James J. Ling in the worlds of business and finance. An outsider unfamiliar with the folklore of American jurisprudence, could have read the record of *U.S. v. LTV* and rationally concluded that the case was "a tale told by an idiot, full of sound and fury, signifying nothing."

The genesis of *U.S. v. LTV* lay in McLaren's Congressional testimony before the House Ways and Means Committee on March 12, 1969, in which he outlined his intended enforcement policy:

Vigorous enforcement of section 7 -- by the Antitrust Division and the Federal Trade Commission -- has resulted in substantial elimination of large-company mergers of a horizontal and vertical nature.

But this decline has been much more than offset by a vast increase in the number and magnitude of *conglomerate mergers; that is, those in which the emerging firms are neither competitors, nor in a customer-supplier relationship, actual or potential.*

* * *

Now, my predecessors at the Antitrust Division took the position that purer forms of conglomerate mergers could not be reached under section 7 because, in their view, where merging firms are commercially unrelated, proof cannot generally be made of a reasonable likelihood of a substantial lessening of competition as called for by the act's provisions. They suggested that conglomerate mergers which threaten undue concentration of economic power should be dealt with through new legislation.

At the Senate Judiciary hearing on my confirmation in January, I stated that I was not persuaded that section 7 will not reach purer types of conglomerate mergers than have been dealt with by the courts thus far. In public statements since that time I have tried to warn businessmen and their lawyers that they cannot rely on the merger guidelines issued by my predecessors in this regard -- that we may sue even though particular mergers appear to satisfy those guidelines -- and that, to be safe, firms desiring to merge should learn our enforcement intentions by applying for a business review letter. I have also stated that I am by no means opposed to amendatory legislation, but I feel that the matter is too pressing to wait, *and we are willing to risk losing some cases to find out how far section 7 will take* us in halting the current accelerated trend toward concentration by merger and -- as I see it -- the severe economic and social dislocations attendant thereon.[14]

McLaren thus made a lottery of § 7. He was on record that he first spoke of challenging "purer types of conglomerate mergers" during his confirmation hearing before the Senate Judiciary Committee in January 1969. By the government's own admission, LTV had acquired control of more than 60% of LTV's stock in June of 1968, *i.e.*, long before the 1968 election[15] It had announced its intention to make a tender offer for the balance in December of 1968 -- before Nixon took office.[16] Consequently, the institution of the case not only reflected a 180° turn from all prior § 7 precedent, but it was confessedly retroactive and experimental.

The experiment represented an exhibition of indefensible government recklessness. From LTV's standpoint, it meant that public and private funds would be used for a judicial crap game, in which the company would be compelled to play against its will. McLaren was later rewarded by appointment as a federal judge.

In Ling's view, J&L represented the lawful acquisition of another business to be brought under the LTV umbrella for profit-making purposes, through a technique which he christened "Project Redeployment." This consisted of several steps.

The first was to obtain outside capital needed to acquire the target.[17] The next step was to divide such a company's assets into components consisting of product lines which could function as separately viable businesses. LTV would then transfer each such component to a newly formed corporation in exchange for 100% of its common stock. A minority interest in the new corporation would then be sold to the public. This made the stock retained by LTV a marketable security, valued not solely by its own earnings, but enhanced to some degree by the market's appraisal of the worth of shares in other companies engaged in a similar line of business.[18]

The classic example of a successful LTV "redeployment" was afforded by its acquisition of Wilson & Company -- the meatpacker -- with borrowed funds. It was subsequently divided into three separate corporations. One engaged in meatpacking, another in the manufacture of sporting goods, and the third in the production of chemicals and pharmaceuticals. In exchange for their common stock, LTV transferred a part of the acquired assets to each such corporation, plus a part of the debt incurred for the Wilson acquisition. The subsidiaries then paid off the debt by selling additional shares to the public. It was a tremendous financial success. As a result, LTV's stock surged to new highs, increasing the value of Ling's LTV shares to $70 million.[19]

LTV was to be Ling's ninth acquisition at an offering price of $85 per share in cash, compared with its market price of about $50 per share.[20] According to the Complaint in *U.S. v. LTV*, the total cash cost paid by LTV for 63% of the J&L stock it acquired in June 1968 was $428.5 million[21] Although the financial health of the company was plagued by its "ancient crowded Pittsburgh works", Ling intended to overcome it by the redeployment method.[22]

The announcement of the J&L acquisition pushed J&L's stock to 136.[23] However, as already noted, it proved Ling's personal undoing and, ultimately, LTV's and J&L's. As Brown stated:

> . . . when Ling recently observed "I won eight times and only lost once" he omitted the crucial fact that he parlayed his winnings brilliantly though dangerously, suffering his one loss at the end -- the Jones & Laughlin acquisition, a disaster that cost him almost everything but his nerve."[24]

The antitrust action precipitated the "disaster." While it dragged on, LTV's shares fell to $24 in late 1969 and by mid-1970 to 7 1/8.[25]

The progress and events of the litigation reflected a breach of faith on the part of the Department of Justice, including John Mitchell, the Attorney General, and the lawyers representing the Antitrust Division. From the beginning, Ling had emphasized his desire for the earliest possible final disposition of the case. The Justice Department ostensibly concurred.

I estimated that it could be tried by the fall of 1969 and decided early in 1970. With that timetable in mind, we had pushed the government to agree that a complaint would be filed no later than April 15. We had also agreed to the entry of a preliminary injunction on consent pending final judgment of the case. It incorporated the same hands-off terms prescribed by the agreement with McLaren, plus consent to the divestiture of J&L if the government prevailed.[26] That expedited the matter by dispensing with the need for the hearing otherwise required to support findings of fact and conclusions of law justifying a preliminary injunction.

Both the complaint and the preliminary injunction were filed on April 14, 1969 in the United States District Court for the Western District of Pennsylvania, sitting in Pittsburgh, the headquarters of J&L. Prior to the filing, I received an invitation to witness the assignment of the case to a trial judge -- also on April 14, 1969 -- at the office of the clerk of that court. I should have immediately understood that something out of order was afoot. But I didn't. It was the one and only time I ever received such an invitation, although I have defended a good many cases in both federal and local courts throughout the country.

I knew that my partner, Victor Kramer, had tried a merger case in Pittsburgh against the government.[27] After mentioning the invitation, I told him that his knowledge of the Pittsburgh court might be helpful, particularly if anything out of the ordinary occurred, and asked that he join me. (There was no added cost to LTV since we were to travel on one of its Falcon jets). He agreed. During the flight, he predicted that the case would be assigned to Judge Louis Rosenberg, who had ruled against him in the *Pennzoil* case and was notoriously pro-government.

En route, Vic told me more about Judge Rosenberg's history and peculiarities. He was a long-time Democratic worker who had been rewarded by appointment as Police Commissioner of Pittsburgh by Mayor David Lawrence, the entrenched Democratic boss of the city. When Rosenberg proved utterly inept as Commissioner, Lawrence had him "kicked upstairs" to his post as United States District Judge.

Vic also told me of Rosenberg's habit of opening every court day with a paean to the wonders of the United States -- notably the fact that an ordinary person could rise to the semi-deified position of United States District Judge, or words to that effect. Vic also warned me that it was very difficult to communicate with Rosenberg. He suggested that I retain Harold Schmidt, a local Pittsburgh attorney, who somehow seemed able to converse on the judge's peculiar wavelength.

Upon arriving at Pittsburgh, we went straight to the clerk's office and identified ourselves. The clerk was a cartoonist's caricature of a low-level politician, right down to the derby hat positioned on his coatrack. After welcoming us, he produced a large black book stating that we would now ascertain the identity of the judge who would try the LTV-J&L case. After ceremoniously turning a number of pages in the volume, the clerk announced -- as if greatly surprised -- "It's Luigi!" Vic was right. The Antitrust Division had handpicked Rosenberg. The invitation to attend was a transparent effort to cover up the fact -- a pure charade. (To comment peripherally: for a time, I could not reconcile Judge Rosenberg's strange orations on the bench with the lucidity of his written work. I later learned that it was the product of a very talented woman law clerk -- in her thirties -- whom he had retained from the day of his appointment).

Of course, there wasn't a thing I could do about the Antitrust Division's prearranged assignment of Judge Rosenberg. I consoled myself with the thought that the case would eventually be resolved by the Supreme Court, whatever its outcome in the trial court.

We did play one other card to hurry the case along. It involved a step unprecedented for an antitrust defendant. On April 23, 1969, we hand-delivered a letter to Attorney General Mitchell, requesting that he file a "certificate" with the court, stating "that in his opinion the case was of a general and public importance." Pursuant to an antitrust procedure then in force, but since repealed, such a certificate would require that the judge "cause the case in every way to be expedited."[28] By letter of May 2, 1969, Mitchell refused the "certificate", but pointed to the early judicial assignment of the case and noted that the trial decision could be appealed directly to the Supreme Court. His letter concluded:

> . . . Moreover, given the expressed desire of all parties for an expeditious hearing, we are confident that the court will cooperate fully to promote that objective.

> Accordingly, it is our view that the determination of this case can be expedited without resort to the unusual procedure of 15 U.S.C. § 28. We shall cooperate with you in every appropriate way to accomplish this goal.

Mitchell and the Antitrust Division turned out to be unvarnished prevaricators. They did just the opposite.

At this point, Ling was counting on my estimate that the trial would be finished in the fall of 1969, with the likelihood of a decision in early 1970. At first, this seemed a feasible schedule. The government had completed its pre-trial depositions of about a dozen LTV and J&L representatives, including Gustave Levy, by mid-July 1969, and was prepared to finish off with Ling. It did so in three sessions, from July 16 through 18, 1969. During the concluding session of Ling's deposition, the government's lead counsel, Paul Owens, stated: "We are trying to get to trial by December."[29]

In this day and age of client concerns about excessive legal fees, I can't help adding the following excerpt from Brown's book, quoting Ling's first person reaction to the setting of his deposition and further indicating the extent of his celebrity:

> Norm and some other lawyers sat at one long table and Paul Owens, the Justice Department's Chief lawyer on the case, sat at another table with his associates. There were maybe a couple of dozen other chairs in the room behind those tables, for whoever wanted to come and watch the proceedings. I am told that the spectators were mostly Arnold & Porter's young lawyers who wanted to take a look (Norm reassured me that we wouldn't be charged for their time) . . .[30]

At this point I have to interject an incident which illustrates Ling's unassuming character and, indeed, basic humanity. Prior to the depositions of Ling and Paul Thayer, President of LTV's subsidiary -- LTV Aerospace Corporation -- Dennis Lyons and I had gone to the company's headquarters to prepare them for their appearances. I worked with Thayer and a court reporter on one floor, while Dennis prepared Ling at the Chairman's office, with another reporter.

After some three or four hours, a messenger informed us that Dennis and Ling had finished and that we were invited to join them downstairs for a drink when we were through. In about a half an hour or so, Thayer and I finished up and went down to Ling's office. Our reporter left with us and took a seat outside Ling's office. When we entered, Ling asked "Where's your reporter?" I replied, "He's waiting outside", meantime noticing that a third person, apparently the reporter who had worked with Dennis and Ling, was in the room. Ling then remarked, "Maybe he'd like a drink"; then opened the door and invited our reporter to join the group. When the reporter was agreeable to a drink, Ling asked his preference and personally poured it for him.

After Ling's deposition, the Antitrust Division let the air out of LTV's balloon. Instead of working towards a trial in the upcoming fall, it cut loose with a further barrage of pre-trial discovery which foreclosed any such possibility. As Brown put it:

> But the Justice Department did not bring the case to trial in the fall. Instead, the antitrust people asked for a lot more information from LTV, so much in fact that somebody in the corporation figured it would take

a couple of hundred man-years or a million dollars' worth of payroll and computer time to come up with the answers. Word from Washington seemed to indicate that the government's lawyers were having trouble establishing a case against LTV on reciprocal dealings with suppliers and customers and on concentration of "control of manufacturing assets," in the words of the complaint . . .[31]

Moreover, between September 9 and December 18, 1969, the Antitrust Division noticed nine additional third party depositions. For some unfathomable reason, these included representatives of Westinghouse, Time, Inc., and General Motors.

In the fall of 1969, trial seemed a long way off. Meanwhile LTV was carrying a huge long-term, consolidated debt of $1.2 billion plus a $200 million increase in bank debt. Its interest obligations were monumental compared to the slumping earnings yielded by J&L.[32] Nor could LTV do anything about turning J&L around, since the voting trust ordained by the Antitrust Division kept control in the hands of J&L's management. LTV's hands were tried, although "the way the steel company was performing indicated that it was going to take some fancy redeploying by Ling and his financial people to get the debt-ridden machine running properly again."[33]

In mid-November 1969, Ling directed me to seek a settlement of the case by a decree divesting LTV subsidiaries, other than J&L.[34] I undertook the project despite my doubt that J&L's divestiture could be avoided. Ling had known better. He had ascertained through Attorney General Mitchell that the government wanted out of the case.[35] Ling's decision was prudent, particularly in light of the financial plight of LTV. In his final opinion, eventually rendered in June of 1970, Judge Rosenberg made this finding regarding the government's discovery program up to the start of the settlement negotiations:

> That discovery procedure up to the time when the settlement negotiations began required the turn over to the plaintiff of more than 36,000 pages of documents and the conduct of depositions totaling more than 4,400 pages of oral testimony transcript, while the defendants (sic) discovery was far from complete . . .[36]

After lengthy negotiations -- in which Dennis Lyons, Jim McAlee and I represented LTV -- the Antitrust Division agreed to a settlement acceptable to Ling. It gave LTV the option of divesting either J&L or two other subsidiaries -- Braniff Airways and Okonite Company. As previously noted, Ling wanted to sell them for his own reasons.

But the terms of the settlement did not sit well with Judge Rosenberg. Rather than sign the settlement, he noted that resolution of the case had to "accord with the purposes of Congress for the best interests of the public" and ordered "counsel to make suggestions for such procedure as will accommodate [that] requirement( )."[37]

Subsequently, on May 13, 1970, the judge ordered a hearing to consider whether the proposed settlement was in the public interest. In the process he revealed his own dissatisfaction with the settlement terms. In its edition of May 14, 1970, *The Pittsburgh Press* so reported under the following headlines:

HEARING SET FOR
LTV-J&L MERGER SUIT

*Federal Judge Here
Dissatisfied with Settlement*

Among other things, the article then reported:

"It was the Justice Department's first attempt to use the Clayton Antitrust Act to halt economic concentration in giant conglomerates, such as Dallas-based LTV.

The J&L stock owned by LTV has since been held in trust.

The settlement was to have been effective April 10, but final judgment had to be entered by Rosenberg.

He has balked at signing the order without adequate reassurances that the public interest was being protected by the settlement.

A joint legal statement by the government and the corporations filed Friday apparently did not appease the judge."

On May 17, 1970, at a meeting of LTV's board, Ling was demoted from CEO to president. No successor CEO was appointed. Instead, Robert Stewart III, a banker with no industrial experience, was named chairman and Ling as president.[38]

The lack of a CEO left what Brown terms "a power vacuum" at the top of LTV.[39] It was filled by Ling, who handled one of the last problems delaying effectuation of the settlement. This was the concern of the leaders of the Pittsburgh local of the United States Steel Workers about the members' job security at J&L. That problem was resolved when Ling wrote this to the union:

> You have my personal assurance that LTV has no plans to close the Pittsburgh works, or any other facility, or to decrease the hourly paid work force.

> *   *   *

> It is my intention to obtain an independent study of ways and means by which the efficiency and viability of the entire S&L operation -- including the Pittsburg works -- can be improved.[40]

Brown characterized this as "a rather sweeping commitment considering that the Pittsburgh works was one of J&L's chief problems"[41] Nevertheless, it got the job done. The judge signed the order the following week -- to be precise on June 10, 1970.[42]

But Brown and Ling were surely unaware about the circumstances under which Judge Rosenberg signed the order. The judge had been adamantly opposed to the takeover of J&L by an outsider -- *i.e.*, "the cowboy."[43] His principal concern was it would mean the loss of pensions and jobs to the Pittsburgh steelworkers.[44]

What ensued when Judge Rosenberg was presented with the agreed final judgment by Jim McAlee and me for Arnold & Porter, and John Fricano for the Antitrust Division, was probably unique in the judicial history of the United States and maybe in the entire annals of jurisprudence anywhere, anytime. When Fricano presented the judgment for his signature, the judge bolted from his chambers to the elevator bank. Fricano ran right behind him, physically grabbed Rosenberg before he could enter an elevator, wrestled him back to his chambers and literally forced him to sign the document.

On July 8, 1970, Ling was removed as President of LTV.[45] After that, the company struggled for some sixteen years before filing for reorganization under Chapter 11 of the Bankruptcy Act. As the *Wall Street Journal* reported:

LTV Corp., the one-time Dallas high-flyer, filed for protection from creditor lawsuits under Chapter 11 of the federal Bankruptcy Code, becoming the largest industrial concern to make such a filing.

The concern, which hasn't had a profitable year since 1981, said it concluded in the past two weeks that it wouldn't be able to meet future obligations, including certain big debt and pension payments. It cited deteriorating operating results in its *steel* and energy operations, a drying-up of credit and reduced liquidity.[46]

*   *   *

In my opinion, the LTV case represented an irresponsible use of the Antitrust Division's authority. The fact is that LTV's acquisition of J&L could only have made it a more competitive factor in the steel industry.   While its own management had been lethargic and disinterested and its Pittsburgh mill was obsolete, J&L did have state of the art mills at Cleveland and Aliquippa, Pennsylvania -- northwest of Pittsburgh -- and a new mill at Hennepin, Illinois.[47] Who's to say that Ling's flair for innovation, his imagination and his energy would not have rejuvenated J&L's steel operations and enhanced competition within the steel industry?

As it turned out, the case was an exercise in futility. To my knowledge, no purely conglomerate merger has ever been successfully prosecuted to judgment after trial on the merits. It seems safe to characterize the notion that a purely conglomerate combination violates the Clayton [Anti-Merger] Act as a fleeting antitrust anachronism. The epilogue of McLaren's ill-starred experiment might accurately read that Ling was struck by a hit-and-run bureaucrat.

I must add my disappointment at the debacle caused by the government's delay. Had it kept its word, I'm convinced we'd have promptly won. We had a top-notch staff. Dennis Lyons, Jim McAlee, Gerry Stern and Pat Macrory were on our team.

CHAPTER TWENTY-THREE

WHAT GOES AROUND COMES AROUND

Paul Porter was full of maxims -- seemingly one for every conceivable context. I'm not sure whether he originated all or any of them. But I heard them first from him and they were always exquisitely pointed to the subject at hand.

But one he especially emphasized was "never score on a Member of Congress." Paul himself proved that even his maxims -- like all other precepts -- are subject to exception. He scored a direct hit on a sanctimonious member of the House of Representatives -- Charles Wolverton of New Jersey -- during a highly charged legislative hearing.

The context was the post World War II scramble for television licenses from the Federal Communications Commission (the "FCC"). The lure of potential profits from this new medium excited enormous interest. There were multiple applications to the FCC for each available TV channel in every community. The Commission held competitive hearings to determine the successful licensees. The stakes were so high that *ex parte* approaches to influence the votes of the seven commissioners became a tactic routinely used by the various applicants. The FCC's rules were silent on the subject.

The frenzied competition for the licenses provoked hearings before the Subcommittee on Legislative Oversight of the House Committee on Interstate and Foreign Commerce.[1] Its members included Charles Wolverton of New Jersey. During the hearings Wolverton repeatedly moralized about the impropriety of the *ex parte* representations to individual commissioners. His sanctimony took center stage to the point where he attracted widespread media coverage.

Before the hearings were over, Paul caught the pious Wolverton with his hand in the same cookie jar as the applicants the Congressman had been denouncing. Specifically, Paul disclosed that Wolverton -- using his official position -- had asked the Commission, in writing, to prefer one of his constituents by granting its application in knowing derogation of the Commission's rules.

In both the FCC and in the Congressional hearings Paul represented Frank Katzentine -- a radio licensee -- who had applied for the license to operate Channel 10 in Miami. Among the other applicants for that channel was Ted Baker, President of National Airlines, then a major north-south carrier on the east coast. *Ex parte* representations on his behalf from numerous influential sources were notorious. Katzentine had responded in kind.

While Katzentine was in the witness chair, Wolverton intoned, among other things:

> During the evening I had given considerable thought to just what can be done about this situation that has been shown to exist.

*   *   *

> I do not believe that you would have ever thought of appearing before the judge of a Federal court in any such backstage surreptitious manner as we have found exists with respect to this particular Commission.

> Why can we not have that same attitude toward our commissions that exercise judicial powers as we have toward our courts of justice?

* * *

> Now, do you know, and maybe you can consult with someone who would know, whether the Federal Communications Commission has ever adopted a code of ethics?

> MR. KATZENTINE: If so, I do not know about it. They have established a formal criterion -- Mr. Porter is a member of the FCC bar. He ought to know, I don't know, sir.

> MR. WOLVERTON: Maybe he could advise you.

MR. KATZENTINE: Mr. Porter said that as far as he knows there are no rules or regulations with respect to ex parte representations to the Commissions (sic).

MR. WOLVERTON: That is a bit discouraging to me.

The Interstate Commerce Commission, which was brought to my attention by another newspaperman last night, has adopted a code of ethics . . .

*   *   *

Under the heading "Standard of ethical conduct in courts of United States to be observed," then these words --

these canons are in furtherance of the purpose of Commission's rules of practice which enjoin all persons appearing in proceedings before it to conform as nearly as may be the standards of ethical conduct required of practitioners before the courts of the United States.

Attempts to exert political influence on the Commission.

Under that heading is this canon:

It is unethical for a practitioner to attempt to sway the judgment of the Commission by propaganda or by enlisting the influence or intercession of Members of the Congress or other public officers or by threats of political or personal reprisal.

* * *

Finally under the heading "Private communications to the Commission":

To the extent that it sits in a quasi-judicial capacity, it is grossly improper for litigants directly or through any counsel or representative to communicate privately with the Commissioner, representative or examiner or other representative of the

Commission about a pending case or to argue privately the merits
thereof in the actions of their adversaries or without notice to
them.[2]

*   *   *

[MR. WOLVERTON:] Now I only want to say in conclusion, Mr.
Chairman, I had intended and I went to a great length in this last
evening in going through the record, but I will pass over it for the time
being, by merely saying that I was surprised with the testimony in the
case with reference to Judge Anderson and that side of it, which might
be termed the National Airline's side, but with the testimony that was
given yesterday, and the letters that were introduced that show such a
widespread use of outside influence as has been shown by this witness
in his endeavors as he terms it, to present the merits of his case, is so
strikingly wrong that it shocks me, and moreover, I am certain that it
shocks most any person who has ideals of morality in the practice of
law.[3]

*   *   *

MR. WOLVERTON. I am merely drawing attention to the fact that
as you have corroborated and as you and others have stated the facts in
the case, it has developed that you did utilize the services, I would say
of at least 15 individuals in one way or another to bring it to the
attention of the Commission and not on the basis of a hearing but on the
basis of friendships and contacts of one kind and another, that is the sort
of thing I am objecting to.[4]

The quoted extracts are only part of Congressman Wolverton
preachments. Unwittingly, however, he was digging himself into a
deeper and deeper hole. Following one of Wolverton's sermons Paul
applied another of his maxims. This is it: "If you're going to cut off
a cat's tail, do it at the stump in one fell swoop; if you do it inch by
inch, you'll always have a sore tail and a mad cat." Instead of a
lengthy presentation about the general use of off-the-record
representations by all applicants, Paul demolished Wolverton by a
single stroke. He produced an exchange of correspondence between the
Congressman and the Commission. In a letter of March 30, 1953 the
Congressman had asked the Commission to grant special treatment to
a constituent who was seeking a license for Channel 17 in Camden,
New Jersey. Specifically, after calling attention to withdrawal of a

competing application by Westinghouse on March 26, 1953, he requested the Commission to waive its seven day waiting period before acting on any application, even if apparently unopposed, by granting the license on April 1.[5] In so requesting, Congressman Wolverton expressly acknowledged his awareness of the seven day rule, stating:

It is my understanding that you have a "practice" requiring an application for a "passed over" city to be "in the clear" for at least 1 week before it will be acted upon by the Commissioners.[6]

The Commission's reply of April 16 to the Congressman stated in part:

. . . This is with reference to your letter of March 30, 1953 concerning the application of South Jersey Broadcasting Co. (BPDT-1522) for a permit to construct a new television broadcast station on Channel 17 in Camden, New Jersey. In your letter you requested that the above application be considered by the Congressman on April 1, 1953.

* * *

The South Jersey application first became eligible for processing on March 26, the date Westinghouse requested dismissal of its competing application. To have taken action on the application on April 1 would have been contrary to the policy which the Commission has been following of not considering an application unless it has been in noncompetitive status for at least 7 days.

In this connection it should be pointed out that in two cases pending before the Commission, formal protests have been filed pursuant to section 309 (c) of the Communications Act of 1934, as amended, respecting questions concerning the legality of the Commission's action in granting applications without hearing where the noncompetitive status existed for only 7 days.

The facts set forth above were considered by the Commission when your letter was brought to its attention on April 1.

However, in light of the above facts, the Commission concluded that action by it on that day with respect to the South Jersey application would constitute a deviation from the procedure previously followed and might raise serious questions concerning the legality of any such action. As you may know on April 6 1953, a competing application for channel

17 was filed by Patrick Joseph Stanton, the licensee of a standard broadcast station in Philadelphia.

I regret that the Commission was unable to comply with your request and trust that you will understand the basis for the Commission's judgment in light of the facts outlined above.[6]

In the ensuing colloquy Paul demonstrated his finesse in delicately fencing with a highly embarrassed legislator -- whose acute discomfort was intensified when the national press delightedly and prominently reported his humiliation. More particularly, immediately after reading the correspondence into the record, Paul explained his purpose, to the Congressman's utter dismay. In Paul's words:

[PORTER] Mr. Wolverton, I contend that there is absolutely no impropriety in any Congressman even though this case was in contested status, making that kind of representation on behalf of a constituent.

I insist equally that my client and the Senators who interested themselves in his behalf are not subject to criticism of the actions that they took, and I brought that to the committee's attention, Mr. Chairman, solely for the purpose of illustrating that this is not uncommon practice.

MR. WOLVERTON. Why did you select my letter to prove your point?

MR. PORTER.   Because, sir, I thought that would be an unimpeachable source as to what was occurring at the time.

MR. WOLVERTON. I wish I could agree with you that was your reason. Did you inquire yourself for that letter? And if not, how did it come to your attention?

MR. PORTER.   It was in the public reference room at the Commission, Mr. Wolverton.

MR. WOLVERTON. What was that?

MR. PORTER. In the license files and the public reference room at the Commission.

MR. WOLVERTON. Who advised you to look in that particular file?

MR. PORTER. Nobody advised me to, sir.

MR. WOLVERTON. Why did you do it?

MR. PORTER. Because I felt that it might produce the results which I have just read into this record, sir.

MR. WOLVERTON. What results?

MR. PORTER. That you as well as many Members of Congress have made ex parte representations in contested proceedings on behalf of a constituent.

MR. WOLVERTON. Did you make an inquiry with respect to any other Member of Congress?

MR. PORTER. No, sir, I did not.

MR. WOLVERTON. Why did you select me?

MR. PORTER. Because, sir, I thought if you had indulged on behalf of a constituent in this practice, it could not be questioned as to the propriety as far as those who intervened on behalf of my client are concerned.[7]

*   *   *

More of the same followed with Wolverton repeatedly asking: "Why was I selected instead of any other member of this committee." Meanwhile, Porter kept insisting that Congressman Wolverton had been chosen because "I felt that your stature was such that nobody could challenge the propriety of this practice."[8]

The reaction of the press ended Wolverton's career as the avenging knight on a white horse engaged in slaying the malevolent transgressors of public morality. The front page of the *New York Times* of Saturday, March 22, 1958, highlighted Wolverton's stumble with the following headlines:

INFLUENCE CRITIC LISTED
AS SEEKER OF ACTION BY F.C.C.

Wolverton Agrees He Wrote '53 Letter Asking Quick Approval in TV Case

This was the front page headline of the *New York Herald Tribune* for the same date:

LETTER BACKFIRES ON F.C.C. PROBER

Rep. Wolverton Urged Agency In
'53 to Act on Camden TV Channel

The same event was also front page news in *The Washington Post* and *Times Herald* of March 22, 1958:

WOLVERTON FCC PLEA REVEALED BY PORTER

To Congressman Wolverton's everlasting humiliation, he became a caricature of self-pronounced self-righteousness. He had learned the truth of the street smart adage: "What goes around comes around."

CHAPTER TWENTY-FOUR

THE PACKRAT PAYOFF AND "MR. FRED"

As any lawyer versed in litigation knows, the outcome of any legal proceeding can hang on peculiar quirks. A strange impulse proved our salvation in a brief joust with the National Production Authority ("NPA"). That agency regulated the distribution and use of various "controlled" materials during the Korean War. In the late summer of 1951, Federated Department Stores -- a major client -- had decided to build a chain of seven middle class stores modeled on the Sears type. They were to be named "Fedway" and located in the southwest.

Before construction could begin, the NPA regulations intervened. Federated's Chairman was Fred Lazarus, Jr. -- known to all as "Mr. Fred". Many regarded him as the greatest retail genius of his time. He personally asked Abe Fortas to submit an analysis of the legalities governing the procurement and use of the components needed for the building program. Fortas asked me to study the regulations and provide a concise written analysis -- a somewhat complex assignment.

After careful review of the outstanding NPA regulations and press releases, I drafted a document reciting my understanding of their meaning as applied to construction projects. I then arranged to meet with one Henry Heymann, Counsel, NPA's Facilities and Construction Branch. He read the paper and said it was accurate except for a few minor items. I don't know what motivated me to ask him if he would note the corrections on my document. He acquiesced and made the corrections in ink. Nor do I know why I didn't do a clean copy, with his changes incorporated, instead of retaining the original with his handwritten notations. But that's what happened. It sure paid off later.

The gist of my analysis was that if Federated could obtain the needed materials by October 1, 1951, it could proceed with construction. In mid-September 1951, Abe and I met with Mr. Fred at the Mayflower Hotel to advise him of our conclusions (after which

269

I confirmed by letter). No sooner had I completed my statement than Mr. Fred was on the phone to various Federated personnel directing the immediate procurement of all necessary building personnel and materials.

Proceeding in accordance with our advice, Federated promptly commenced work on the construction projects. Not long afterward, during the winter of 1951-52, a number of the contractors engaged in the work began reporting on-premises interrogations by government people. These involved detailed questions about acquisition of the materials being used for the structures. Fortas and I decided that Federated was on the NPA's hot seat. We agreed that I should promptly interview each of the sources of the reports to get the low-down on what was going on. I took off immediately and stalked every move the government people had made. It wasn't fun. All were located in the dusty, red clay country around Houston, where the first Fedways were under construction. I returned with a complete report of what was clearly a compliance investigation, with potentially severe penalties if Federated were found in violation of the NPA controls.

Within two or three days, NPA Compliance blew the whistle by a hard-nosed letter, followed by a press release, claiming that Federated had violated the agency's regulations on controlled materials. According to the grapevine, it was to be the prized and widely publicized target of the NAP enforcement program. Fortas and I immediately arranged to meet with Rintels, head of NPA Compliance.

My strange notion of having the NPA attorney, Heymann, correct my memorandum paid a big dividend. Its impact is best indicated by our file copy of a letter, dated March 18, 1952, from Abe Fortas to Ralph Lazarus, Federated's Executive Vice President, reporting on our meeting with Messrs. Rintels and Ganse of NPA Compliance:

> After the review of the individual transactions, Mr. Rintels brought into the meeting Mr. Henry Heymann, counsel to the Construction Controls Division, for the purpose of establishing whether he had actually approved a written opinion submitted for his review by Norman Diamond on September 17, 1951. This memorandum outlined our understanding of the effect of the outstanding NPA regulations with specific reference to the circumstances under which a project might be undertaken after October 1 without a controlled materials allotment. (Our letter of September 17, 1951 to Mr. Fred reflects this memorandum as reviewed by Mr. Heymann.) Mr. Heymann stated that he was deluged with meetings about that time and could not remember

the specific conference with Diamond. However, he agreed that several corrections on the memorandum were in his own handwriting. Furthermore, Mr. Heymann conceded that the memorandum, as corrected, reflected the thinking of his unit at that time. He stated also that it had not been considered until a considerably later time that the inventory regulations applied to construction. At this point, Rintels said that he didn't believe Heymann could have sneaked into Diamond's office and inscribed the notations on the memorandum. Rintels commented further that in view of Heymann's statement, he did not see how the inventory regulations had any bearing on the procurement activities in the Fedway operation.

NPA terminated the matter by a face-saving press release, of no concern to Federated.

As I think back on my suggestion to Heymann and his acquiescence I'm reminded of the cliche that "It's better to be lucky than good." There was no similar incident in all my years of practice, which date back to 1939.

It is impossible for me to write about Federated without expressing my personal admiration and affection for Mr. Fred. He was short, a bit on the stocky side, round in face and always smiling. He suffered from palsy but it didn't seem to disturb him. He was always friendly toward me when we occasionally met on my many trips to Federated headquarters.

On one such trip, I was asked to join Abe to attend a board of directors meeting at the company's headquarters. As I recall it, our purpose was to explain proposed amendments to the Fair Labor Standards Act, pending in 1961. Their purpose was to subject retail employees for the first time to the minimum wage and overtime requirements of the Fair Labor Standards Act.

In discussions with Mr. Fred, we had advised him that the amendments would likely pass notwithstanding the objections of virtually the entire retail industry. The opposition included the two major trade associations whose membership included all high grade department stores, including Federated. Their representatives were especially active and vociferous in voicing the industry's objections.

Mr. Fred agreed with our recommendations that the practical course would be to try to ensure that the amendments recognized the special conditions affecting certain employees of retail department stores. The object would be to achieve the adoption of statutory language which would take account of them. After acquainting us with the problems, Mr. Fred authorized us to undertake a low key effort to get the job done in Congress.

We so reported to the Board of Directors, which acquiesced. Incidentally, I was truly impressed by the businesslike way Mr. Fred conducted the meeting. The Board included a number of prominent outside directors. He kept their comments and inquiries strictly on target, but always tactfully.

As the meeting broke up, Mr. Fred invited me to attend the traditional Directors' dinner, which followed its meetings. Meantime, I lost touch with Abe who had evidently been engaged in a discussion with one of the Board members. When I arrived back at the hotel, where we had shared a room, Abe was changing clothes and said: "I'll see you back in Washington tomorrow. I've got to go to the Board of Directors' dinner tonight." I must confess that I enjoyed replying: "If you'll wait a little bit, Abe, I'll be along with you. Mr. Fred invited me to the dinner." I had a feeling that this deflated Abe just a little bit or, perhaps more accurately, raised his appraisal of my standing with Federated.

The major responsibility for achieving the desired changes in the pending amendments was delegated to me. To that end, I met with the staffs of the House and Senate Labor Committees to draft amendments addressed to special problems of three classes of retail employees: They concerned overtime pay specifications for employees compensated by commissions; exemption for assistant buyers who mainly performed exempt managerial functions but also devoted part of their time to other work; and the application of less stringent minimum wage requirements for full-time students who were employed in retail establishments.

In the course of this undertaking, I met personally with Chairman Adam Clayton Powell of the Committee on Education and Labor of the lower House, who proved very helpful. I may also have met with one or two members of the Senate's Committee on Labor and Public Welfare. But in major part I worked with the committee's staffs.

Our efforts were successful. The bill was enacted on May 5, 1961.[1] The special retail exceptions remain in force to this day.[2] Incidentally, it was the only time, in my memory, that I registered as a lobbyist.

Another of Mr. Fred's impressive talents was his ability to stay on top of the numerous legal problems we handled for Federated. We rarely discussed them with him, but he somehow knew even their minor features. He'd occasionally spot me at Federated's headquarters and recall an incident in one of the matters we had litigated or negotiated for it. This was a source of constant wonder to me, considering his tremendous merchandising responsibilities.

One such incident happened a good while after Mr. Fred had retired. He still maintained an office at the Federated Offices. Having evidently heard that I was in the building, he asked that I drop by. Of course, I was happy to do so. After we chatted a bit, he said: "Remember the trouble we had with that Baltimore department store in the AMC case?" That astonished me. What he referred to was an unorthodox procedure we had followed in a major matter which ultimately led to the dismissal of a government complaint against Associated Merchandising Corporation ("AMC"). The members, technically stockholders, were leading department stores for which AMC performed a variety of activities important to their business, particularly research projects. Federated was its largest member.

AMC also operated a group-buying subsidiary on behalf of its members, called "Aimcee Wholesale Corporation." The FTC had charged them and each AMC member with violating Section 2(f) of the Robinson Patman Act,[3] by inducing various suppliers to grant them pricing favors which substantially injured their competitors.[4] We represented Federated.

The matter was serious. It affected the competitive capability of every store operated by AMC members. By far the greatest number were Federated establishments.

After the complaint was filed, we were advised that the Commission counsel proposed to call hundreds of witnesses in support of the complaint. We invoked the Commission's rule allowing respondents to take pre-hearing depositions of all such persons and others in order to examine them concerning evidence relevant to the complaint or which might lead to such evidence. Our notices of deposition were accompanied by subpoenas which demanded related documents, likewise permitted by the FTC's rules of procedure.

The Hearing Examiner initially authorized us to proceed. However, on motion of the Commission counsel, he reversed himself. The Commission then denied our appeal from his ruling. This moved us to recommend a suit to sue to enjoin the hearing on the ground that we had been denied the right to take depositions in violation of the Commission's own rules, the Administrative Procedure Act and the Due Process clause of the Fifth Amendment to the Constitution.

In proposing to seek such an injunction, we had in mind the same novel strategy which had proved successful in an FTC matter involving another client, the Kroger Co. -- namely, suit against the agency's hearing officer in his home district, as described in the preceding CHAPTER EIGHTEEN, *INDECENT EXPOSURE*. As there noted, under the legislation then in force, the FTC itself could be sued only in the District of Columbia federal court where most of the judges had a strong pro-government bias.

We soon ascertained that the hearing officer in the AMC case was a resident of Maryland. That meant we could sue him in the United States District Court in Baltimore to enjoin the hearing, which we did.[5]

It was a most inviting prospect. It will be recalled that in CHAPTER SIXTEEN. *"THE DISCOUNTER"*, we had enjoyed good fortune in two cases before that bench, which sat only in Baltimore. The judges in those matters -- Chesnut and Watkins -- were exceptionally able. It was common knowledge that the Chief Judge of that Court, Rozell Thomsen, was also extraordinarily competent. My secret hope was that we might draw him for the AMC case.

That was the context of one of Mr. Fred's amazing revelation of his conversance with Federated's legal problems. I still can't forget his reference to the recalcitrant Baltimore member of AMC.

It was named Hutzler Brothers. The store of that name was located in Baltimore. For some reason, the Hutzler management thought that its business would be adversely affected by publicity concerning the law suit. I never could understand it.

At any rate, Hutzler's resistance was soon overcome and suit for an injunction to prevent prosecution of the proceeding was filed against William K. Jackson, the Hearing Officer.

The Baltimore offensive worked perfectly. Chief Judge Thomsen took personal charge of the case. As anticipated, the first move in the matter was a motion by the FTC to dismiss the case on the ground that the case should have been filed against the Commission itself in the District of Columbia federal court. For this purpose, it claimed that the Commission was "an indispensable party" -- meaning that the case therefore could proceed only if the agency was a defendant and could be heard only in that court. I distinctly remember the opening line of the argument by Harold Rhynedance, the FTC's Assistant General Counsel, and Judge Thomsen's instant reply:

Mr. Rhynedance: I don't know what we are doing in this Court.

Judge Thomsen: I don't happen to believe that every case against the federal government has to be tried in Washington, D.C.

Rhynedance next made a hardship plea. He urged that if the FTC could be sued any place but Washington, depositions could be held all around the country and stretched out *ad infinitum*. Authorization of such proceedings, he asserted, would disable the agency from conducting its business efficiently for lack of sufficient time and manpower.

Judge Thomsen then threw a hard fast ball right past Rhynedance. Depositions are pre-trial oral examinations customarily attended only by lawyers for the parties. However, Judge Thomsen offered to consider the merits of each Notice of Deposition, to preside at each one in person and to conduct each of them at a time and place agreeable to the Commission lawyers. This was sweet music to me and Murray Bring, who provided invaluable assistance in our prosecution of the matter.

The Commission was now disabled from using its customary tactic of grinding down respondents to its complaints by one-sided proceedings. Instead, Judge Thomsen had confronted it with the necessity of facing formidable opposition.

That was the end of the case. The Commission dismissed its complaint.[6] The Hearing Officer, Jackson, then filed a motion requesting dismissal of the court case as moot -- *i.e.*, academic -- in light of the dismissal of the administrative proceeding. Chief Judge Thomsen granted that motion, without prejudice to our right to refile our complaint against the FTC, if it renewed its charges.[7]

Chief Justice Earl Warren

CHAPTER TWENTY-FIVE

JUSTICE ICARUS

On July 28, 1965, Abe Fortas was appointed to the Supreme Court by President Johnson. After speedy confirmation by the Senate, he took his seat on the Court at the beginning of the October 1965 term. While serving as an Associate Justice, he taught a six-week summertime seminar at the Washington College of Law at American University on subjects described as "law and contemporary society". His compensation was $15,000, almost 40% of his judicial salary of $39,500.[1] It represented one-half of a total of $30,000 raised by Paul Porter from five of Abe's former clients and friends, all prominent businessmen. The balance was applied to administrative costs.[2]

On June 26, 1968, LBJ nominated Fortas as Chief Justice, following the resignation of Earl Warren, to take effect as soon as his successor qualified.[3] The nomination failed in the Senate. It was blocked by a filibuster which succeeded for several reasons, drawing some support from both parties. One was the unpopularity of the Vietnam War. That fueled the opposition of Republicans who hoped to win the presidential election in 1968 and thereby the prerogative of appointing the next Chief Justice. Another was the hostility of conservative southern democrats to the Warren Court's liberal decisions with respect to racial discrimination, the rights of criminal defendants and the scope of civil liberties. A third factor, in my mind was the exposure, at a congressional hearing, of the source of his compensation for the seminar.[4] With Johnson hamstrung as a lame duck President, those factors generated the successful Senate filibuster. Abe consequently requested withdrawal of his nomination.[5] He had come as close to the apex of our judicial system, as Icarus had to the sun in attempting to

277

escape from Crete. But as the heat had melted Icarus' wings of wax, I feel that Abe's flight had been afflicted by an incurable monetary infirmity, which lent crucial support to those opposed to his confirmation.

Unhappily before another year had passed, Abe's troubles on the Court would worsen to the point of forcing his resignation for suspected violation of law, however unfounded the suspicion. He was the first and only Justice ever to endure that disgrace.

In my mind, it was a needless result of Abe's supreme self-assurance which impelled him to deal with the difficulty on his own. As I see it, he thereby exposed himself to the groundless, but widely circulated, belief that during his service on the bench he had unlawfully accepted fees for providing legal advice to Louis Wolfson, one of his former clients. After Abe's appointment to the bench, Wolfson -- a wealthy industrialist -- had twice been convicted of securities fraud, a felony for which he had been sentenced to prison.[6]

Before summarizing the events which caused the debacle, let me state my conviction that had Thurman been asked to represent Abe, the Justice's status and reputation would have been salvaged. As it was, the Nixon Administration, in particular Attorney General Mitchell and his subordinates, were able to bluff Abe into resigning. This fulfilled the purpose of their intervention in the matter -- to open the way for a Republican successor to Abe's seat on the Court.

In fact, following his appointment, Abe's contacts with Wolfson were entirely within bounds. Their only communication of even a remotely legal nature concerned Wolfson's fruitless plea on the eve of his imprisonment, that Abe enlist LBJ's support of a pardon from Nixon.[7] Abe declined to do so.

What ultimately proved the *coup de grace* was Abe's acceptance of a fee of $20,000 in January of 1966 for agreeing to act as a consultant to the Wolfson Family Foundation -- a charitable organization dedicated to helping all kinds of "do-good" causes.[8] It was the only payment he ever received and was returned in December of that same year. But Abe forfeited the opportunity for an effective and truthful explanation by his misleading statements about his financial arrangement with the Foundation, when it first came to light.

These were the circumstances which precipitated the tragedy: In 1968 rumors about a questionable relationship between Fortas and Wolfson began circulating. There were some intimations that William Lambert, an investigative reporter for *Life Magazine*, would do a piece on it. That had some substance. At the instance of a rank and file government employee, Lambert had begun to investigate the matter.[9] Abe discussed the subject with Ramsey Clark, LBJ's Attorney General. When Abe mentioned that he had returned the $20,000 to the Foundation, Clark suggested that communication of that fact to Lambert would likely resolve the problem. Abe chose Paul Porter to relay that information to Lambert.[10]

Lambert was unimpressed by Porter's statement that due to the press of his court duties, Abe had been unable to find time for the Foundation's work, had therefore returned the funds, and consequently no taxable income was involved. Instead, Lambert's investigative instinct was intrigued by the delay in returning the fee until December, after Wolfson had twice been indicted.[11]

However Lambert believed that he needed further confirmation before going with the story. Meantime, the Department of Justice, particularly Will Wilson, head of the Criminal Division, was gunning for Fortas, based on a score that he wanted to settle with LBJ. As the rumors ballooned, Wilson met with Lambert, but failed to provide him with satisfactory confirmation. At that point, Wilson brought the matter to the attention of Attorney General John Mitchell of the Nixon Administration, the new Attorney General.[12]

Soon afterward, a Justice Department official -- apparently lacking actual proof -- nevertheless confirmed the fact that Fortas had accepted the $20,000 for one year's work on Wolfson's behalf. That satisfied Lambert who broke the story in *Life's* issue of May 5, 1969.[13]

Featuring two large pictures of Fortas and Wolfson, the article was entitled: "Fortas of the Supreme Court a Question of Ethics" [and] subtitled "The Justice . . . and the Stock Manipulator." Among other things, Lambert reported that Fortas had received a single fee of $20,000 in January of 1968 and had kept it until December of that year. The article asks: "why would a man of his legal brilliance and high position do business with Louis Wolfson, a well-known corporate stock manipulator known to be under federal investigation." The innuendo of the article was that Wolfson had paid Fortas to provide him with legal advice -- prohibited conduct for a federal judge. Lambert further suspected that Fortas had returned the money because of Wolfson's subsequent indictment.[14]

Following *Life's* publication, Fortas issued a brief statement to the press. In it he denied that he had served Wolfson in any legal capacity while serving on the Court or that he had accepted anything from Wolfson or his Foundation. However he admitted that he had been "tendered a fee," which he had returned when he could find no time for the Foundation's affairs. There was no mention, however, of the actual arrangement which provided an annual payment of $20,000 to him during his lifetime and for his wife, Carol Agger, if she survived him. So far that had not been disclosed.[15]

Fortas' statement soon ballooned the matter into a real "*cause celebre*". Liberals joined in the chorus of criticism. Some agreed with Republicans that the Justice should resign.[16]

Subsequently, Wilson and two FBI agents met with Wolfson -- then in prison in Florida -- per an arrangement made by Mitchell with Wolfson's attorney. The meeting disclosed nothing of an incriminatory nature. Wolfson swore that Fortas "had never helped him . . . had made no offer of assistance nor did he indicate he would do anything one way or the other in connection with the matter."[17] But this did not resolve Abe's problem.

Upon receipt of the *Life* issue carrying Lambert's story, the Internal Revenue Service had issued a subpoena to the Wolfson Family Foundation for all correspondence involving Fortas. It was soon in the hands of the Department of Justice. Among the documents was Abe's contract with the Foundation. It disclosed, for the first time, the lifetime and survivorship benefits for Abe and Carol if she survived him.[18] Two decisive events followed.

Will Wilson and Henry Peterson -- top criminal lawyers at the Justice Department -- agreed that Mitchell should contact Abe's attorney. Since Abe had not officially designated anyone to represent him, the sly decision was reached that Chief Justice Warren came closest to occupying that position.[19]

Mitchell went along. He met with the Chief Justice and disclosed the six documents he had received from the Internal Revenue Service, including the previously suppressed contract. Although none of the documents supported any legal violation by Abe or Wolfson -- merely the exchange of the consulting fee and cancellation of the agreement[20] -- Fortas was, in reality unable to continue further service on the Court. The revelation of the full details of the Fortas-Wolfson arrangement convinced Warren that Fortas could not remain.[21]

A follow-up article in *Newsweek* concerning Mitchell's meeting with the Chief Justice fed the flames, creating the false public impression that there had been real skullduggery. Mitchell contributed to that misconception, publicly stating that he had delivered "certain information" to the Chief Justice. This cryptically implied that it was invidious without saying so.[22] The author has a personal recollection of a television appearance by Mitchell in which he ominously told inquiring reporters: "There is more." I felt a tremor as I heard it.

Meantime, his half-truths had caught Abe in a trap of his own making. He had no way of knowing what communications had passed between Wolfson and the Department of Justice representatives, and he was in no position to inquire. A direct inquiry to Wolfson would have exposed him to a charge of attempting to exert undue influence. Yet, he had reason to wonder whether his hands-off attitude towards Wolfson's legal problems -- especially with regard to the pardon -- might have impelled adverse comments.

Abe had placed himself in the same position as the Nixon men later assumed in the Watergate scandal. He had in effect anticipated their turnover of partial transcripts of the tapes, while withholding the "smoking gun" -- *i.e.,* Nixon's prompt participation in the break-in cover-up -- until the Supreme Court ordered full production. Similarly, the full scope of Abe's contract with the Foundation only came to light in response to the Internal Revenue's subpoena. To continue the Watergate playbook, it was Abe's recourse to a "modified, limited hang-out" -- in answer to Lambert's *Life Magazine* piece -- which left "him twisting in the wind."

But if Abe ever was in the mood for the last laugh, he ultimately had reason. Mitchell went to jail. Nixon needed a pardon to escape the same fate.

As the chorus for Abe's resignation swelled, he decided to speak to the Court in person. Upon doing so, he sensed that the Chief Justice was also of that mind. He promptly acceded.[23]

In the views of a leading liberal, Joseph ("Joe") Rauh, and of Justice Black, it would have been much better to have made a full and complete disclosure of the Wolfson connection as soon as the matter arose.[24] When it was similarly disclosed that Justice Douglas was on the payroll of the Parvin Foundation (a do-good organization headed by a man with Las Vegas gambling connections), nothing came of Republican talk of impeaching him.[25]

To my mind, the ineradicable stain on an otherwise brilliant career was at bottom the product of Abe's conviction that he could, on his own, effectively address any difficulty that confronted him. It is my

conviction that the whole tragedy could have been avoided if he had
simply asked Thurman to act as his counsel when the Wolfson problem
first erupted. Abe's troubles devastated Arnold. To quote Kalman:

> Fortas's fall left his other former partner "heartbroken." When
> Eugene Rostow dropped by to commiserate, Thurman Arnold acted as
> if he were in mourning. He believed Fortas had made an error in
> judgment, but Arnold remained loyal to his friend. In fact, while Fortas
> and Porter were in Europe, Arnold worked on a project he had begun
> the day after his friend resigned: finding Fortas a job. On May 16,
> Arnold wrote the former justice that "Paul has just left the office to tell
> you of our irrevocable decision to welcome you back to the firm . . . "[26]

However, as later events proved, the younger partners nevertheless
blocked Abe's return.

I have trouble understanding why, in his hour of need, Abe did not
enlist Thurman's aid. It is all the more puzzling in light of their
mutual respect and affection for each other.

Arnold's reputation for integrity and intellect was impeccable.
There had never been a breath of criticism about his character or his
official or personal conduct, let alone any suggestion of scandal. He
carried the prestige of outstanding service at the Department of Justice
and on the nation's second highest court.

Arnold could have persuasively emphasized that judges need not be
hermits. Soon after his appointment Abe himself had embarked on the
lecture circuit, speaking for a fee of $1750, plus expenses.[27] No one
ever questioned the propriety of that "extracurricular" activity. Justice
Brennan taught a summer course at the New York University Law
School.[28] A search would doubtless have yielded other examples.

Most of all, the Judge was gifted with an unmatched and instinctive
expertise for putting matters in perspective, coupled with a mind that
was at once, quick, creative and pragmatic. Hindsight is always 20-20.
But I can't imagine that Thurman would have neglected to uncover and
disclose the whole picture as soon as the Fortas-Wolfson connection
became public knowledge -- which Rauh and Justice Black believed to
be the right course. Although Wolfson was in jail, Arnold could
readily have arranged to visit him and learned that he had not said
anything incriminating about Fortas to any government representatives.

Arnold's advice to the Chief Justice so affirming -- following his
prompt disclosure of the arrangement with the Foundation -- would

have overridden any conflicting assertions from Mitchell or his staff members. From every standpoint, particularly in legal stature, Thurman was a giant, Mitchell a pygmy. Actually, according to Kalman: "Mitchell later admitted that Fortas had committed no crime."[29]

Finally, had Thurman represented Abe, Mitchell would have had to communicate with him, as Abe's counsel, instead of discussing the matter with the Chief Justice. In my opinion, Arnold would have quickly foreclosed Mitchell from any implication of serious misconduct, if only by pointing to the exculpatory dialogue between Wolfson and the Department of Justice personnel.

In these circumstances, Warren might have been more tolerant. Abe would not have been vulnerable to justified accusations of prevarication. There would have been no extended interval for the buildup of a hostile public and congressional opinion. The absence of any illegal activity would have been promptly disclosed. If Murphy is right about Warren's reaction to the documents Mitchell delivered, it is my sense that prompt intervention by Arnold would have changed the outcome. This is what Murphy says:

> Despite all of Mitchell's dramatic evidence, there was something very encouraging about it for the chief justice. First, there was no question now that long ago Fortas had indeed canceled the arrangement and returned the money. Then, too, there was not one shred of evidence that Fortas had done anything improper by way of intervening in the legal troubles of Wolfson. But Warren knew that action now had to be taken.[30]

In my view prompt and candid disclosure of all of the facts, coupled with a presentation by Arnold, would have made all the difference. The key word in Murphy's recitation of Warren's reaction is "now." By the time Mitchell delivered the Fortas/Foundation documents to the Chief Justice, Abe's deception had been exposed and widespread suspicion of unlawful misconduct had circulated to the point that liberals as well as conservatives had joined in demanding his resignation. In this focus the actual events marched to the familiar beat in criminal law: the acquittal rarely catches up with the indictment. Here it meant that the truth was revealed too late to undo the initial dissembling and concomitant suspicions.

The sad end of Abe's career on the Court had all the elements of a Greek tragedy. Abe never wanted to serve on the Supreme Court, as

LBJ well knew. Nevertheless, he ambushed Abe into permitting his nomination to the court to go forward by stating simultaneously that he was sending 50,000 more American boys to Vietnam and forwarding Abe's nomination to the Court for confirmation by the Senate.[31]

Abe's subsequent career could not have been happy. Because the younger lawyers resisted, the firm's veterans, including me, were unable to arrange his return. I'm not sure exactly why they objected. There were probably a variety of reasons based on individual experiences.[32]

Before closing out this unhappy interlude, I must commend the admirable conduct of his wife during that trying period. She remained a partner of the firm throughout what must have been a tortuous time for her. She never missed a day's work. She never once injected, even remotely, her thoughts on the firm's course of action.

Abe later set up a profitable Washington counseling firm with a Chicago lawyer, Howard Koven, known as Fortas & Koven.[33] He died suddenly of a ruptured aorta at age 71 in 1982. I'm convinced that the stress of his Supreme Court troubles shortened his life.

The full extent of the personal disaster that befell Abe Fortas is apparent from the editorial of *The Washington Post* of April 7, 1982, following Abe's death. This is what it said:

> The appreciations of Abe Fortas come with no small degree of agonizing, from the legal peers he so dazzled to the admirers he did deeply disappoint. But there should be no denying that the legacy of Mr. Fortas, who died late Monday at the age of 71, is replete with significant contributions to the history of civil liberties and civil rights in this country -- moments of great distinction in his service to the public both as a lawyer and as a Supreme Court justice.
>
> It was these very strengths -- of the lawyer, the scholar, the teacher and the champion of liberties -- that made so distressing to so many the nevertheless necessary resignation of Mr. Fortas from the court when improprieties involving outside fees became public.

The net of the entire matter is that Abe's misfortune could easily have been avoided. He had only to heed the wisdom of that age-old legal homily: "A lawyer who represents himself has a fool for a client."

CHAPTER TWENTY-SIX

LAW AND REMEMBRANCE

As I look back upon the happenstance of the events that brought me to the firm of Arnold, Fortas & Porter, I have a hard time resisting the idea that some undefinable force was responsible. Suppose New Haven was not my mom's hometown? To which law school would I have thought to go? Couldn't the Yale Law School have easily rejected me? Would Abe Fortas have noticed me if I had written on some other subject for the *Yale Law Journal* than the one that caught his eye?

Whatever the reason, I'll always be grateful that I landed on the doorstep of Arnold, Fortas & Porter. As a result, for half a century, I have enjoyed a rare combination of challenging projects, intellectual stimulation and the pleasure of association with companionable and talented colleagues in the practice of law.

The enjoyment of all three of the founders' company subsisted until Abe's departure for the Supreme Court in 1965. I regret that Fortas did not rejoin us after his resignation from the Court in 1969. That would have added 13 years to his gifted service to the firm, before his death in 1982 at the age of 71. Thurman's incomparable contributions endured until he died in 1969. He was then 78. Paul was with us until he passed on at age 70, in 1975.

During the recent move of our office to a new location, a memorandum turned up which I had long since forgotten. It speaks of the compensation system instituted by the second generation of the firm's partners. Circulated under date of October 21, 1976, it reflects the harmony that prevailed under the partnership's original compensation system. The subject is the suggestion that our

285

compensation system should be reconsidered. Let me refer to three
extracts. To quote:

I. *The 100 Ceiling*

A.   The 100's [*i.e.*, the most senior partners] have always operated
under a voluntary ceiling foreclosing any addition of any points to their
shares. Nothing in the partnership agreement so requires. None of the
original 100's [Arnold, Fortas, and Porter] has ever received one
additional point. No 100 has ever proposed a breach of the 100 ceiling.

B. The ratio of a 100 shares to the firm's net profit has consistently
declined in recent years. It averaged about 9% from 1960-1965. It will
be about 4% in 1976. This reflects the intervening point distributions.

C.   During 1968-1971, the dollar value of a 100 share declined from
$199,000 to $141,000--or about 30%. It was $157,000 in 1972 and
$170,000 in 1973. It never reached $200,000 until 1974.

D.   No percentage partner below 100 has ever suffered a reduction in
his shares. All but those admitted at year-end 1974 and 1975 have
received share increases. Every non-equity partner has always received
an annual dollar increase.

II. *The De-Emphasis of Business Origination*

The firm is unique in that business origination has never been a factor
in advancement.

*   *   *

IV.   *The Merit Promotion Standard.*

This allows recognition of the lawyers making outstanding contributions
to the firm in terms of talent and dedication. It constitutes a reward for
outstanding performance. It is not designed to penalize anyone else.

The merit system reflected an effort to perpetuate the tradition of
emphasizing unselfishness, generosity and extraordinary performance
which characterized the environment that prevailed during the
generation of the merit formula. But it was impossible to maintain as
the years went by, because of developments, both within the firm and

the profession in general. When the third generation took control of the firm in the mid-1980's, it had changed significantly. By that time we had grown into a bureaucracy with some 300 lawyers plus a support staff of close to 1,000 men and women. It needed more definitive controls. Watching the process evolve taught me that Parkinson's law was not just a witticism. A formal governing system was established. An elected "Policy Committee" made all major decisions except as to partners' compensation, admissions to partnership and decisions to take on experienced outside lawyers, described as "lateral" entries. An elected Compensation Committee made recommendations for changes in partnership status and remuneration. Those matters were subject to review at an annual partnership meeting. Day-to-day activities were supervised primarily by a Management Committee. An Office of Practice Development was established. In all, twenty committees dealt with every conceivable aspect of the firm's operations ranging from "Art" to "Training."

Before long, bulletins, memoranda and reports flooded the office on such subjects as budgets and billing and realization reports, on a partner-by-partner basis. There was regular circulation of quarterly income reports, comparing actual income and expenses with budget projections. Billable hour reports were compiled and distributed, covering each partner and associate. A "Partners Handbook" was composed. It contains 700 pages and weighs 7 pounds.

Specialists replaced generalists for allocation of the firm's work. Twenty "Practice Groups" were established reflecting the various legal subjects which comprise the firm's major practice areas.

In the transformation process, "Rainmaking" -- *i.e.*, business getting -- became the most significant measure for distribution of the firm's income. Records reflecting that factor were instituted. The "100 share" ceiling was broken. A bonus pool was established. Its principal use was to reward the top income producers but excellent performance was also recognized, albeit more modestly.

In substantial part, the change from the merit system of compensation reflected the transformation of the legal profession. It had become more competitive. A major reason was the erosion of the tradition that the firm lawyers first joined were "families" with which they spent their entire careers. "Lateral" movements within the profession became commonplace as firms raided one another's major income producers by the promise of increased earnings. To retain their services, it was frequently necessary to meet fire with fire.

In short, Arnold & Porter is no longer distinctive in its compensation system or its informal management. It has also outgrown its earlier collegial atmosphere. Its warm and friendly ambiance were irretrievably lost with the passage of Thurman and Paul. Yet they left a legacy of informality and absence of protocol that survives to this day.

Most importantly, through it all, the exciting character of the firm's work has remained constant. So has the excellence of the service provided by its lawyers. The proof is in the pudding of the loyalty of long-term clients and the regular acquisition of new ones. The founding fathers had established an institution which achieved prestige in the profession by reason of national recognition of the quality of its service, rather than the presence of nationally known "trophy" celebrities within the partnership. Because of them, the firm enjoys a special cachet to this day.

The metamorphosis of the firm's ambiance from its earlier years to its current atmosphere was well described in the written comments of two "experts" on the firm -- an outsider and an insider. One is a letter I received, under date of March 4, 1992, from George Leonard, for many years the General Counsel and Vice President of the Kroger Co., now retired. The other is a "farewell" note dated April 12, 1995, from one of our departing stars. Its author was Robert Pitofsky, former Dean of the Georgetown Law School. He recently left his position as Counsel to our firm to become Chairman of the Federal Trade Commission.

Leonard wrote:

Dear Norman:

I simply cannot tell you how much I enjoyed being with you for a few hours last week. One of the most delightful aspects of visiting with you is that we never seem to run out of things to talk about. I have also noted that you seem never to forget anything, and I remember best those things that never happened.

*   *   *

I never cease to be surprised at how much at home I feel when I am in the Arnold & Porter offices. I keep bumping into people with whom I have worked over the years and who have become friends of mine. I would only hope that the atmosphere of years ago would never be lost, but it seems to be disappearing everywhere.

Take good care of yourself. I am looking forward already to the next reason for me to get to Washington and another chance for us to have dinner together.

Very best regards,

Bob's good-bye said:

TO: Arnold & Porter

FROM: Robert Pitofsky

RE: *Another Farewell*

After over 20 years of Counsel to the firm, I will be leaving to serve as Chairman at the Federal Trade Commission.

The firm has changed enormously in my years here. But there are some constants. It still includes the best lawyers I know, practicing in a way that allows people to retain their individuality and special qualities.

I have often said that I doubt an academic like myself could achieve a more congenial or rewarding or delightful professional relationship in law practice that I have enjoyed at Arnold & Porter. Year in and year out, the firm and its members have respected my prior commitment to an academic life, and have allowed me to enjoy what I regard as the best of both worlds.

Both George and Bob know the firm intimately. I share their sentiments. I can't agree with the French maxim: *"La plus ca change, las plus c'est la meme chose."* The more time passes, the more I realize the truth of Paul's maxim that "Things aren't what they used to be, and what's more, they never were." I'm just happy that I was there when the "things that used to be" included the magical men who founded Arnold, Fortas & Porter.

An effort is now under way at Arnold & Porter to recapture the spirit of the firm's youthful days. I hope it succeeds. But in concluding, I'm reminded of Senator Moynihan's moving response when asked to comment on the effect of President Kennedy's assassination, during the television dirge that followed. Then a virtually unknown and youthful Assistant Secretary of Labor, he said: "We'll laugh again, but we'll never be young again." Neither will Arnold & Porter.

EPILOGUE

The bond among the founders of the firm was deeper than their mutual personal affection and professional admiration. Thurman, Abe and Paul shared a loyalty so profound as to be worthy of the motto of the Three Musketeers: "All for one and one for all."

As soon as Abe resigned from the Court, Thurman's immediate reaction was to have him rejoin Arnold & Porter. By letter of May 16, 1969, Arnold wrote the former Justice that "Paul has just left the office to tell you of our irrevocable decision to welcome you back to the firm."[1] To Thurman, any other outcome was inconceivable.

To be sure he lifted Abe's spirits, Thurman continued:

> . . . I came down to the office this morning with all my worries and cares rolled away, with a feeling of triumph. Never in my long experience with you have I ever been so proud of being your friend and associate. Your support of the Court which was under heavy artillery fire was magnificent. You have been a great credit to the profession and the Court, and your manner of leaving the Court will insure you recognition which you might have missed if you had just kept on writing opinions . . . .[2]

Following his resignation, Abe in fact felt rejected and dejected, although he tried to show a stiff upper lip. He was ignored by many of his Washington friends. Just a week after his resignation, the American Bar Association denounced Abe's relationship with Wolfson. It was declared to be a violation of the requirements of Canon 5 of the Judicial Ethics that a judge's conduct must avoid the "appearance of impropriety." It also induced a revision of those canons designed to deter judges from accepting outside income.[3]

Abe's condition was so worrisome to Mercedes Eichholz, Carol's closest friend, as well as a longtime family stalwart, that she raised the matter with Joseph Hirshhorn -- whom Abe had persuaded to donate his great art collection to the National Gallery. She suggested that he offer his home at Cap d'Antibes to Abe and Carol as a refuge at which they could escape the relentless pressure of the media. Hirshhorn readily agreed. When Mercedes so informed them, Carol, who detested airplanes, first resisted. She finally agreed, when Mercedes said "you

have to do this to save Abe. He's just about at the end of the road."
The Porters joined them for two relaxing weeks in France.[4]

When Abe resigned from the Court on May 14, 1969, he was not
yet 60, still youthful and vigorous, except possibly to the extent that the
ordeal had exacted its toll. His return to the firm had been blocked.
When Thurman died on November 7, 1969, Abe lost a major anchor
of his life. Leaving his own problems, he rushed to the Arnold home
after receiving a call from Frances Arnold in the wee hours of that
morning and remained all day. So did Porter. Abe then took charge
both of the services in Washington and the funeral in Laramie,
Wyoming, which the whole firm attended. Kalman relates:

> . . . Elizabeth Black [wife of Justice Black] thought Fortas and Porter
> were "magnificent. They would tell funny stories about Thurman and
> everybody laughed and cried." Fortas took charge of the services at the
> National Cathedral and in Laramie, Wyoming. He personally arranged
> for rental cars to transport everyone from the Denver airport to Laramie.
> "He was meticulous," Thurman Arnold, Jr., recalled.[5]

Paul was no less determined than Thurman to bring Abe back to the
firm. Following the funeral service in Laramie, he told Abe that he
"would go to any length to bring him back" and then began playing
"hardball."[6] He wasn't kidding. In Kalman's words:

> . . . He threatened to reconstitute the firm without Fortas's opponents.
> Alternatively, he warned that the firm would lose its founders' names,
> as he would withdraw his and persuade Frances Arnold to retire her
> husband's . . . .[7]

When none of this worked, Paul tried another tack, which involved
substantial personal sacrifice. He proposed that Abe be brought back
on terms which would reduce both of their financial interests in the
firm to equivalence with those of partners holding 100 shares. Those
were significantly less than half of the amounts held by the founders.
Even this did not get the job done. When Abe later learned of the
proposal, he said that he would not have permitted Paul to absorb such
a monetary loss under any circumstances.

In retrospect, I first appreciated the full measure of the devotion of
the founding partners to one another when Abe's troubles on the Court
began, and particularly after his resignation. The sorrow each felt

probably exceeded the pain either of them would have suffered had he been the one in Abe's shoes.

Their emotions were directed solely at rejuvenating Abe regardless of the possible impact on the firm's and their own incomes. During the discussions concerning Abe's return, some of the most talented younger partners were emphatic that they would leave the firm if he came back. Others were convinced that the firm would sustain a substantial loss of clients and revenue. But such contingencies were of no concern whatever to Thurman and Paul. Abe's welfare was their sole concern.

APPENDIX

Because of space limitations it proved impossible to include all of my assignments while the founders were engaged in active practice at the firm. This prevented identification of all the splendid lawyers with whom I had the privilege of working during that period. This list has therefore been compiled to name them. I hope I have not inadvertently omitted anyone.

Alex Bennett
Peter Bleakley
David Bonderman
Brooksley Born
Jeffrey Burt
Brad Butler
Mike Curzan
James Dobkin
Melvin Garbow
Patrick Grant
John D. Hawke, Jr.
Richard Hubbard
David Kentoff
Stuart Land
Ken Letzler
Jack Lipson
David Lloyd
Tom McGrew
Nancy Mintz
Bruce Montgomery
Irv Nathan
Tom Nurmi
Walter Rockler
William Rogers
Robert Rosenbaum
Cary Sherman
Tom Silfen
Michael Sohn
Mark Spooner

ENDNOTES

PROLOGUE

1.   Gene M. Gressley, *Voltaire and the Cowboy*, Colorado Associated University Press (1977) at 72 (*"V.C. "*).

2.   *Masters of Deceit*, Henry Holt (1958).

3.   Bontecou, *The Federal Loyalty Security Program*, Cornell University Press (1953) at 82-90.

4.   *Harper's* Magazine , *Arnold, Fortas, Porter & Prosperity* (Nov. 1951) at 70 (*"Harper's"*).

5.   McCullough, *Truman*, Simon & Schuster (1992) at 551 ("McCullough").

6.   McCullough at 553.

7.   Henry VI, Part 2.

Part I - How We Happened

CHAPTER ONE
The Founding Fathers and Me

1.   *V.C.* at 68.

2.   *Harper's* at 64.

3.   *Id.*

4.   Kalman, *Abe Fortas*, Yale University Press (1990) at 185 ("Kalman").

5.   Andrews, *Washington Witch Hunt*, Random House (1948) at 16 (*"WWH"*).

6.   *V.C.* at 374-77; *WWH* at 20.

7.   Douglas, *The Court Years 1939-1975,* Random House (1980) at 66.

8.   *Harper's* at 66.

9.   Res. 280, 81st Cong., 2d Sess. (1950), *Employment of Homosexuals And Other Sex Perverts in Government, Interim Report, Submitted to the Committee on Expenditures in the Executive Department,* by its Subcommittee on Investigations, at 9, 11, Appendix III.   According to Appendix III, dismissals for "sex perversions" from the State Department accounted for more than 50% of the total in the entire government.

10. *Webster's New Universal Unabridged Dictionary,* Barnes & Noble (1994) at 887.

11.   *Coleman v. Brucker,* 257 F. 2d 661 (D.C. Cir., 1958).

12. *Coleman et al. v. Brucker,* 156 F. Supp. 126 (U.S. D.C. 1957); Arnold, *Fair Fights & Foul,* Harcourt Brace & World (1965) at 210 - 213 *("FFF").*

13.   *Coleman v. Brucker, supra,* 257 F.2d at 662.

14.   *Id.*

15.   *FFF* at 213.

16.   *WWH* at 214-15.

17.   Kalman at 161.

18.   Goulden, *The Superlawyers,* Weybright and Talley (1972) at 122.

19.   47 Yale L.J. (1937-38) at 229 *et seq.*

20.   Report on Protective Committee reorganization, *H.R. Report on Protective Committee Reorganization,* H.R. Report No. 35, 74th Cong. 2d Sess. (1936).

21.   Shogan, *A Question of Judgment,* Bobbs Merrill (1972) at 44 ("Shogan").

CHAPTER TWO
THURMAN ARNOLD
A Singular and Plural Mind

1.   The Autobiography of William O. Douglas, *Go East, Young Man*, Dell Publishing Company (1974) at 171 (emphasis in original).

2.   *Folklore of Capitalism,* Yale University Press (1937) at 35 (*"Folklore"*).

3.   *Id.*

4.   *Id.* at 36-37.

5.   *Id.* at 113-14.

6.   *V.C.* at 482-84.

7.   Schwarz, *The New Dealers*, Knopf (1993) at 162.

8.   *State of Vermont v. Vernham News Corporation*, Sup. Ct. # 1305 (1959), Brief for Respondent-Appellant at 3.

9.   *Id.* at 6.

10.   *Id.* at 6-8.

11.   *HMH Publication Company, Inc. v. Arthur J. Summerfield, Postmaster General*, Civil Action No. 5041-55 (D.D.C. 11/16/55); restraining order issued 11/18/55.

12.   S. Res. 202, 81st Cong. 2d. Sess. (5/3/50).

13.   Reprinted in *FFF* at 197-203 (emphasis added).

14.   *Id.*.

15.   Kalman at 141.

16.   *Ballard v. United States*, 329 U.S. 187, 195 (1946).

17.   *Folklore* at 55-56, 57.

18.   Joseph H. Beale was Professor of *Conflict of Law* at Harvard Law School.   Sayre and Thayer were other distinguished members of the same faculty.   In a partial reprinting of the verse, the author of a recent volume reported that it "was written while Thurman Arnold was a budding humorist at the Harvard Law School.   White, *Trials and Tribulations,* Catbird Press (1989) at 223.

CHAPTER THREE
Abe Fortas
Elder Prodigy

1.   372 U.S. 335 (1963).

2.   214 F.2d 862 (D.C. Cir. 1954).

3.   Kalman at 183.

4.   *Id.* 214 F.2d, *supra* n.2, at 835.

5.   *Id.*

6.   *FFF* at 233-36.

7.   *Yale Law Report*, Spring/Summer 1982 at 10.

8.   *Id.* at 11.

9.   Kalman at 193.

10.   *Id.* at 220-21.

11.   *Id.* at 187.

12.   *Id.* at 189.

13.   *Id.* at 188.

14.   *Id.*

15.   *Id.* at 184.

16.   Kalman at 70.

17.   *Id.* at 187.

18.   *Id.* at 210.

CHAPTER FOUR
Paul Porter
Toujours L'Ami

1.   *Bailey v. Richardson*, 182 F.2d 46 (D.C. Cir. 1950).

2.   *Id.*, 341 U.S. 918 (1951).

3.   *Kalman* at 138-39.

4.   *Harper's* at 67.

5.   *Kiefer-Stewart Co. v. Joseph E. Seagram & Sons*, 340 U.S. 211 (1951).

6.   *Dean Milk Co. v. Madison*, 340 U.S. 349 (1951).

7.   *Kiefer-Stewart Co. v. Joseph E. Seagram & Sons*, 182 F.2d 228 (7th Cir. 1950).

8.   *The Washington Star*, Section B at 1 (4/26/79).

9.   *The Washington Star*, Section B at 1, 3 (4/26/79); Encyclopedia Britannica, Vol. 3, *Micromedia*, 15th Ed., at 113-14.

10.   *Harper's* at 65.

11.   *Id.*

12.   Kalman at 184.

13.   McCullough at 990.

CHAPTER FIVE
The Formation of the Firm

1.   *V.C.* at 62; *Kalman* at 114.

2.   *FFF* at 156.

3.   See also *Harper's* at 64.

4.   *FFF* at 159.

5.   *"The Growth of Awareness: Our Nation's Law and Law Among Nations, International Lawyer* Vol. I (July 1967 at 534-47.) (*"Awareness"*). This is a rare example of the full text of an Arnold speech.

6.   *V.C.* at 92-93.

7.   *"Awareness"* at 544.

8.   *Harper's* at 63-64; see also Schwarz at 162.

9.   *V.C.* at 64.

10.   Kalman at 154.

11.   *FFF* at 33-34.

12.   *Fortas: The Rise and Ruin of a Supreme Court Justice,* Morrow (1988) at 76 ("Murphy").

13.   Allen, *Secret Formula,* Harper Business (1994).

14.   *Id.* at 162.

15.   *United States v. Pullman Co.,* 50 F. Supp. 123 (E.D. Pa. 1943).

16.   *V.C.* at 64, 66.

17.   *Id.* at 66; *United States v. Pullman Co.,* 64 F. Supp. 108 (E.D. Pa. 1948).

18.   *FFF* at 154.

19.   *United States v. Pullman Co.,* 330 U.S. 806 (1947).

20.   *V.C.* at 66.

21.   *Id.* at 64, 66.

22.   Kalman at 114.

23.   *Id.*

24.   *Id.*, note 116 at 427-28.

25.   *FFF* at 23-24.

26.   *Id.* at 33-34.

27.   Kalman at 153.

CHAPTER SIX
Naval Support

None.

Part II - How We Lived

CHAPTER SEVEN
The Founders' Workshops

1.   Space limitations prevent reference to all the matters I worked on and all the wonderful lawyers who worked on them with me during the early days at Arnold, Fortas & Porter. What I hope is a complete list of those lawyers appears at Appendix 1.

CHAPTER EIGHT
The Management

1.   Paul (co-authored with Jacob Mertens, Jr.), *The Law of Federal Income Taxation,* Callaghan (1934).

CHAPTER NINE
Life With the Fathers

1. *United States v. Scophany Corporation*, 333 U.S. 705 (1948).

2. *Harper's* at 70.

3. Kalman at 186-187.

4. *Id.* at 190-191.

5. *Id.* at 184.

6. *Id.* at 49-50, 126; V.C., at 38.

7. Kalman at 192.

8. 15 U.S.C. § 19.

9. *United States v. W.T. Grant Co., et al.*, 112 F. Supp. 336 (S.D.N.Y. 1952).

10. *Id.*, 345 U.S. 629 (1953).

11. Judy Hennessee, *The Washington Legal Establishment*, *The Washingtonian* (August 1967) at 34.

12. Kalman at 187.

13. Kramer, *Selections From The Letters and Legal Papers of Thurman Arnold* (1961) at preface.

14. *FFF*, fly page.

CHAPTER TEN
From New York To New York

1. *United States v. Paramount Pictures, Inc., et al.*, 334 U.S. 131 (1948).

2. *Twentieth Century Fox Film Corporation v. Goldwyn*, 328 F.2d 190 (9th Cir. 1964).

CHAPTER ELEVEN
The Burma Theatre

1.   *United States v. Paramount Pictures, Inc., supra,* 334 U.S. 131 (1948).

2.   *Loew's, Inc., et al. v. Cinema Amusements, Inc.,* 210 F.2d 86, 95 (10th Cir. 1954); *cert. denied,* 347 U.S. 976 (1954).

CHAPTER TWELVE
The Queen of Diamonds

1.   Frances Russell, *The Shadow of Blooming Grove, Warren G. Harding in His Times,* McGraw Hill (1968) at 443, 445-459.

2.   *FFF* at 246, 247-48, 249.

3.   *Id.* at 250.

4.   *Id.* at 250-51.

5.   *In re Estate of Evalyn Walsh McLean, Appraisal* (D.D.C., 12/8/47).

6.   *Id., First Account* (D.D.C., 7/16/48).

7.   *Id., Second & Final Account* (D.D.C., 9/30/49).

8.   *Legal Times,* 1/9/95, at 1.

9.   *Id.* at 6.

10.   *FFF* at 246-47.

11.   *Id.* at 247.

12.   *In re Estate of Evalyn Walsh McLean, Petition to Sell Household Effects* (D.D.C. 3/15/48).

13.   *Id., Second and Final Account* (D.D.C. 9/30/49).

14.   *Id., Appraisal* (D.D.C. 12/8/47) at 96.

15. *Id., Petition to Sell Jewelry and Order Authorizing Sale of Jewelry* (D.D.C., 3/18/49).

16. *U.S. News & World Report*, Vol. 121, No. 6 at p.14 (8/12/96).

17. Whittlesey House (1949).

CHAPTER THIRTEEN
The Loyalty Lunacy

1. Bontecou, *The Federal Loyalty Security Program*, Cornell University Press (1953) at 238.

2. McCullough at 551-52.

3. *Id.* at 553.

4. *Id.*

5. Kalman at 127-151.

6. Kalman at 145.

7. *FFF* at 214

8. *Id.* at 215.

9. *Id.*

10. *Id.* at 217.

11. *United States v. Lattimore*, 112 F. Supp. 507, 516 (D.D.C. 1953); *aff'd in part and rev'd in part*, 215 F.2d 847 (D.C. Cir. 1954).

12. *Id.*, 127 F. Supp. 405, 409-410 (D.D.C. 1955).

13. *Id.*, 125 F. Supp. 295, 296 (D.D.C. 1954).

14. *Id.* at 296.

15. *Id.*, 127 F. Supp. 405, 408 (D.D.C. 1955), *aff'd, equally divided court*, 232 F.2d 334 (D.C. Cir. 1955).

16.   *FFF* at 217-18.

17.   *Id.* at 219-20.

18.   *V.C.* at 87-88 (brackets in original); 401-403.

19.   *Id.* at 410-11.

CHAPTER FOURTEEN
Court Fright

1.   *Peters v. Hobby*, 349 U.S. 331 (1955).

2.   *Id.* at 333.

3.   *Id.*, at 334-5.

4.   *Id.* at 335-6.

5.   *Id.* at 337, n.2.

6.   *Id.* at 337 (emphasis added).

7.   Kalman at 143; *FFF* at 209-10.

8.   *FFF* at 210.

9.   *Estate Of Dr. Beatrice Braude v. The United States*, 35 Fed. Cl. 99 (1996) (*"Braude v. U.S."*).

10.   *Braude v. U.S.*, at 101 n.1, 106.

11.   *Id.* at 102.

12.   *Id.* at 106, 108, 114.

13.   *Id.* at 104.

14.   *Id.*

15.   *Id.*

16.   5 U.S.C. § 552a.

17.   *Braude v. U.S.*, at 105.

18.   *Id.* at 102.

19.   *Id.*

20.   *Id.* at 106, 114.

21.   *Id.* at 114.

CHAPTER FIFTEEN
The Ineffable Justice Frankfurter

1.   *V.C.* at 75.

2.   *Bruce's Juices v. American Can Co.*, 330 U.S. 743 (1946).

3.   *Clyde-Mallory Lines v. Steamship "Eglantine" and the United States of America*, 317 U.S. 395 (1943).

4.   257 U.S. 419, 433 (1922).

5.   *The Siren*, 7 Wall. 462 (1868).

6.   Harvard University Press (1941).

7.   *Williams v. Fanning*, 332 U.S. 406 (1947).

8.   *California v. United States*, 320 U.S. 577 (1944).

9.   *Id.* at 583.

10.   *Id.* at 583-584.

11.   See *Black's Law Dictionary*, Rev. 4th Ed. (1968), at 692.

12.   *Phelps Dodge Corp. v. National Labor Relations Board*, 313 U.S. 177 (1941).

13.   *Id.* at 189.

14.   29 U.S.C. §§ 152(B), 160(C).

15.   Emphasis added here and in balance of discussion of *Phelps Dodge* case.

16.   *Phelps Dodge Corp. v. National Labor Relations Board, supra,* 313 U.S. at 188.

17.   *Id.* at 192-93.

18.   *California v. United States; supra,* 320 U.S. at 582.

19.   18 *V.C.* at 75.

20.   *Youngstown Sheet and Tube Co. v. United States,* 343 U.S. 579, 634-35 (1952) (emphasis added).

CHAPTER SIXTEEN
The Discounter

1.   66 Stat. 632 (1952), repealed Pub. L. 94-145, 89 Stat. 801 (1975).

2.   *General Electric Co. v. Masters, Inc.,* 307 N.Y. 229, 237-39, 120 N.E. 2d 802, 804 (Ct. App. 1954); *appeal dismissed,* 348 U.S. 892 (1954).

3.   *Schwegmann Bros. v. Calvert Distillers Corp.,* 341 U.S. 384 (1951).

4.   *Sunbeam Corp. v. Wentling,* 185 F.2d 903 (3rd Cir. 1951).

5.   See note 2, *supra,* 348 U.S. 892.

6.   *Id.*

7.   *General Electric Co. v. Masters Mail Order Co. of Washington, D.C.,* Inc., 145 F. Supp. 57, 59 (1956); *rev'd, id.,* 244 F.2d 681 (2d Cir. 1957); *cert. denied, id,* 355 U.S. 824 (1957).

8.   *Sunbeam v. McMillan,* 110 F. Supp. 836 (1953).

9.   *Revere Camera Company v. Masters Mail Order Company of Washington, D.C.,* 128 F. Supp. 457 (D. Md. 1955).

10.   *Bissell Carpet Sweeper Co. v. Masters Mail Order Co.*, 140 F. Supp. 165, 174 (D. Md. 1956).

11.   *Bissell Carpet Sweeper Company v. Masters Mail Order Company of Washington, D.C., Inc.*,   240 F.2d 684 (4th Cir. 1957).

12.   *General Electric Co. v. Masters Mail Order Co.*, 145 F. Supp. 57, 61 (S.D.N.Y. 1956).

13.   *Id.*, 244 F.2d 681 (2d Cir. 1957).

14.   *Id.*, 355 U.S. 824 (1957).

15.   *Sunbeam Corporation v. Masters, Inc.*, 157 F. Supp. 689 (S.D.N.Y. 1957).

CHAPTER SEVENTEEN
Gilbert & Sullivan To The Rescue

1.   The Clayton Act, 15 U.S.C. § 18.

2.   The Robinson-Patman Act, 15 U.S.C. § 13a.

3.   The Federal Trade Commission Act, 15 U.S.C. § 45.

4.   15 U.S.C. §§ 1, 2.

5.   *Federal Trade Commission v. Motion Picture Advertising Service Co., Inc.*, 344 U.S. 392, 394-95 (1953).

6.   *Consolo v. Federal Maritime Commission*, 383 U.S. 607, 620 (1966).

7.   *The Kroger Co., Complaint*, 74 F.T.C. 1129, 1134-35 (1959).

8.   *The Kroger Co., Order Terminating Proceeding* 74 F.T.C. 1129, 1134 (1968).

9.   2 CCH Trade Reg. Rep. ¶ 4525 (1971) [rescinded 50 Fed. Reg. 21,508 (1985)].

10.   *Id.* ¶ 4525 at 6904-05 (emphasis added).

11. *Id.* at 6905 (emphasis added).

12. *Id.* at 6906.

13. *Id.* at 6907 (emphasis added).

14. *Id.*

15. *The Kroger Co.,* FTC Docket No. 7464, *Motion for Continuance* (1/20/60).

16. *Id., Order Substituting Hearing Examiner* (6/13/63).

17. *Id., Motion for Extension of Time* (7/26/63).

18. *Id., Order to Show Cause* (9/26/63); (emphasis added).

19. *Id., Motion to Amend Complaint* (10/7/63).

20. *Id., Certification* ((10/30/63).

21. *National Tea Co.,* 69 F.T.C. 226 (1966).

22. *Id., The Kroger Co.,* FTC Docket No. 7464, *Request for Ruling on Motion to Amend Complaint and Return of Matter to Hearing Examiner for Completing Proceeding* (7/22/66).

23. *Id., Order Amending Complaint* (8/10/66).

24. *Id., Subpoena Duces Tecum,* (11/23/66)

25. *Id., Transcript, Pre-Hearing Conf.* (3/1/66) at 23.

26. *Id., Motion to Quash, etc.; Motion to Dismiss* (12/30/66).

27. 5 U.S.C. § 1005(a) (1964 Ed.).

28. *The Kroger Co.,* Docket No. 7464,, Motion to Dismiss (12/30/66) at 8, 9.

29. 2 CCH Trade Reg. Rep. ¶ 4525 (1971) [rescinded, *supra,* n.9, 50 Fed. Reg. 21,508 (5/24/85)].

30. *Id.* at 6905.

31. 15 U.S.C. § 45(a)(1).

32. *Texaco Inc. v. FTC*, 336 F.2d 754, 759 (D.C. Cir. 1964).

33. Id. at 760.

34. Hearings, *Appropriations*, House of Representatives, 89th Cong., 2d Sess., Part I at 402; (emphasis added).

35. *Texaco Inc. v. FTC, supra*, at 764.

36. *The Kroger Co.*, FTC Docket No. 7464, (2/16/67).

37. *Id., Certification* (2/16/67) at 17; (emphasis added).

38. *The Kroger Co.*, FTC Docket No. 7464 (3/1/67).

39. *Id.* (3/30/67).

40. *Id.*

41. *Id.*, at 2 (emphasis added).

42. *In the Matter of the Kroger Co.*, 74 F.T.C. 1129, 1134-35 (1968).

CHAPTER EIGHTEEN
Indecent Exposure

1. *Oklahoma Press Publishing Co. v. Walling*, 327 U.S. 186, 209 (1946). Hannah v. Larche, 363 U.S. 420, 448-49 (1960).

2. *In the Matter of the Investigation of the Kroger Co.*, FTC Investigational File No. 621 0823 (1962).

3. See cases cited in n.1, *supra*.

4. *Hall, et al. v. Lemke*, Civil Action No. 62 C 942 (N.D. Ill. 1962), *Plaintiffs' Memorandum of Points and Authorities in Support of Motions for Temporary Restraining Order and Preliminary Injunction at 4-5. ("Hall v. Lemke").*

5.   *Id.*, *Complaint*, Exhibit 4 (emphasis added).

6.   *Id.*, Exhibit 1 (emphasis added).

7.   *Id.*, *Plaintiffs' Reply Memorandum in Support of Motion for Preliminary Injunction and Opposition to Defendant's Motion for Summary Judgment at 45-6* (emphasis added).

8.   *Id. Complaint*, filed 5/4/62.

9.   *Williams v. Fanning*, 332 U.S. 490 at 494 (1957).

10.   *Hearts of Oaks Assurance Co., Ltd. v. Attorney General* (1932) A.C. 392 (*"Hearts of Oaks"*).

11.   *Id.* at 397.

12.   *Id.* at 402-04 (emphasis added).

13.   *Hall v. Lemke, supra, TEMPORARY RESTRAINING ORDER*, (5/7/62).

14.   *Id., Affidavit of Norman Diamond in Support of Plaintiffs' Motion for Preliminary Injunction and in Opposition to Defendant's Motion for Summary Judgment* (5/28/62) at 3.

15.   *Id.*, attached Exhibit 4 (emphasis added).

16.   *Id., Plaintiff's Supplemental Memorandum on Defendant's Motion to Dismiss as Moot* (6/28/62).

CHAPTER NINETEEN
Fox Hunting

1.   *SuperX Drug Corporation v. State Board of Pharmacy*, 372 Mich. 22, 46-47 (1963) (*"SuperX v. State Board"*); *SuperX v. Michigan Pharmacy Board*, 233 F. Supp. 705, 706-07 (W.D. Mich. 1964) (*"SuperX v. Board"*).

2.   *SuperX v. State Board*, 372 Mich. 22, 47-49, 57-58, 61, 125 N.W. 2d 13, 26-27, 30, 31.

3.   *SuperX v. Board*, 233 F. Supp. at 707.

4.   28 U.S.C. § 1657 (1993 Ed.).

5.   *Lewis v. City of Grand Rapids Michigan*, 222 F. Supp. 349 (W.D. Mich., 9/13/63), (*"Lewis* v. *Grand Rapids"* or *"Lewis"*).

6.   *SuperX v. Board*, 233 F. Supp. at 706.

7.   *Id.* at 712.

8.   *SuperX v. State Board*, 378 Mich. 430, 146 N.W. 2d 1 (1966).

9.   *Lewis v. Grand Rapids* at 352.

10.   *Id.* at 382.

11.   *Id.* at 384.

12.   *Id.*

13.   *Id.* at 386.

14.   *Id.* at 391.

15.   *Id.*

16.   *Id.* at 383-84, 385, 386, 387, 391 (emphasis added).

17.   *SuperX v. Board, supra*, 233 F. Supp. 705.

18.   *Id.* at 708.

19.   *Id.* at 707.

20.   *Id.* (emphasis added).

21.   *Id.*

22.   *Id.*

23.   *Id.* at 708 (emphasis added).

24.   *Id.*

25. *Id.*

26. *Id.* (emphasis added).

27. *Id.* at 709.

28. *Id.* (emphasis in original).

29. *Id.* (emphasis added).

30. *Id.*

31. *Id.*

32. *Id.* at 709-10.

33. *Id.* at 710.

34. *Id.* at 712.

35. *Id.* at 707.

36. *Id.* at 712.

37. *SuperX Drugs Corporation* v. *State Board of Pharmacy and David M. Moss*, Sup. Ct. Mich., No. 50087, Petition for Affirmation That Decision of December 5, 1963 is Res Adjudicata.

38. *SuperX* v. *State Board*, 132 N.W. 2d 328 (Mich. 1965) (emphasis added), [not reported in Michigan state reports].

39. *Id.*, 375 Mich. 314, 134 N.W. 2d 678 (1965).

40. *Id.*, 378 Mich. 430 at 457-460; 146 N.W. 2d 1 at 6-10 (1966).

41. *Id.*, 378 Mich. at 460; 146 N.W. 2d at 10.

42. 324 U.S. 439 (1945).

43. *Id.* at 450-51, 466, 468.

44. *Id.* at 466.

45.   326 U.S. 693 (1945).

CHAPTER TWENTY
Unintended Consequences

1.   29 U.S.C. §§ 101 *et seq.*

2.   *Id.* § 104.

3.   *Id.* §§ 107(a)(b)(e) (emphasis added).

4.   *Id.* § 107(a).

5.   *Tri-Plex Shoe Co. v. Cantor*, 25 F. Supp. 996 (D.C. Pa. 1939); *Knapp-Manurich Co. v. Anderson*, 7 F. Supp. 332 (D.C. Ill. 1934).

6.   *The Evening Star Newspaper Company v. Washington Newspaper Guild, et al.*, Civil Action No. 3083-58 (D.D.C. 5/5/58).

7.   Certified Record of Official Court Reporter at 20-22.

8.   *Id.* at 24-25.

9.   *Id.* at 26-27 (emphasis added).

10.   *Id.* at 52.

CHAPTER TWENTY-ONE
Citizen Poynter

1.   *U.S. News & World Report*, (3/19/90) at 42; *Washington Post*, (3/4/90) at H1, 4-5.

2.   *Wall Street Journal*, (8/20/90) at B8; (8/19/93) at B6; *New York Times*, (2/8/90) at D25; (2/17/90) at 37; (8/18/90) at 33.

3.   *Id.*

4.   Times Publishing Company, *Evening Independent, News Printing Co.* and St. Petersburg Typographical Union, Local 860, Affiliated with I.T.U. *(AFL)*, 72 NLRB 676 (1947) (*"Times Publishing Company"*).

5.   29 U.S.C. § 158.

6.   Times Publishing Company, 72 NLRB at 690 (references from 688 are to Intermediate Report of the Trial Examiner).

7.   *Id.* at 691-692.

8.   *Id.* at 692.

9.   *Id.*

10. *Id.* at 684 (references from 676 to 687 are to Board's decision, reversing Trial Examiner's decision).

11. *Id.* at 686.

12. *Id.* at 693.

13. *Id.*

14. *Id.* at 694.

15. *Id.* at 695.

16. *Id.* at 696.

17. *Id.* at 681.

18. *Id.* at 683, 697.

19. *Id.* at 698-702.

20. *Id.* at 698.

21. *Id.* at 691.

22. *Id.* at 692.

23. *Id.* at n.4.

24. *Id.* at 683.

25. 29 U.S.C. § 158(b)(3).

26.   72 N.L.R.B. at 683.

27.   *Id.* at 684.

28.   *Id.*

29.   *Id.* at 686.

30.   *Id.* at 698.

31.   National Labor Relations Board, Complaint, Case No. 10-CA-1487, *The Times Publishing Company & International Printing Pressman and Assistants Union of North America* (4/29/53) at 2.

32.   *Id.*, *Order Rescheduling Hearing* (6/17/53).

33.   *The Times Publishing Co. and International Printing Pressmen & Assistants' Union of North America, A.F.L.*, Case No. 10-CA-1487.

CHAPTER TWENTY-TWO
The Swing At Ling

1.   *United States v. Ling-Temco-Vaught*, Civil Action No. 69-438 (W.D. Pa. 1969) (*"U.S. v. LTV"*).

2.   Brown, *Ling*, Atheneum (1972) at 4 ("Brown").

3.   Brown, at 151, 170.

4.   *U.S. v. LTV, Deposition of Gustave Levy* at 4-5, 19-20.

5.   15 U.S.C. § 18.

6.   Brown at 169, 171.

7.   *Id.* at 19.

8.   *Id.* at 211.

9.   *Id.* at 173, 176.

10. *U.S. v. LTV; Memorandum of Agreement*, 3/26/69; *Letter Amendment*, 3/27/69.

11. Brown at 176.

12. *Business Week* (6/6/70) at 110-111.

13. Brown at 249.

14. Hearings, *Tax Reform 1969*, Committee on Ways and Means, House of Representatives, 91st Cong., 1st Sess. (3/12/69), at 2388-89 (emphasis added).

15. *U.S. v. LTV, Complaint*, (5/14/69) ¶ 6.

16. Brown at 170.

17. *Id.* at 135-136.

18. *Id.* at 116-119.

19. *Id.* at 132-37.

20. *Business Week* (6/6/70) at 110; Brown at 149-151.

21. *U.S. v. LTV, Complaint*, ¶ 6.

22. *Business Week* (6/6/70) at 110, 112; Brown at 167-168.

23. Brown at 166.

24. *Id.* at 43.

25. *Id.* at 242, 244, 246, 266.

26. *U.S. v. LTV, Memorandum of Agreement*, 3/26-27/69.

27. *United States v. Pennzoil Company and Kendall Refining Company*, 252 F. Supp. 962 (W.D. Pa. 1965).

28. 15 U.S.C. § 28 (1982 Ed.).

29. *U.S. v. LTV, Ling Deposition* (7/18/69) at 329.

30.   Brown at 211.

31.   *Id.* at 246-247.

32.   Brown at 167, 239; *Business Week* (6/6/70) at 110.

33.   Brown at 167.

34.   *Id.* at 247-248.

35.   *Id.*

36.   *U.S. v. LTV, Opinion,* (6/70) at 14.

37.   *Id., Memorandum and Order,* (4/13/70) at 3, 4.

38.   Brown at 261-263.

39.   *Id.* at 267.

40.   *Id.* at 268.

41.   *Id.;* see also *Business Week* (6/6/70) at 110.

42.   *U.S. v. LTV, Stipulation and Opinion and Final Judgment,* (6/3&10/70).

43.   *Business Week* (6/6/70) at 210.

44.   *U.S. v. LTV, Opinion* (6/10/70) at 4.

45.   Brown at 276.

46.   Emphasis added.

47.   *Business Week,* (7/18/980) at 3.

CHAPTER TWENTY-THREE
What Goes Around Comes Around

1. *Investigation of Regulatory Commissions and Agencies,* Hearings Before a Subcomm. of the House Comm. on Interstate and Foreign Commerce, 85th Cong., 2nd Sess.

2. *Id.*, Part 2 (February 1958) at 723-25.

3. *Id.* at 725.

4. *Id.* at 726.

5. *Id.* Part 5 (March 1958) at 1876-77.

6. *Id.* at 1877-78.

7. *Id.* at 1878.

8. *Id.* at 1880.

CHAPTER TWENTY-FOUR
The Packrat Payoff and "Mr. Fred"

1. Public Law 87-30, 87th Cong., First Sess. (May 5, 1961).

2. 29 U.S.C. §§ 207(h); 213(a)(1); 214(b).

3. 15 U.S.C. § 13a(f).

4. *Associated Merchandising Corporation, et al.*, FTC Docket No. 8651, *Complaint* (11/24/64) ("AMC, Docket 8651").

5. *Associated Merchandising Corporation, et al. v. Jackson,* Civil Action No. 18993 (D.Md. 1967) *("THE AMC CASE").*

6. *AMC,* Docket 8651, *Order Withdrawing Complaint,* 74 FTC 1555, 1560-61 (1968).

7. *AMC v. Jackson, Memorandum and Order* (2/25/69).

CHAPTER TWENTY-FIVE
Justice Icarus

1.   Kalman at 322, Murphy at 500.

2.   Kalman at 326; Murphy at 499.

3.   Kalman at 328.

4.   Kalman at 351; Murphy at 503.

5.   Kalman at 351-55; Murphy at 522-25.

6.   Kalman at 363; Murphy at 554-55.

7.   Kalman at 363; Murphy at 552.

8.   Shogun at 189.

9.   Murphy at 546.

10.   *Id.* at 547, 549.

11.   Murphy at 549; Kalman at 361-62.

12.   Murphy at 551-53.

13.   Kalman at 364; Murphy at 555.

14.   Kalman at 364-65; Murphy at 556.

15.   Kalman at 365; Murphy at 557-58, 563.

16.   Kalman at 365-66; Murphy at 559-560.

17.   Kalman at 369; Murphy at 568, 573.

18.   Kalman at 367.

19.   *Id.* at 368.

20.   Murphy at 568.

21.   Kalman at 368; Murphy at 562-64.

22.   *Id.* at 369.

23.   Kalman at 373; Murphy at 528.

24.   Kalman at 365; Murphy at 565.

25.   Kalman at 374; Murphy at 579.

26.   Kalman at 380.

27.   *Id.* at 326.

28.   Murphy at 503.

29.   Kalman at 369.

30.   Murphy at 363 (emphasis added).

31.   Shogun at 108, 111-12.

32.   Kalman at 380-81.

CHAPTER TWENTY-SIX
Law And Remembrance

None.

Epilogue

1.   Kalman at 380.

2.   *Id.*

3.   *Id.* at 379.

4.   *Id.* at 380.

5.   *Id.* at 381.

6. *Id.*

7. *Id.*

INDEX

Acheson, Dean, 35-6

Agger, Carol, 10, 31,
    40, 64, 280
   Attorney, income tax, joined
    Arnold, Fortas & Porter
    1960; Wife of Abe Fortas,
    90-1

Agricultural Adjustment
   Administration ("AAA"), 52,
   82, 96

American Association of
   Railroads, 63

American Civil Liberties
   Union ("ACLU"), 143-4, 204

American Law Institute, 20

Anderson, Clinton, 41, 54, 69,
   73, 135, 145

Anderson, Marion, 41

Andewelt, Roger B., 150
   see Braude, Beatrice Estate of,

Andrews, Bert, 6, 8
   see Arnold, State Department
   "security risks",

Arnall, Ellis, 222-3

Arnold, Fortas & Porter, 5, 14,
   24, 44, 58, 72, 83, 91, 95, 98,
   102, 111, 118, 147, 163, 285,
   289
   accomplishments of founders
    before establishing firm,
    remarkable scope, xiv
   advantages of entry by Arnold
    and Fortas into private
    practice; Arnold
    uncomfortable as Judge; 59

   Fortas ready to retire as Under
    Secretary of Interior; 64
    both knew ways of Washington;
    wives liked living there, 64-5
   at all times subordinated
    monetary considerations to
    integrity, excellence and courage
    of services, xiv
   courageous defense of
    civil liberties and many victims of
    the red-baiting frenzy from 1947
    to 1958 before and throughout
    horror of McCarthy era, all
    without compensation, xiv, 5, 7
   cowed reactions of many
    law firms fearing loss of clients, 8
   dictionary definition of
    "McCarthyism", 6
   humor and wit of Arnold
    and Porter kept office relaxed
    despite long hours hard word;
    morale high; protocol unknown to
    them, xv, 30 90, 93, 98-9
   name partners mutual respect
    affection and admiration;
    extraordinary bond, "Three
    Musketeers", xv, 291
   relations between lawyers
    and staff highly informal, first
    name basis, xv
   social occasions often
    included staff, notably annual
    Christmas party, 95, 100